The Bear Book

Bear Trust

A Bear Trust International Conservation Publication

A Bear Trust International Conservation Publication

Edited by Julie Lange

Printed by
FALCON BOOKS
San Ramon, California

ISBN: 978-0-9798645-0-6

Bear Trust International is a 501(c)(3) nonprofit wildlife conservation organization founded in 1999 to protect all eight species of bears through wild bear research, habitat protection, and conservation education. *www.beartrust.org*

PRINTED IN THE UNITED STATES OF AMERICA

The Bear Book

TABLE OF CONTENTS

Foreword

It all began at an informal breakfast gathering in San Diego in 2004, during the Fifteenth International Conference on Bear Research and Management sponsored by the International Association for Bear Research and Management (IBA). Gathered at the conference were bear researchers from around the world, making presentations and discussing their work. The formal presentations were highly technical and informative, heavy on statistical analysis and the specialized language of wildlife biology. Most of the attendees, after all, were biologists and agency people who spend their lives in the scholarly and professional pursuit of bear research and management.

But scratch a field biologist and you'll find a story-teller. During breakfast on the third day of the conference, one of the previous day's presenters sat back sipping coffee and told a story about a bear he knew of that broke into a building at the county fairgrounds year after year, and stole peach pies that had been entered into the pie-baking contest. The bear never touched another thing. Then someone told a story about a bear that broke into a cabin and ate 12 boxes of D-Con rat poison, and washed it down with a gallon of cooking oil, which no doubt saved its life.

Soon, practically everyone at breakfast had a story to tell about a bear they knew—a troublesome bear, a clever bear, a friendly one, an ornery one, a bear that inspired, that amused, that provoked. No statistics, just personal stories. This, and the coffee, got everyone fired up. Spectacled bear expert Bernie Peyton mused, "Wouldn't it be great if someone compiled a book of bear stories?"

Three representatives of Bear Trust International happened to be sitting at that breakfast. And the idea of a bear book stuck with them long after they returned from San Diego. So Bear Trust decided to compile a book of stories, soliciting story contributions from biologists, agency people, conservationists, writers, wildlife photographers and artists, and anyone else who might have something interesting and worthwhile to say about bears.

The first step was to find the funding to compile and publish the book. As a nonprofit organization, Bear Trust found this step to be on familiar territory. At the end of July 2005, Bear Trust received a grant from a generous donor to launch the book project. At this time, Bear Trust established the following five goals for the compilation to ensure the project remained consistent with the organization's mission: to compile a book of nonfiction stories about all eight species of bears that were highly entertaining and accessible to a general readership; to raise public awareness of the need to protect wild bears and their habitat; to increase interest in wildlife biology as a career choice; to provide classroom teachers and students with a highly readable and accurate resource about wildlife; and to raise funds for wild bear projects through book sales.

With funding in hand, Bear Trust was able to move forward with the project, and the results have been worth the effort. The stories, essays, and photos have exceeded our expectations. *The Bear Book* has become much more than we had envisioned that morning back in San Diego. Bear Trust hopes the reader gets as much enjoyment out of the book as we did in compiling it.

I would like to extend a special thanks to my wife Melissa for her love and enduring encouragement, and to my children Molly, Arthur, and Gretchen for their unconditional support. With a caring family, much can be accomplished. Also, my deepest gratitude to all of our donors, with a very special thank you to the Puelicher Foundation, whose generosity over the years has been instrumental in the success of Bear Trust. And finally, I would like to thank Julie Lange for all her efforts on behalf of Bear Trust, and the members of the Bear Trust Board of Directors for their guidance over the years.

A.C. Smid
Founder and President
Bear Trust International

Acknowledgements

BEAR TRUST WOULD LIKE TO THANK FRED AND KAREN SCHAUFELD FOR THEIR GENEROSITY AND PATIENCE IN MAKING THIS BOOK POSSIBLE. WILD PLACES ARE MADE BETTER, AND WILDLIFE MORE SECURE, BY CONSERVATIONISTS LIKE THE SCHAUFELDS.

****

THE CHARLES ENGELHARD FOUNDATION HAS HELPED SUPPORT THE PRODUCTION OF THIS COMPILATION, AND BEAR TRUST IS GRATEFUL FOR THEIR ASSISTANCE IN BRINGING THIS PROJECT TO COMPLETION.

****

BEAR TRUST WOULD ALSO LIKE TO THANK THE DISTINGUISHED MEMBERS OF THE BEAR TRUST EDITORIAL BOARD FOR THEIR GUIDANCE AND SUGGESTIONS IN COMPILING THIS BOOK: JACK WARD THOMAS, KAREN NOYCE, AND HARRY REYNOLDS.

****

FINALLY, BEAR TRUST THANKS ALL OF THOSE WHO CONTRIBUTED STORIES AND PHOTOGRAPHS TO THIS BOOK. THEIR WILLINGNESS TO SHARE THEIR WORK, THEIR EXPERIENCES, AND THEIR PASSION FOR BEARS HAS MADE THE TASK OF COMPILING THIS BOOK A TRUE PLEASURE FOR BEAR TRUST INTERNATIONAL. ALSO, BEAR TRUST THANKS EVERYONE WHO REVIEWED THE FACTUAL INFORMATION PROVIDED ON THE EIGHT SPECIES OF BEARS, INCLUDING MELISSA REYNOLDS-HOGLAND AND ANDREW DEROCHER.

Primer on Bear Species

There are eight species of bears. Each species has a story or two in this book, as well as several photographs. The following is some basic taxonomic and geographic information about the eight species. You will note that all eight species are of the Order Carnivora and Family Ursidaie, while the four species of Bears of the North all share the genus *Ursus*. In contrast, the four species of Bears of the South have different genera. There is additional information on each bear species following individual stories and in the glossary at the end of the book.

Bears of the North:

Order Carnivora
Family Ursidaie
Genus Ursus

Species	*Ursus Americanus*	**American Black Bear**	Canada, United States, Northern Mexico
	Ursus Thibetanus	**Asiatic Black Bear**	Southeast Asia, Northeast China, Japan, Far Eastern Russia
	Ursus Arctos	**Brown Bear (Grizzly)**	Eastern and Western Europe, Northern Asia and Japan, Western Canada, and Western United States (Alaska, Wyoming, Montana, Idaho, and Washington)
	Ursus Maritimus	**Polar Bear**	Canada, Alaska, Russia

Bears of the South:

Order	Carnivora		
Family	Ursidaie		
Genus	Ailuropda		
Species	*Ailuropoda Melanoleuca*	**Giant Panda Bear**	Southwest China
Genus	Melursus		
Species	*Melursus Ursinus*	**Sloth Bear**	Sri Lanka, India, Bangladesh, Bhutan, Nepal,
Genus	Tremarctos		
Species	*Tremarctos Ornatus*	**Spectacled Bear**	Bolivia, Colombia, Ecuador, Peru, Venezuela
Genus	Helarctos		
Species	*Helarctos Malayanus*	**Sun Bear**	Burma, Bangladesh, Eastern India, Southern China, Laos, Cambodia, Vietnam, Thailand, Malaysia, Sumatra, Borneo

Nelun
Shyamala Ratnayeke, Ph.D
Sloth Bear

This is a story about Nelun, a sloth bear that Shyamala Ratnayeke studied in Wasgomuwa, Sri Lanka. "Nelun" means lotus flower in Sinhala. As Dr. Ratnayeke explains, "People who study sloth bears think all sloth bears are beautiful, majestic and precious and we gave our bears names that reflect the honor and pride with which we regard them."

This afternoon we saw Nelun. Very exciting because we walked in on her quietly and found her fast asleep on the ground where a fallen tree covered with lianas had created a shady thicket. We had followed the signal from her radio collar for nearly an hour through dry scrub forest. My heart was beginning to pound as the receiver and antenna I was carrying suggested we were close.

Karu and Rohan were ahead, moving too quickly for my comfort, but I didn't want to scare the bear away by speaking to them. Neither did I want a confrontation with an irate sloth bear and her offspring. The moment of truth arrived when Rohan and I smelt the bear and paused. I saw her a split second later. Rohan was squatting, searching the scrub beyond her prone body now scarcely ten feet from him. Grasping Rohan's shoulder, I pointed at the bear's belly gently moving up and down as she slept. A muffled gasp followed as Rohan immediately got up and backed away quietly, followed by Karu wringing his hands in horror.

I was choking with a mixture of laughter and relief. Hadn't I told them to stay behind the person carrying the antenna? Karu was mad at us for getting him into this situation, and Rohan and I somewhat aghast at this close call.

Why were we here? In an immediate sense, we wanted to know whether this sloth bear and her cub were still united after their capture and release more than a month ago. Previous attempts to see her had met with little success because she either heard us or picked up our scent, sneaking off quietly, giving brief and unsatisfying glimpses of white snout and shaggy black fur beating a hasty retreat. But today, on a hot September afternoon at Wasgomuwa, she had slept soundly through the approach of three humans at her daybed.

I first visited Wasgomuwa in 1999 in search of sloth bears. Wasgomuwa, according to local wisdom, is a derivation of the old name Walasgomuwa, meaning "Bear Country." Most people fail to realize that, and no one is more at fault for this sad state of affairs than the bears themselves. After a couple of years in these jungles, I realized that sloth bears might be the most secretive and elusive of any of Wasgomuwa's carnivores.

A pair of leopards

Elephants peacefully feeding at Wilmitiya grassland, Wasgomuwa, Sri Lanka

Golden Palm Civet

To most visitors, the national park, Wasgomuwa, is better known for its magnificent and temperamental elephants that terrorize people with spectacular displays of rage. The rich diversity of mammalian carnivores, sloth bears included, and other abundant animal life sheltered by the dense jungles, is less apparent.

As I grew to know Wasgomuwa, I realized it was a place of wonderful secrets that take time, patience, and familiarity to discover. Even more unforgettable were the people at Wasgomuwa whose fellowship and generosity of spirit made an old expatriate like me feel more Sri Lankan than I had ever felt before.

Two years after my first visit, I pitched a tent next to a small range outpost on the eastern edge of Wasgomuwa, a prelude to establishing a small field station and field crew a few months later. Field assistant Rohan was an avid naturalist with a seemingly endless capacity for fieldwork. His wife and baby daughter lived in the capital and had an unlimited amount of patience with his long absences from home.

Karu was a slip of a lad with a smile who could light up the grayest of mornings, a great sense of humor, and a shout that can stop a charging elephant in its tracks. He also carried a shot gun, which I later learned needed special equipment like a screw driver or pliers to remove the empty shell after it was fired. He was one of the three wildlife officers who lived at the range outpost.

Karu

Rohan

The other half of the range outpost building was an abandoned, bat-infested space that eventually became our field station after much cleaning and repairs. The crew ate together, and if we returned to the field station after dark, we went down to the river for baths carrying a hurricane lamp, a couple of flashlights, accompanied by Karu armed with his one-shot shot gun in case we ran into wild elephants along the trail to the river.

Shortly after we set up our field station, we were on the trail of the first radio-collared sloth bears in Sri Lanka. The sixth bear we captured had a small cub clinging to her belly when we pulled her drugged and passive body out of a barrel trap. Our permit would not let us handle the cub so we left the terrified little fellow inside the barrel trap in a shady spot surrounded by trees and shrubs while we tagged, collared, and measured the adult bear. She was fat, well-muscled, with fur that was surprisingly short and thick for a sloth bear.

After receiving an antidote less than an hour later, she staggered up and with roars of fury charged headlong, barreling into our research truck with such force that she left a small dent in the front bumper. She crashed into the jungle, heading north. The pandemonium was followed by the cub running out of the trap with loud cries of distress and disappearing into the jungle behind her. We named the mother bear Nelun, which means lotus flower in Sinhala, and is a name some may find odd for a bear that looks rather comical and has a reputation for being extremely pugnacious. But people that study sloth bears think all sloth bears are beautiful, majestic and precious and we gave our bears names that reflect the honor and pride with which we regard them.

Not just another pretty face

Female sloth bears typically carry their young

Now, fifty or so feet from Nelun's daybed, Rohan, Karu and I debated in whispers. What should we do? Karu was never enthusiastic about getting close to bears and wanted to leave immediately, but we hadn't seen the cub yet, which was the reason we were here in the first place. Rohan's suggestion that we climb a tree was a good one, but after several years of teaching biology at a very proper college for women, this was a psychological leap for me.

I eventually—and proudly—achieved this feat. Perched in the crotch of an old *Weera* tree, I watched Rohan and Karu climb an adjacent tree and settle down to wait for the bear to emerge. We were now about thirty feet from the daybed, and inexplicably, the bear had slept through all this commotion, including frequent muttering and clearing of the throat from Karu who was very unhappy with the whole arrangement. Rohan could see the bear from his position and after about an hour, he signaled that she was getting up.

A few minutes later, Nelun emerged from the thicket and slowly shuffled towards the foot of the *Weera* tree, followed by her cub. A magical moment followed when she paused at the foot of the tree, waiting for the cub that was now chasing a large beetle. I was scarcely a dozen feet from a wild sloth bear and she looked as magnificently fat and healthy as the day she was first captured. Had she smelt us? I couldn't imagine that she hadn't, and thought that she might look up any second and see me.

But the cub eventually gave up his beetle-chase and caught up with her, and the two lumbered off together. We waited until she was at a safe distance before dismounting to examine her daybed, a meter-wide circle of sand, scraped clean of leaves and other debris, with several fresh bear scats containing the remains of termites and *ehela* pods next to it.

Two years later, we talked with a gentle 36-year-old man called Leelaratne who had a terribly disfigured face. We met him along a dirt road in his village and he graciously invited us to his home to hear his story. We sat and talked in the neatly kept yard of a typical village home with floors and walls of *matti*, a mixture of dirt and ground termite mounds commonly used as a building material for walls and floors in rural homes. Leelaratne's wife and daughters prepared hot sweet tea for us, their visitors.

Leelaratne was mauled by a sloth bear when he was 13 years old, when he and his father entered the forest in a national park to cut fence posts for their chena. If the rains and wild animals permitted, the chena, a patch of jungle which had been cleared and tilled with great labour, would provide vegetables and millet for the family to eat or trade for other necessities. The young Leelaratne strayed some distance to search for berries to eat and wandered into a thicket in which a female bear and her cubs were resting.

He described the bear lying on her back as the cubs fed from her belly. She charged out of the thicket with guttural roars, barreling into him, and knocking him off his feet before biting most of the lower part of his face, removing his entire nose and left cheek, causing multiple fractures to the bones in his face, breaking his lower jaw and removing much of his scalp.

Leelaratne's father heard the commotion and came running to find the bear lying on top of his son. The cubs attempted to attack his father, who then killed one of the cubs with his axe. He then used the axe to break the she-bear's back, and seizing the bear by the scruff of her neck and rump, he lifted her clear of the boy's prone body. He then carried his gravely injured son to the village.

The villagers returned to the site shortly afterwards, and finding the injured mother bear, hacked her to death with machetes. Perhaps this was a mercifully expedited death for what might have otherwise been a slow and painful end for the she-bear.

Leelaratne's story had the familiar theme of poor rural farmers who depend on forests for various reasons, including additional means of income such as bushmeat, fuel or timber, and who risk the potentially dire consequences of encountering a sloth bear. There is no forest now left in the vicinity of Leelaratne's village, but he had a small plot of land cultivated with pumpkins, maize and moong beans. In any case, he told us, he never went into the forest again after that one unforgettable experience.

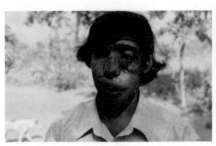

Leelaratne

Leelaratne and family outside their home

Villagers in Sri Lanka consider the sloth bear a dangerous adversary. The bear's reputation for inflicting serious injury, especially to the heads or faces of the people it attacks, may result in horrifying mutilation making it one of the most feared animals in the dry-zone jungles. Sloth bears are already experiencing gradual loss of their habitat, but this is compounded by humans who fear and frequently kill them on sight. By wearing radio collars, Nelun and nine other sloth bears have given us a glimpse into their secretive, solitary lives and a better understanding of the behavior and biology of sloth bears.

We had several more close encounters with Nelun, including a recapture a year later, shortly after she had dropped her radio collar. The bear in the trap had a pair of number-six ear tags, so we recognized our shy old friend. We released her without further ado to conform as closely as possible to the requirements of our research permit, which instructed that we were not to recapture any bears. It seemed as if we had grown to know this bear especially well because she often slept or foraged within a short distance of the Kadurupitiya bungalow where the bungalow keeper, Piyal, frequently revived our weary crew with cups of hot sweet tea.

Sloth bears have a reputation for avoiding areas used by humans, but for the bears that lived in the vicinity, the buildings occupied by wildlife staff, along with their human sounds and smells, seemed as much a part of their habitat as the surrounding jungle. Nelun frequently bedded down within earshot of the national park's office and officer's quarters, although the staff never saw her. This secretive behavior was very typical of sloth bears at Wasgomuwa, so much so that Piyal and some wildlife staff at Wasgomuwa had never seen a bear, despite living amongst what was possibly Sri Lanka's most abundant population of sloth bears. Newspaper reports of the first sloth bear study in the island drew more visitors to Wasgomuwa, but they left with some added irritation that not one of those damned bears had made an appearance.

In the years following their capture, two of the ten bears we studied fell victim to poachers. National parks such as Wasgomuwa are patrolled by wildlife staff and allow visitor access only with a permit and an accompanying wildlife officer, constituting what should be the highest level of protection afforded to wild animals. The loss of two bears from a seemingly small sample of study animals is a bleak warning of what the future may hold for sloth bears in a small country with a teeming human population and widespread poverty.

We were still to lose another bear. I visited Nelun's old haunts at Wasgomuwa two years later.   The staff said they had found the decomposing carcass of a bear in the middle of an open patch of grassland a few weeks before.   Two metal ear tags bearing the number six were found with the remains and given the circumstances, they suspected the bear had been shot.   The life of this old she-bear had finally passed, leaving a question.   Had she come to an untimely end at the hands of poachers in a place that was supposed to protect her, and where she had clearly felt safe among the humans who lived there?

More about Sloth Bears
from Bear Trust International
Bear Trust is solely responsible for the information in this section. Opinions about this information may vary.

Sloth Bear - *Melursus Ursinus*

Appearance:
Sloth bears are small, and usually black with a long shaggy coat, especially over the shoulders. There is a distinctive whitish or yellowish chest patch in the shape of a wide "U" or sometimes a "Y." They have a light colored snout, and two-to-three-inch-long front claws used for digging.

Size:
Adult males weigh between 175 and 310 pounds (79 and 140 kg), while female sloth bears weigh 120 to 240 pounds (54 and 109 kg). Birth weight averages 10 to 17 ounces (28 to 48 grams).

Reproduction:
The family unit generally consists of an adult female with cubs. Sloth bears breed in June and July, and cubs are born from November to January. A typical litter is two cubs. Cubs stay with the mother for a year and a half or longer.

Social Life:
Sloth bears generally live as solitary individuals, except for females with cubs. However, sloth bears sometimes congregate where food sources are abundant. Several adults may use a common rock outcrop as a daytime retreat, and during the breeding season, estrus females may be accompanied by several males. Home ranges overlap extensively among individuals of the same sex as well as between sexes.

Food:
Sloth bears specialize in termites, but fruit is another important component of their diet through much of their range. Sloth bears will eat eggs, insects, honeycombs, carrion, and vegetation other than fruit.

Habitat:
Sloth bears inhabit forested areas and grasslands in India, Sri Lanka, Bangladesh, Nepal, and Bhutan. They seem to prefer lower elevations and drier forests with rocky outcrops.

Wild Population:
Estimated between 10,000 and 25,000 and declining due to loss of habitat.

FYI:
Special physical adaptations allow sloth bears to feed extensively on termites, and the nostrils can be closed voluntarily to keep termites from entering.

Cubs ride on the mother's back.

Sloth bears have been used in circuses, and called "the juggling bear."

Sloth bears show aggressive behavior towards humans and other natural predators.

Baloo of Rudyard Kipling's *Jungle Book* is a sloth bear.

Yinda, a Strange Family Member
Bernie Peyton, Ph.D.
Spectacled Bear

This is spectacled bear expert Bernie Peyton's unforgettable story of Yinda, the Peruvian spectacled bear, and the Ecological Reserve of Chaparri that is Yinda's legacy.

The Beginning

In October 1999, I received a phone call from Heinz Plenge, Peru's most respected wildlife photographer. I had just returned to California after spending several weeks with Heinz while filming bear worshipers at 5000 meters elevation in southern Peru.

"There's a bear living in the house of the Huaynate Diaz family in Oxapampa. What do we do about it?" Heinz said excitedly.

"What you mean by what do WE do about it?" I replied. "That one bear will cost us more than five Peruvian park budgets."

Heinz explained the circumstances. He had received a tip from INRENA, Peru's government agency in charge of wildlife and parks. They told him they were poised to confiscate a spectacled bear that was living as a pet with poor farmers on the jungle side of the Central Andean Range. Heinz told INRENA he knew a gringo field biologist who was "sure to help." Just to be sure, Heinz raced off to Oxapampa to check out the bear.

This was no ordinary pet bear. This was Juana Diaz's four-legged daughter! She and her husband, Oscar Huaynate, her children, and grandchildren lived in two shacks at the edge of the cloud forest. When I first visited Oxapampa in 1977 to start learning about spectacled bears, the steep hillsides surrounding the village were covered with cloud forests. Two decades later the hillsides were nearly bare. Remnant forest patches provided cover for spectacled bears, who now ate corn and cattle, which had replaced their natural foods.

This reality was not lost on Oscar. He considered bears dangerous, and a competitor for the crops farmers could provide their family. And now he had one in his own house! "What's worse," Oscar said, "is she escapes and makes a mess of the neighbor's squash, oranges ... everything she eats." But Juana didn't feel the same way about this, which placed Yinda in the middle of a family crisis.

"My other kids are trash," Juana told Heinz. "My son Oscar beat one of my youngest daughters right by my side after she ran off with a man! My other daughters had already run off, and now I care for them and their kids. But this last daughter of mine, my Yinda, will turn out right."

Yinda punctuated this last remark by grabbing one of the Huaynate Diaz dogs by the ear and lifting it up to a platform she was tethered to, making the dog yelp. The tables certainly had turned on those dogs. Last year they set upon something when the family was harvesting corn. Juana tore the dogs off to find a small bear cub. She carried the cub off in a sack. She nursed it on her breast and put it in her bed. She named it "Yinda" (perhaps a variant of "Linda" meaning "beautiful" in Spanish). When Heinz caught up with Yinda, she was approximately 45 pounds heavy and 18 months old. What Heinz didn't know then was that Yinda was starting to come into heat two years earlier than her wild counterparts. Juana had sped up Yinda's maturation by stuffing her last daughter with yucca, corn, beans, squash, even Coca-Cola. She was a feisty teenager, and she was becoming more rambunctious and harder to control by the day.

"She's absolutely beautiful, Bernie," Heinz said. "Black coat, white markings around the eyes and under her chin. And a blotch of yellow on the side of her white nose." I was sure she looked comical, but the description of her eye rings was consistent with why the species was named "spectacled." Every individual of the species had his own pattern of markings around the eyes, chin, and chest.

"I have no doubt she's special," I remarked disinterestedly to Heinz. Of course, from a conservation perspective, I knew she *was* special. This was the only species that remained of the bears that came over the land bridge from Asia to North America, before the brown and black bears arrived with their longer rostrums. Although spectacled bears live in the Andes Mountains from Venezuela to northern Argentina, the hurricane rate at which their forest habitat was being cut down alarmed conservationists. Most of the forests I had worked in at the beginning of my career were now gone. I considered the job of saving the forest as hopeless. Perhaps I could help slow deforestation down a bit and still provide farmers their needs. Little did I know how much hope Yinda would shed on this possibility.

"Juana does everything with Yinda," Heinz explained to me. "The family has a long rope attached to Yinda's neck to control her. When Juana cooks for everyone, Yinda is tied up nearby. She puts Yinda up a tree, rope and all, while she tends the crops. While she washes all their clothes in the river, Yinda swims. Her kids do nothing to help her!"

I could see the trap jaws shutting. Cute bear, really cute bear. Noble mother, like every mother I have met in Peru. She does everything for the family, and only the bear reciprocates her love. Tragic. Oscar probably wasn't a bad father, just busy with the crops. He's watching their food creating more bear, who will eat even more food. Who could blame him for wanting to sell Yinda to a circus, I thought. The kids were angry about the attention their mother gives Yinda. This increases her isolation from them. It's a job for a psychiatrist, not a biologist!

"You know what is going to happen when INRENA confiscates that bear?" Heinz asked triumphantly.

"No, what?" I lied.

"They are going to put her in some cement pit."

"Oh brother!" I said, half seriously.

"They were here just recently. Ricardo Jon Llap told Juana that the bear was listed on the CITES list of endangered species, and it was against Peruvian law for her to keep it. Problem is, as you know and I know, there is not one facility here in Peru that can house confiscated wildlife," Heinz announced.

"That's for sure," I replied. For the next ten minutes we discussed the state of zoos in Peru. Though improving, the keepers still eat the wild pigs, the bears have open sores and flies, etc., etc.

I could have let the whole conversation die right there if Heinz hadn't innocently baited the trigger with Juana. After spending almost two decades working on spectacled bears with little success, I was looking for a story about bears that could appeal to the hearts of South Americans. Spectacled bears didn't need one more scientific article. They needed a spokesman to encourage them to adopt bears as part of their extended family. A spokeswoman!

I don't recall any rational conversations during the next two weeks. I bought the bear for $700. The sale was held up another ten days because the police in Oxapampa were upset about not receiving their cut of the sale price. I also got a 45-year-old woman in the bargain, even though I was already married to one! Juana was determined to go with her furry child wherever it went. Heinz and I thought that was a good idea because it would reduce the bear's stress during the voyage.   But how were we going to take care of it?

The irony of that question wasn't lost on me when we asked INRENA if we could buy the bear. Since 1993, I had criticized a Peruvian law that allowed the government to sell endangered wildlife to captive breeding centers. The law lacked provisions for sufficient background checks on these facilities and their administration.   To me it sounded like the government had found a legal way to participate in the black market.

Now I was going to be that market. Any background check would reveal I didn't know the first thing about captive husbandry. Heinz wasn't much better, but he had grand visions for Yinda that ignorance was not going to stop. He had been ready for years when Yinda popped into his shutter, and this gringo Bernie Peyton was going to help him achieve it. Peruvians are among the most "can do" people I have ever met. This adventure was certain to be reckless.

The Journey

Heinz thought the best place to take Yinda was Santa Catalina de Chongoyape, a community of some 3000 people in northern Peru near the coast. Yinda could educate the community not to fear or hate the wild bears that inhabited the community's desert and dry forest.

I had no idea that Heinz wanted to house the bear in the same dry forest where we saw our first wild spectacled bear in 1977. It was a spot where Heinz started his career by photographing condors on a massive knife ridge known as Chaparri. The sheer walls were enough to elicit awe and fear in anyone who approached. Chaparri's mystical powers were enhanced by artesian springs that bubbled from its foothills, even when the rest of the landscape was dry. Whether it was the topography or the water, Chaparri was the mountain most revered by the shamans of northern Peru.

Nobody but powerful healers lived there because of the supposed powers of the mountain's spirit.

These beliefs had spared Chaparri's dry forests from being turned into wooden boxes to contain the lemons that farmers grew in the desert below. It was at one of these coastal lemon farms that Heinz planned to store Yinda temporarily until he could build a large outdoor enclosure in Chaparri. He called Gustavo del Solar, a former hunter of bears and the person who introduced lemons to Peru's coast. Gustavo had one of the few captive breeding zoos in the country, at his lemon farm in Olmos.

The same year that Heinz and I saw our first wild bear, Gustavo rediscovered the white-winged guan, a large member of the pheasant family that was believed to have gone extinct more than 100 years before. He devoted the next 20 years to raising these guans in captivity with the idea of eventually releasing them back to the dry forest. He instantly agreed to house Yinda. But how were we going to get Yinda 1000 kilometers over the Andes to Gustavo's farm?

I called Mark Rosenthal at the Lincoln Park Zoo in Chicago. His staff faxed us plans to construct an animal transport crate. In November, Juana bid her grandchildren a tearful goodbye as her ungrateful daughters realized their mom was leaving them for the first time ever, to go anywhere. Yinda had been coaxed into her crate with cooked yucca, and loaded on the back of a rental truck. A veterinarian was hired to accompany Yinda to Olmos. Also on the trip were Juana's oldest son Oscar, Heinz, and Heinz's publicist Maria Cecelia Astengo Moreno, or Ceci for short. She was as comfortable in high heels as she was covered in grease taking apart an engine. Ceci had no equal behind the wheel.

I created a film company while these preparations were underway. I hired soundman Jose Balado to be the sixth person in the truck to record the journey. Sometime down the road we would find the story in the editing room.

The journey from the foothills near the jungle, over the Andes to the desert, and then up the coast to Olmos, took two days. On the way, the truck drove past burned forests that once where strongholds of spectacled bears, and snowcapped peaks almost 6000 meters high. The pass at Ticlio, the highest point in the road, is over 5000 meters in elevation. The veterinarian kept an eye on Yinda, who could be seen through the truck's back window nervously chewing on nothing. Juana faced her unknown future, and that of her daughter, rigidly, in silence. Jose and I would discover that of the pair, the bear was far easier to film. As a spokeswoman, Juana was as endearing as a truck spring.

On the second day, Ceci veered off the Pan American highway to the beach. It was the first time in perhaps 1000 years that a spectacled bear had visited the Pacific Ocean. Yinda tucked her head behind Juana's wind-blown dress as the two approached the surf. She reached up to tug on the rope end held by her adopted mother. While Yinda might have been scared by this biggest of rivers, Juana was starting to relax. "None of my daughters has taken me anywhere," Juana confided in Heinz. "But this, what people call the daughter with four paws, has taken me far away. I am so grateful."

Later, by the soft light of evening, our tired party swung inside the gate of Gustavo's farm. The mesquite trees in Olmos were a welcome greeting after a day spent squinting at the desert devoid of greenery. The sounds of oven birds and Gustavo's guans were a welcome change from the rattling and grinding of the car.

A tired Juana led Yinda slowly toward a cement corral that would be Yinda's temporary lodging. Yinda promptly climbed the faique tree in the middle of the corral while Juana secured the tin door.

"Don't worry," Heinz explained to Juana. "Yinda will have a large space to run in, with many trees, cacti, water, and most importantly, there are also wild bears." But privately Heinz was very concerned about the monumental task ahead. He would have to use all the political capital and contacts he knew to create a sanctuary for Yinda at the base of Chaparri's cliffs.

Yinda's escape from her temporary corral on the 7th of December, and her subsequent recapture four farms down the road, added urgency to our mission to build a more secure facility.   Juana spent a melancholy Christmas with Yinda, away from her family.   But Heinz told me her stress was starting to unwind, that she was beginning to relax.

On the other hand, my stress was about to begin. I studiously had avoided dealing with captive bears. I didn't understand why anyone would spend so much money on them when a fraction of those funds could protect so much natural habitat for a whole population of bears.

"Preserve the habitat and prevent most of the hunting mortality, and bear populations would take care of themselves," I argued to Heinz. "First you need good scientific data on bears and habitat."

 Heinz agreed in principle, but a science-based approach was not the way he was going to make it happen.   He would leave me to solve the technical aspects of the project while he massaged the political opinion of the community toward conservation.   We agreed the answer lay in community-based initiatives that would provide jobs for local residents in return for their stewardship of bears and bear habitat.

We would start with the creation of a large enclosure for Yinda on the steep hillsides of Chaparri.   Later we would reintroduce or encourage colonization of species that were locally extinct.   The condors that Heinz photographed as a young adult no longer nested in Chaparri's cliffs.   Gone also were white-winged guans and guanaco, a camel that once roamed Chaparri's foothills.   Chaparri still had wild bears, but these were being killed by hunters at an alarming rate.   We hoped Yinda would educate local residents that bears were not dangerous to them or to their livelihood as long as sufficient wild food existed. Heinz and I were convinced that we could make this bear the focus for conservation in the entire region.

The stakes were high. The El Niño floods of 1997-1998 created a temporary lake 80 kilometers long, and washed out all the roads and bridges in the Department of Lambayeque where Santa Catalina is located. Some residents of Santa Catalina were aware they needed to preserve their forests to prevent flooding, but how were they going to do it?

The community had other more immediate problems. The 3000 residents were divided into a dozen hamlets spread out over an area of roughly 100,000 hectares (250,000 acres). There were few roads and no telephones to keep hamlets in contact with each other. To go from one hamlet to another sometimes took a whole day on foot. Just getting people together to make decisions in their common interest was difficult.

The town also had little ability to manage its resources. The 3000 cattle that trampled the hillsides around Chaparri were owned by outsiders who paid nothing to the community for the pasture. Residents of Santa Catalina had no water rights, not even to the streams that flowed through their land. What they had—fantastic species diversity—they so far hadn't been able to make money from.

The northern coast was one of the three richest areas in Peru for unique species that lived in one local area and in no other. Scientists call these species "endemic." Of the many reasons why this is so, two stand out. The lack of water had prevented humans from colonizing all but a few places along rivers, leaving the vast majority of the land untouched by agriculture. Also, a gradient of humidity developed along Peru's coast that made each valley's microclimate slightly different than that of its neighbors'. As populations of plants and animals evolved under these different climates, they differentiated into separate species.

Approximately one-third of the vertebrates that inhabited Lambayeque were endemic. These included large species such as white-winged guans, the Sechuran fox, and the macanche, a huge boa constrictor. What excited me about making conservation viable in Santa Catalina was that we might be able to encourage neighboring communities to do likewise. There were only about 20 communities between Santa Catalina and the Ecuadorean border, each community with few people and huge amounts of dry land. Perhaps an entire ecosystem could be preserved!

The whole concept rested on setting Yinda up to work her magic on Santa Catalina's residents. Heinz's plan was to start with just the residents in the hamlet of Tierras Blancas where Chaparri was located, and then expand from there. I had doubts it would work. These residents, like Oscar Huaynate, distrusted bears and feared them. Some of the neighboring communities to Santa Catalina might be anything but cooperative. In 1978, I was actually tied up by guerillas who terrorized a community above Chaparri. I suppose they released me because they had never caught a "CIA agent" with a rucksack full of bear excrement. No bear crap would save me on this side of the Andes. The locals gave it to their cattle to make them strong like bears.

They also drank the blood of newly slaughtered bears to give them strength. This they learned from the mestizo descendants of the Spaniards, who lassoed bears in the desert from horseback and clubbed them to death. Now, in all but a few desert areas like Chaparri, nothing remains to tell the story of bears except the scars of their claws on tall cactus.

I spent November and December researching an electric fence that would become Yinda's new home. I called Harry Reynolds, who managed the brown bear population in the interior of Alaska for the Fish and Game Department. He put me in touch with several suppliers of electric fence parts. I also contacted animal rights organizations that had used these fences to house confiscated circus bears in Eastern Europe. However, their staff wanted a hefty fee to show us how to construct them. So I flew Heinz up to the States and together we went to the suppliers to learn how to make the fence.

While I gathered fence parts in California, Heinz convinced Peru's military to bulldoze an 11-kilometer road to the base of Chaparri. The bulldozer operator threatened to quit until Heinz put some oil in his palm to go the last and most rugged kilometer. A dozen community members cleared brush and carried gasoline for that project. Yinda was already creating jobs!

In mid-December, I mailed 1200 pounds of wire and plastic insulators to Peru. Insulators are plastic gizmos used to attach wires to fence posts without conducting the 8000 volts of electrical charge we would put through them. A regulator limits the charge so it occurs for only 3 milliseconds every second, enough to give a nasty shock, but not to kill.

Complications arose. Peruvian customs agents wouldn't let Ceci take possession of the fence parts because I had put Heinz's full family name on the bill of lading, but not on the customs form. Somehow an extra hundred dollars identified these two names as belonging to the same person. Ceci sent the coils of wire and insulators on a truck bound for Chiclayo, the nearest major city to Santa Catalina. In January 2000 Heinz sent me a message that he had run out of both wire and insulators.

No way, I thought. I had sent him enough of both to enclose a soccer field! In mid- January, I bought another 600 pounds of fence supplies and flew with them to Peru. The customs officers could barely contain their glee for charging me an import duty of 20 per cent of the value of the fence parts. I acted like I had gotten a terrible drubbing. Somehow Customs had missed a large BetaCam video camera, tripod, monitor, and 12 brick-sized batteries that I smuggled in with the fence parts. Now we were really set up to record Yinda's story!

I was in for a shock when I arrived in Chaparri with the gear. The three-to-four-hour walk from Tierras Blancas to Chaparri had been reduced to a 45-minute drive. Vultures with outstretched wings decorated many of candelabra cactus that dotted the pampas. Red-backed hawks were scooping up locusts. The windshield of Heinz's car was crusted with these grasshoppers when we swung through a new gate.

There, to my amazement, were two adobe houses in mid-construction. One was a caretaker's house with veranda and two bedrooms, and an outdoor kitchen. The caretaker Javier Vallejos, his wife Pepi, and their children were living in a tent nearby until their house could be occupied. Javier had killed several bears over the years. He was handy with everything he touched.

The other house was a slightly bigger construction, for Heinz and his family. It was situated at the edge of the largest pool created by the stream that flowed past both houses. A long stone patio had been laid out above the stream that would later be covered by a roof of mud and thatch, supported by rustic mesquite beams. Heinz was especially proud of one feature. Chaparri had the only sit-down toilets in the entire community!

The landscape around us was magical with palo santo trees. For half the year, palo santo trees looked like rubbery aortas; during the other half, the limbs were resplendent with green leaves and vines. Now, the new leaves were about to sprout. I could tell because everywhere, there was a resinous scent from plants releasing stored energy in anticipation of rains soon to come.

There were bombax trees whose green trunks were armored by thorns. And ironwood, whose leaves cause a nasty rash. Chaparri's cliffs rose vertically for 800 feet from these forested lower slopes, with no apparent transition. I had crawled along the base of Chaparri enough to know that the dark green patches seen here from a distance were fig trees. These trees and the bromeliads that studded the cliffs provided food and water for spectacled bears year-round.

Bears chew the base of bromeliad leaves after using their considerable strength to rip them apart. Like the giant panda, spectacled bears have large, flat molars. They also have muscle attachments on the lower jaw well suited for grinding tough foods like bromeliads.

"It is going to be relatively easy for us to bring bromeliads and figs to Yinda's enclosure," I told Heinz. He and Javier laughed, and led me up the quarter-mile trail past the houses to where they were constructing the fence. My jaw dropped. The enclosure was huge, the side of the fence I could see screaming up a cliff! As we scrambled up along its side, other mesquite posts came into view far to the right. "No wonder you ran out of wire."

Altogether, Javier and his sons had enclosed two hectares (five acres). Within the fence, Yinda would have over a dozen wild foods to choose from, including honey in the hives that hung from the cliffs. There would be no need to bring food to her. Javier's thumbs were split and purple from trying to nail the insulators to the tough mesquite posts. He abandoned that approach, and tied them on with wire. We had a seven-wire construction, four hot wires with three ground wires between them. Yinda would have to touch both a ground and a hot wire to close the circuit and receive a shock. A regulator, battery, and solar panel mounted two meters from the front gate provided the current. And most important of all, a prominent red switch had been installed on the post that supported the gate. When turned off, a person could open and close the gate without getting shocked, while the rest of the fence was still charged with electricity.

Yinda arrived in Chaparri later in January with Juana, her son Oscar, and two of her grandchildren who had come by bus from Oxapampa. The rains had arrived. The dry forest was turning green. Fish were running upstream to spawn. Frogs and toads appeared out of nowhere. Chaparri was a living paradise.

Yinda quickly adapted to her new home in the electrified corral. She bathed in a rock pool Javier built for her. Often she could be seen at the top of the corral high in a tree, sniffing the air. But her favorite place was an old mango tree full of ripening fruit at the bottom of the corral. It had been planted by one of the shamans who lived here 100 years ago.

Juana's routine was to take her Yinda to the corral in the morning, stay with her all day while she played and ate in the mango tree, and then return with Yinda to her tent next to Heinz's house in the evening. Every day Yinda grew stronger. By February, Juana needed Oscar to help her manage the strain on the rope that Heinz and I hoped would eventually be taken off Yinda's neck. But we were both concerned about the separation that we knew would eventually occur. Yinda seemed intensely interested in something that was just beyond the upper end of the fence. She bobbed back and forth testing the air. "I went up to check the fence," Javier told us, "and there are bear tracks all around the perimeter."

We also noticed a change in Javier. Initially he had been timid around Yinda. Now he entered the corral and wrestled with her when Juana wasn't there to scold him. The rest of the cowboys who came to look after their cattle on Chaparri's lower slopes stopped to admire Yinda and ask questions. Juana was pleased to show off her daughter. Even children from the local school trudged up the road to get a glimpse of the beast that, according to their parents, "Whistles like a man to attract cows before it hurls them to their death over a cliff."

One evening in the first week of February, the air around Chaparri became unusually still. Dark purple clouds descended on the ridges. Red-headed parrots returned to their roosts on Chaparri's cliffs a bit earlier than usual. Locusts that normally were hidden during the evening breezes appeared in the still air to feed. Juana was now in the habit of leaving Yinda in the corral overnight. All afternoon, Yinda peeled mango after mango between her paws, and ate the flesh off the stones which she then dropped on Juana and Oscar below. She was a master at coiling her rope in her teeth to avoid getting it tangled in the branches as she searched for more fruit.

Rain fell softly at first, then increased. By the time Juana and Oscar left their natural umbrella under the tree, rivulets of water were scouring the desert. Whether it was forgetfulness or a vengeful act against his mother, Oscar did not turn the fence gate back on when they left.

The Escape

The human residents of Chaparri mopped themselves up after a night of torrential rain. The road was washed out. Tent walls had collapsed. A crab raised its claws in defense on the trail to the corral, as Heinz moved swiftly past to check on Yinda. Probably out feeding in the wet desert, Heinz thought. But then he noticed something odd. A track in the damp trail, like that of a large boa. His heart sunk. Heinz raced to the corral and confirmed his worst fears. The gate was open and Yinda was nowhere to be seen, just a trail left by her rope. "It's as if my whole world had ended," Heinz confided in me.

Urgent word went out to the community, and the residents responded in kind. Cowboys arrived the following morning with their dogs to give chase to Yinda. The party split up. Pedro Cáceres, Valentín Sanchez, his son Edwin, and the Diaz brothers went up above the corral to the cliffs. Juan Alverez, Eduardo, Vicente, Alejandro, and Daniel Vallejos found a spot where they could safely ford the swollen stream, and searched the foothills of Chaparri. Occasionally the men picked up her rope trail.

On the third day, a bear was spotted on the top of a triangular shaped hill, high up above the fence. Yinda had escaped into the most inaccessible part of Chaparri. Horses had to be abandoned, and the party gave chase on foot. On the fifth day, Pedro announced to Heinz: "We have to get dogs that are more accustomed to the altitude and the rough terrain above. Our dogs' pads are bleeding. Javier has left to get them from the sierra."

"Yinda, come back Yinda. Come back little daughter," echoed across the valley as Juana dragged dried fish on the end of a string through the brush, hoping the scent would attract her daughter's attention. Her only source of love was gone. She had been crying; she was determined to get Yinda back.

The situation looked bleak. Pedro and Valentine rode up to meet Heinz, who was repairing the corral should Yinda appear. Their horses' flanks were wet with sweat. Pedro took off his wide-brimmed straw hat and wiped his face with his yellow T-shirt. "Not so good, Mr. Heinz," he said. "We looked for the bear and we didn't find it anywhere. We went all over on horseback, then on foot. Even in the most inaccessible places."

"Well, it's already more than ten days we've been looking for her, right?" Heinz asked.

"More than ten days," he said.

"You've done well," Heinz told him. "We are all grateful for the effort you have given us."

"Thank you Mr. Heinz. We have to get back to our crop fields. But we are ready to help when you need us." Pedro raised his hat in salute and turned his horse.

Heinz watched him go, thinking the world may not be so near the end. A dozen men had given him days of work without once asking for any pay. He left the corral gate open just in case Yinda might come back to feed in the mango tree. Just then, he saw Valentine turn his horse and come back. "That's a bit odd," he thought.

"Señor."

"What's up, Valentine?"

"I met a man. I don't know if you believe in such things, but he took some medicine…"

"A shaman?" Heinz asked.

"Yes. He doesn't come from here. He comes from the jungle. He took some ayahuaska and saw Yinda in a dream. Perhaps he can help."

"Thank you, Valentine," Heinz said. "Why don't you ask him to come here and we'll see what he can do."

My first reaction when Heinz told me about Regulo Mejia and his dream was, "Here we go again." But why not? Everyone felt hopeless by now, and we didn't have any options. Besides, Heinz believed in the power of the shaman. While he was away on a trip, a shaman told him his car at that very moment was being stolen in front of his house. It was true!

Stories of shamans abound in Chaparri. Ernil Bernal, a man Heinz knew, had a recurrent dream of a woman dressed in black holding two globes in her outstretched hands that cast blinding light. The woman descends a pyramid in one of these dreams. Ernil consulted a shaman who told him to pay close attention to the exact location of his dream. On December 21, 1986 Ernil drank three glasses of San Pedro cactus brew instead of eating his lunch. Later that day, while walking near Sipán, he saw the same woman from his dream descending a large pyramid. Then she flew over his head and alighted on a smaller pyramid nearby. The moon was on the left side, and the sun was behind on the right. The two globes!

A few weeks later, on January 17th, Ernil and his brother Chalo dug seven meters down in the smaller pyramid mound and found 25 sacks full of Moche artifacts, many of them gold. When the police learned about Ernil's discovery, they arranged for his murder and stole the gold. These Moche artifacts were considered the archeological find of the century. Heinz took the photographs for *National Geographic* magazine. Stories like these abound around Chaparri.

In my experience, shamans can be everything from charlatans seeking power to very skilled healers. Generally they absorbed the pain in a community and gave people hope. We needed that, so I cabled some funds to Heinz for Regulo to work his magic.

Regulo arrived three days later. He looked as if he had stepped off a cod trawler in Newfoundland, not from a canoe in the jungle. The drugs and alcohol he had consumed on the job had not been kind to his angular features. But he told Heinz and Javier with conviction that they would find "the little animal." He led them above the corral to the place he had seen in his dream. He stopped at the base of a ledge, a place he had never been before.

"See, I told you my powers would work. Nobody believed me, but here they are," he said, pointing to the drag mark of Yinda's rope. "And it looks like she is not alone."

There were several bear prints on top of the drag mark. "Incredible," Heinz said, shaking his head. "She's been here all along and we never suspected it."

"I'll tell you what I'm going to do," Regulo responded. "I'm going to gather some herbs that grow right here in Chaparri, and we'll drink them. Then you can see Yinda, too."

"Tonight?" Heinz asked.

"Yes, in three to four hours. I'll prepare the herbs."

When Regulo was gone, Heinz told Javier that he wished the rope could be taken off Yinda's neck. "It's like an umbilical cord attached to Juana."

Regulo returned at dusk carrying what looked like a large cucumber. It was a San Pedro cactus. The name "St. Peter" should warn anyone about its potent alkaloids. One or two slices of the stuff boiled up is enough to make anyone travel to where Yinda was. What scared me was seeing the huge bites taken out of the sides of San Pedro cactus up on cliffs. I had little fear of bears, but I was somewhat concerned about meeting a bear drugged on San Pedro up on a cliff edge.

"Are you prepared?" Regulo asked Javier. "That's your house. Don't leave to go to another field."

"I'm ready," Javier responded. "I am anointed, and won't go to anyone else's house."

The men had gathered around a roaring fire, the sparks flying from the crackling mesquite logs. Regulo had boiled up a brew of San Pedro near the corral. He was feeding the men this juice using a sea shell as a ladle.

Sometime past midnight, the men walked the remaining distance to Yinda's corral. There in the moonlight, Yinda was clearly visible to them, making her way from the mango tree toward the upper leg of the fence.

"Quick, get the mother!" Heinz said to Javier.

A reluctant Juana arrived later with Javier. She was furious to be included in such chicanery, and didn't have any faith in Regulo's magic. But the next morning when she was shown the fresh tracks, she redoubled her efforts with her dragged fish.

A Community Discovers its Future

On the 23rd of February, Juana walked up the smoothed boulders of the ravine past the fence. It had been three weeks since Yinda's escape, and she wasn't expecting much. Yinda suddenly dashed in front of her.

"Yinda! Yinda. Come to mamacita!" she yelled excitedly.

Yinda loped up the ravine. Then she turned and ran back, and the two embraced. Juana grabbed what was left of the rope around Yinda's neck. When she got back to the corral, there was a small celebration. Regulo and Javier noticed Yinda had been beaten up on her back and neck.

"The boys got her pretty good." Regulo joked to Juana.

"What do you know, you drunk! Leave my daughter alone!" snapped Juana, as she hauled her prize back to her tent.

"No, no, don't make jokes," Heinz said. "Juana's pretty upset with all that has happened. And besides, I just got word that her sons in Oxapampa are spreading rumors that their mother has found another man, that one of her daughters has just run away with a truck driver… Things are not so good. But great work, Regulo! And I think we ought to have a celebration to thank all the people who have helped."

March came, and with it the sprouts of green leaves. On the morning of the celebration feast, Javier came running down the trail from the corral. He was holding an anteater by the tail that was curling up to swat him with its massive claws.

Juana spent the morning swatting Yinda for the grief she had put her through. Cowboys arrived with their families. Pepi's kitchen resounded with laughter, and the chopping sounds of knives slicing hot peppers. A group of women pawed through rice to remove stones. Soon, cubes of meat from a pig and several goats sizzled in large cauldrons.

Heinz gathered the throng in a wide circle for a moment of silence to thank the mountain spirits, and to honor those who have passed away. He then thanked Regulo and the cowboys for their services, saying to them: "Imagine what is happening just with this animal. Imagine the future, when there are more bears, when there are more deer, when there are white-winged guans, when there are more peccaries, when there are condors and guanacos, and all of that. You'll see, there will be more jobs for everyone... and people from other parts of Peru and the world will come to visit us. That's why I want to thank you, and may you now enjoy our party!"

Heinz walked off to the thunderous applause of 70 people of the community, while I filmed the event with soundman Jose Balado and cameraman Cesar Perez. People said they had come to pay their respects to Chaparri's spirit, but what they really wanted was to see Yinda, the object of all this fuss.

Juana tied her daughter up to a tree at the edge of the festivities. She was unusually standoffish toward the interest of the cowboys, who wanted to engage Yinda's attention. In a quiet moment, Juana untied Yinda's rope from the tree, and they slipped off down the main road. I heard a horse whinny and looked up to see Juana take a side path that led to the corral. I alerted the film crew and we followed.

There was no dawdling to let Yinda sniff or play along the trail. Juana yanked her daughter inside the corral and sat down. To our astonishment, she untied the rope from around Yinda's neck and said: "I am leaving you, Yindita, but I won't forget you, because you were like a daughter to me, the last daughter that I love. Have a great life. Do that for all of us. I want to see you happy the day I return. The rest is up to God, my pretty little girl. Are you listening to everything I am telling you? Your brothers would say, 'Why are you crying, Mama? It's just a wild animal.' But I haven't been able to forget you, my child. So many places yet to see because of you, my child, because of you. I am proud to have served you, my child. Don't forget me."

Juana let go of Yinda's paw for the last time and turned. Yinda bounded up a trail inside the fence, then turned around to watch her human mother slowly walk down the slope, dragging the rope behind her, having done the hardest thing she could have done.

Yinda escaped once more on the last day of March, and was again recaptured. Then I got word from Heinz that a circus had arrived in the nearby town of Mocupe. "And they have two bears!"

"What, you don't mean?! Heinz, we have no money to take care of Yinda, let alone two more bears!"

I might as well have been talking to a stone. Heinz not only wanted these two bears, he wanted lots of them: to breed them in captivity, and repopulate the entire region with bears. I thought the repopulation was warranted in extreme cases where numbers were low, but not in Peru, not yet. However, this wasn't about science-based management. This was propaganda. Both Heinz and INRENA could send the message that they were really doing something for bears. The message for the residents of Santa Catalina was also powerful, as I was soon to regret financially.

On the 23rd of April 2000, two heavy crates were hand-carried nearly a kilometer to what now had become known as the Chaparri Bear Sanctuary. Inside the crates were not the two circus bears, but two other captive bears that Heinz earlier had taken me to see at a rice factory in Lima. At the factory, the bears were a dreadful sight. The old male of the pair had a bloated stomach, long claws that curled around and entered his pads, and mangy fur covered in flies. He hadn't even raised his head when his bear caretaker at the factory poured a fresh batch of carrots into the cement pit.

A younger female responded by moving stiffly towards us. She had spent almost all of those eight years in this tiny hole with her older cellmate. And now the pair had come to Chaparri.

Dr. Lydia Kolter had given us instructions about how to introduce the bears to an electrified corral, but despite this the female panicked. She ran through various parts of the fence before she died of a heart attack. Domingo, the old male, got shocked a few times and then settled down.

Yinda, who watched from her separate enclosure as the new bears arrived, bolted through the fence. She went over to an adjacent ravine where workers were finishing a large enclosure made from fishing nets. The nets were stretched across the ravine, where several fig trees grew. When finished, the enclosures would allow Gustavo's captive guans to become adapted to their wild habitat before they would be released. Yinda proceeded to eat all the workers' food, and then spent a week above the corral before wandering off. We were all depressed by what had happened—one dead bear, one escaped. Silently I was elated for Yinda, though concerned that she would be shot in a nearby cornfield. The corn was ripe now and she had been raised on it!

Heinz came up with a brilliant plan to protect her. "We'll start a soccer tournament," he announced. "Men, women, and children, from every hamlet. The rules will be simple. If a player kills a bear or allows a bear to be killed in their hamlet, that team will be disqualified."

Within months, 50 teams were playing in T-shirts with the words "El oso es agua" printed on the back ("The bear is water"). This reinforced the relationship between saving the forest, and preventing spring floods and dry streambeds. The tournament had the added benefit of getting people from distant parts of the community together every Sunday.

Within months, the military and other hunters were being thrown out of community lands by players responding to the no-kill soccer rules. For now, Yinda and her kind would be safer. But their future safety depended on creating jobs, and fast. This wasn't going to be easy. And then, the workers hired to fix the fence snuck past Javier when Heinz was away, and stole the solar panel, battery, and regulator. I responded by telling Heinz, "No more bears! And how come Domingo didn't escape?"

"Oh, he's so happy," Heinz replied. "He hasn't even tried to escape. You wouldn't believe the difference in him. His coat is starting to come back. He looks great. He now walks around."

Barely a week later, on the third of June, I get a call from Heinz. "Guess what?" he says.

"What?" I said stupidly.

"We got two more bears!"

"What!! We don't even have electricity in the corral!"

"Yes, two more bears. Remember that circus I told you about in Mocupe? Well, the townspeople went over and took the bears away, and gave them to us. The bears are in Javier's house. His whole family is taking care of them."

By now, the community was so charged up by newspaper reports of their actions rescuing bears that no captive bear owner was safe. Bears came from everywhere. A cub Heinz named Cha Cha crawled out of the busted crate from an overturned circus truck near Tierras Blancas. Tongo came from Luya, 250 kilometers away. Rosita came from the Lima Zoo, but previously was part of a Chilean circus. Cholita was found in someone's house 60 kilometers away. However, the most amazing story belonged to Milagros (Miracles). This tiny cub was picked up by a rescue team investigating a plane crash on Mt. Coloque in the Chachapoyas region, a day's drive from Chaparri. Her mother was presumed killed in the fireball, but the cub miraculously survived.

Chaparri's reputation had spread widely. The corral was loaded with bears. Male bears were fighting each other for the attention of females. We had, we realized, moved the circus *inside* the corral. I now rued the day I had agreed to buy Yinda, having by now spent, as I predicted, those several national park budgets, many times over.

Heinz was in much worse shape. His eyesight was failing, leaving him no option to go back to his photography. A farm he owned in the jungle, land that could support his family, was overrun by thousands of colonizers. These in turn had bought his property illegally from a few dozen Sendero Luminosa guerillas posing as owners. When he tried to remove them, someone threw a rock and broke his skull.

As was our custom, Heinz and I would meet up in Chaparri and debate about what to do. One Sunday, during a return trip from Chaparri, Regulo leaned into the passenger window of Heinz's car, where I was sitting. A fog of alcohol accompanied his words. "Gringo, Chaparri will survive. Don't despair! It will work."

And work it did. The residents of Santa Catalina gathered and decided to designate almost all of their land to protect Yinda and the forest they both depended on for survival. The Peruvian government responded in kind by creating a new park category for communities, and by giving Santa Catalina rights to their own water. The day after Christmas in 2001, the Ecological Reserve of Chaparri was formerly declared, with 34,412 hectares (86,000 acres).

That same year, Gustavo released eight pairs of guans to the forest from the large netted enclosure. Over 1000 tourists arrived to celebrate these achievements and see the captive bears. Many of these visitors were schoolchildren.

Most of the cattle owned by outsiders were removed from Chaparri's slopes. The forest there started to recover. I released the movie *Hands and Claws,* which told this story, a success story that none of us could have imagined. The rains arrived and people settled into the rhythm of preparing for another year of planting. Valentine continued to look after his cattle on Chaparri's slopes. During the spring, after the park was created, he heard a rustling, looked down, and recognized Yinda from the yellow blotch on her nose. She ambled along by the side of his horse for several minutes, pushing her cub in front of her.

More about Spectacled Bears
from Bear Trust International
Bear Trust is solely responsible for the information in this section. Opinions about this information may vary.

Spectacled Bear - *Tremarctos Ornatus*

Other Names: Short-faced bear, Andean bear, Ucumari

Appearance:
Spectacled bears are small and dark, ranging in color from black to brown; some spectacled bears have a reddish tinge. They have distinctive circular or semicircular creamy white markings (spectacles) on the face around the eyes.

Size:
Male spectacled bears are much larger than female spectacled bears, giving local farmers the impression that they live with more than one species of bear. Male bears weigh from 120 to 340 pounds 54 to 154 kg); females weigh 60 to 180 pounds (27 to 82 kg). At birth, cubs weigh from 10 to 11 ounces (284 to 312 grams). Longevity can be 25 years or longer.

Reproduction:
Females reach sexual maturity between four and seven years of age. Spectacled bears have a variable mating season, and litters range in size from one to three. Most cubs are born from November to February.

Social Life:
Little is known of the social organization in the wild.

Food:
The preferred diet is leaves, bases and hearts of plants of the Bromeliaceae family, and the fruits of other plant groups. Spectacled bears will also predate on a wide variety of foods, including livestock, fish, and rodents.

Habitat:
Spectacled bears are highly adaptable, and inhabit a wide range of habitats including rainforest, cloud forest, dry forest, steppe lands, and coastal scrub desert. They live in a range of altitudes from 600 to 13,800 feet 182 to 4,206 meters), preferring cloud forests between 4,500 and 8,800 feet (1,372 to 2,682 meters), and high elevation grasslands at the upper edge of the forest. They are found mainly in or near forested mountains from Venezuela and Columbia south through Ecuador, Peru, and into Bolivia.

Wild Population:
Estimated at 18,000 and decreasing due to loss of habitat.

FYI:
Spectacled bears often construct tree nests, which they use as sleeping and feeding platforms.

The spectacled bear is the second largest mammal and the largest carnivore in South America. It is the only bear found in South America.

In captivity, females and cubs vocalize using two and five types of calls respectively.

There is no evidence that spectacled bears hibernate.

In the Louisiana Canebrakes
President Theodore Roosevelt
American Black Bear

Theodore Roosevelt, the 26th President of the United States, spent two weeks on a bear hunt in Louisiana during his presidency. This is his account of that experience. Roosevelt was a renowned sportsman and conservationist, and founder of the Boone and Crockett Club. And of course, he was the inspiration for that especially endearing bear, the Teddy Bear, which turned 100 years old in 2002. Thanks to the Theodore Roosevelt Association for their assistance in reprinting this piece.

In October, 1907, I spent a fortnight in the canebrakes of northern Louisiana, my hosts being Messrs. John M. Parker and John A. McIlhenny. Surgeon-General Rixey, of the United States Navy, and Doctor Alexander Lambert were with me. I was especially anxious to kill a bear in these canebrakes after the fashion of the old Southern planters, who for a century past have followed the bear with horse and hound and horn in Louisiana, Mississippi, and Arkansas. Our first camp was on Tensas Bayou. This is in the heart of the great alluvial bottom-land created during the countless ages through which the mighty Mississippi has poured out of the heart of the continent. It is in the black belt of the South, in which the negroes outnumber the whites four or five to one, the disproportion in the region in which I was actually hunting being far greater. There is no richer soil in all the earth; and when, as will soon be the case, the chances of disaster from flood are over, I believe the whole land will be cultivated and densely peopled. At present the possibility of such flood is a terrible deterrent to settlement, for when the Father of Waters breaks his boundaries he turns the country for a breadth of eighty miles into one broad river, the plantations throughout all this vast extent being from five to twenty feet under water. Cotton is the staple industry, corn also being grown, while there are a few rice fields and occasional small patches of sugar cane. The plantations are for the most part of large size and tilled by negro tenants for the white owners. Conditions are still in some respects like those of the pioneer days. The magnificent forest growth which covers the land is of little value because of the difficulty in getting the trees to market, and the land is actually worth more after the timber has been removed than before. In consequence, the larger trees are often killed by girdling, where the work of felling them would entail disproportionate cost and labor. At dusk, with the sunset glimmering in the west, or in the brilliant moonlight when the moon is full, the cottonfields have a strange spectral look, with the dead trees raising aloft their naked branches. The cottonfields themselves, when the bolls burst open, seem almost as if whitened by snow; and the red and white flowers, interspersed among the burst-open pods, make the whole field beautiful. The rambling one-story houses, surrounded by outbuildings, have a picturesqueness all their own; their very looks betoken the lavish, whole-hearted, generous hospitality of the planters who dwell therein.

Beyond the end of cultivation towers the great forest. Wherever the water stands in pools, and by the edges of the lakes and bayous, the giant cypress loom aloft, rivalled in size by some of the red gums and white oaks. In stature, in towering majesty, they are unsurpassed by any trees of our eastern forests; lordlier kings of the green-leaved world are not to be found until we reach the sequoias and redwoods of the Sierras. Among them grow many other trees--hackberry, thorn, honey locust, tupelo, pecan, and ash. In the cypress sloughs the singular knees of the trees stand two or three feet above the black ooze. Palmettos grow thickly in places. The canebrakes stretch along the slight rises of ground, often extending for miles, forming one of the most striking and interesting features of the country. They choke out other growths, the feathery, graceful canes standing in ranks, tall, slender, serried, each but a few inches from his brother, and springing to a height of fifteen or twenty feet. They look like bamboos; they are well-nigh impenetrable to a man on horseback; even on foot they make difficult walking unless free use is made of the heavy bush-knife. It is impossible to see through them for more than fifteen or twenty paces, and often for not half that distance. Bears make their lairs in them, and they are the refuge for hunted things. Outside of them, in the swamp, bushes of many kinds grow thick among the tall trees, and vines and creepers climb the trunks and hang in trailing festoons from the branches. Here, likewise, the bush-knife is in constant play, as the skilled horsemen thread their way, often at a gallop, in and out among the great tree trunks, and through the dense, tangled, thorny undergrowth.

In the lakes and larger bayous we saw alligators and garfish; and monstrous snapping turtles, fearsome brutes of the slime, as heavy as a man, and with huge horny beaks that with a single snap could take off a man's hand or foot. One of the planters with us had lost part of his hand by the bite of an alligator; and had seen a companion seized by the foot by a huge garfish from which he was rescued with the utmost difficulty by his fellow swimmers. There were black bass in the waters, too, and they gave us many a good meal. Thick-bodied water moccasins, foul and dangerous, kept near the water; and farther back in the swamp we found and killed rattlesnakes and copperheads. Coon and 'possum were very plentiful, and in the streams there were minks and a few otters. Black squirrels barked in the tops of the tall trees or descended to the ground to gather nuts or gnaw the shed deer antlers--the latter a habit they shared with the wood rats. To me the most interesting of the smaller mammals, however, were the swamp rabbits, which are thoroughly amphibious in their habits, not only swimming but diving, and taking to the water almost as freely as if they were muskrats. They lived in the depths of the woods and beside the lonely bayous.

Birds were plentiful. Mocking-birds abounded in the clearings, where, among many sparrows of more common kind, I saw the painted finch, the gaudily colored brother of our little indigo bunting, though at this season his plumage was faded and dim. In the thick woods where we hunted there were many cardinal birds and winter wrens, both in full song. Thrashers were even more common; but so cautious that it was rather difficult to see them, in spite of their incessant clucking and calling and their occasional bursts of song. There were crowds of warblers and vireos of many different kinds, evidently migrants from the North, and generally silent. The most characteristic birds, however, were the woodpeckers, of which there were seven or eight species, the commonest around our camp being the handsome red-bellied, the brother of the red-head which we saw in the clearings. The most notable birds and those which most interested me were the great ivory-billed woodpeckers. Of these I saw three, all of them in groves of giant cypress; their brilliant white bills contrasted finely with the black of their general plumage. They were noisy but wary, and they seemed to me to set off the wildness of the swamp as much as any of the beasts of the chase. Among the birds of prey the commonest were the barred owls, which I have never elsewhere found so plentiful. Their hooting and yelling were heard all around us throughout the night, and once one of them hooted at intervals for several minutes at mid-day. One of these owls had caught and was devouring a snake in the late afternoon, while it was still daylight. In the dark nights and still mornings and evenings their cries seemed strange and unearthly, the long hoots varied by screeches, and by all kinds of uncanny noises.

At our first camp our tents were pitched by the bayou. For four days the weather was hot, with steaming rains; after that it grew cool and clear. Huge biting flies, bigger than bees, attacked our horses, but the insect plagues, so veritable a scourge in this country during the months of warm weather, had well-nigh vanished in the first few weeks of the fall. The morning after we reached camp we were joined by Ben Lilley, the hunter, a spare, full-bearded man, with mild, gentle, blue eyes and a frame of steel and whipcord. I never met any other man so indifferent to fatigue and hardship. He equalled Cooper's Deerslayer in woodcraft, in hardihood, in simplicity--and also in loquacity. The morning he joined us in camp, he had come on foot through the thick woods, followed by his two dogs, and had neither eaten nor drunk for twenty-four hours; for he did not like to drink the swamp water. It had rained hard throughout the night and he had no shelter, no rubber coat, nothing but the clothes he was wearing, and the ground was too wet for him to lie on; so he perched in a crooked tree in the beating rain, much as if he had been a wild turkey. But he was not in the least tired when he struck camp; and, though he slept an hour after breakfast, it was chiefly because he had nothing else to do, inasmuch as it was Sunday, on which day he never hunted nor labored. He could run through the woods like a buck, was far more enduring, and quite as indifferent to weather, though he was over fifty years old. He had trapped and hunted throughout almost all the half century of his life, and on trail of game he was as sure as his own hounds. His observations on wild creatures were singularly close and accurate. He was particularly fond of the chase of the bear, which he followed by himself, with one or two dogs; often he would be on the trail of his quarry for days at a time, lying down to sleep wherever night overtook him; and he had killed over a hundred and twenty bears.

Late in the evening of the same day we were joined by two gentlemen, to whom we owed the success of our hunt. They were Messrs. Clive and Harley Metcalf, planters from Mississippi, men in the prime of life, thorough woodsmen and hunters, skilled marksmen, and utterly fearless horsemen. For a quarter of a century they had hunted bear and deer with horse and hound, and were masters of the art. They brought with them their pack of bearhounds, only one, however, being a thoroughly stanch and seasoned veteran. The pack was under the immediate control of a negro hunter, Holt Collier, in his own way as remarkable a character as Ben Lilley. He was a man of sixty and could neither read nor write, but he had all the dignity of an African chief, and for half a century he had been a bear hunter, having killed or assisted in killing over three thousand bears. He had been born a slave on the Hinds plantation, his father, an old man when he was born, having been the body-servant and cook of "old General Hinds," as he called him, when the latter fought under Jackson at New Orleans. When ten years old Holt had been taken on the horse behind his young master, the Hinds of that day, on a bear hunt, when he killed his first bear. In the Civil War he had not only followed his master to battle as his body-servant, but had acted under him as sharpshooter against the Union soldiers. After the war he continued to stay with his master until the latter died, and had then been adopted by the Metcalfs; and he felt that he had brought them up, and treated them with that mixture of affection and grumbling respect which an old nurse shows toward the lad who has ceased being a child. The two Metcalfs and Holt understood one another thoroughly, and understood their hounds and the game their hounds followed almost as thoroughly.

They had killed many deer and wild-cat, and now and then a panther; but their favorite game was the black bear, which, until within a very few years, was extraordinarily plentiful in the swamps and canebrakes on both sides of the lower Mississippi, and which is still found here and there, although in greatly diminished numbers. In Louisiana and Mississippi the bears go into their dens toward the end of January, usually in hollow trees, often very high up in living trees, but often also in great logs that lie rotting on the ground. They come forth toward the end of April, the cubs having been born in the interval. At this time the bears are nearly as fat, so my informants said, as when they enter their dens in January; but they lose their fat very rapidly. On first coming out in the spring they usually eat ash buds and the tender young cane called mutton cane, and at that season they generally refuse to eat the acorns even when they are plentiful. According to my informants it is at this season that they are most apt to take to killing stock, almost always the hogs which run wild or semi-wild in the woods. They are very individual in their habits, however; many of them never touch stock, while others, usually old he-bears, may kill numbers of hogs; in one case an old he-bear began this hog killing just as soon as he left his den. In the summer months they find but little to eat, and it is at this season that they are most industrious in hunting for grubs, insects, frogs, and small mammals. In some neighborhoods they do not eat fish, while in other places, perhaps not far away, they not only greedily eat dead fish, but will themselves kill fish if they can find them in shallow pools left by the receding waters. As soon as the mast is on the ground they begin to feed upon it, and when the acorns and pecans are plentiful they eat nothing else, though at first berries of all kinds and grapes are eaten also. When in November they have begun only to eat the acorns they put on fat as no other wild animal does, and by the end of December a full-grown bear may weigh at least twice as much as it does in August, the difference being as great as between a very fat and a lean hog. Old he-bears which in August weigh three hundred pounds and upward will toward the end of December weigh six hundred pounds, and even more in exceptional cases. Bears vary greatly in their habits in different localities, in addition to the individual variation among those of the same neighborhood. Around Avery Island, John McIlhenny's plantation, the bears only appear from June to November; there they never kill hogs, but feed at first on corn and then on sugar-cane, doing immense damage in the fields, quite as much as hogs would do. But when we were on the Tensas we visited a family of settlers who lived right in the midst of the forest ten miles from any neighbors; and although bears were plentiful around them they never molested their corn-fields--in which the coons, however, did great damage.

A big bear is cunning, and is a dangerous fighter to the dogs. It is only in exceptional cases, however, that these black bears, even when wounded and at bay, are dangerous to men, in spite of their formidable strength. Each of the hunters with whom I was camped had been charged by one or two among the scores or hundreds of bears he had slain, but no one of them had ever been injured, although they knew other men who had been injured. Their immunity was due to their own skill and coolness; for when the dogs were around the bear the hunter invariably ran close in so as to kill the bear at once and save the pack. Each of the Metcalfs had on one occasion killed a large bear with a knife, when the hounds had seized it and the man dared not fire for fear of shooting one of them. They had in their younger days hunted with a General Hamberlin, a Mississippi planter whom they well knew, who was then already an old man. He was passionately addicted to the chase of the bear, not only because of the sport it afforded, but also in a certain way as a matter of vengeance; for his father, also a keen bear-hunter, had been killed by a bear. It was an old he, which he had wounded and which had been bayed by the dogs; it attacked him, throwing him down and biting him so severely that he died a couple of days later. This was in 1847. Mr. W. H. Lambeth sends the following account of the fatal encounter:

I send you an extract from the 'Brother Jonathan,' published in New York in 1847:

" 'Dr. Monroe Hamberlin, Robert Wilson, Joe Brazeil, and others left Satartia, Miss., and in going up Big Sunflower River, met Mr. Leiser and his party of hunters returning to Vicksburg. Mr. Leiser told Dr. Hamberlin that he saw the largest bear track at the big Mound on Lake George that he ever saw, and was afraid to tackle him. Dr. Hamberlin said, "I never saw one that I was afraid to tackle." Dr. Hamberlin landed his skiff at the Mound and his dogs soon bayed the bear. Dr. Hamberlin fired and the ball glanced on the bear's head. The bear caught him by the right thigh and tore all the flesh off. He drew his knife and the bear crushed his right arm. He cheered the dogs and they pulled the bear off. The bear whipped the dogs and attacked him the third time, biting him in the hollow back of his neck. Mr. Wilson came up and shot the bear dead on Dr. Hamberlin. The party returned to Satartia, but Dr. Hamberlin told them to put the bear in the skiff, that he would not leave without his antagonist. The bear weighed 640 pounds.'

"Dr. Hamberlin lived three days. I knew all the parties. His son John and myself hunted with them in 1843 and 1844, when we were too small to carry a gun."

A large bear is not afraid of dogs, and an old he, or a she with cubs, is always on the lookout for a chance to catch and kill any dog that comes near enough. While lean and in good running condition it is not an easy matter to bring a bear to bay; but as they grow fat they become steadily less able to run, and the young ones, and even occasionally a full-grown she, will then readily tree. If a man is not near by, a big bear that has become tired will treat the pack with whimsical indifference. The Metcalfs recounted to me how they had once seen a bear, which had been chased quite a time, evidently make up its mind that it needed a rest and could afford to take it without much regard for the hounds. The bear accordingly selected a small opening and lay flat on its back with its nose and all its four legs extended. The dogs surrounded it in frantic excitement, barking and baying, and gradually coming m a ring very close up. The bear was watching, however, and suddenly sat up with a jerk, frightening the dogs nearly into fits. Half of them turned back-somersaults in their panic, and all promptly gave the bear ample room. The bear having looked about, lay flat on its back again, and the pack gradually regaining courage once more closed in. At first the bear, which was evidently reluctant to arise, kept them at a distance by now and then thrusting an unexpected paw toward them; and when they became too bold it sat up with a jump and once more put them all to flight.

For several days we hunted perseveringly around this camp on the Tensas Bayou, but without success. Deer abounded, but we could find no bear; and of the deer we killed only what we actually needed for use in camp. I killed one myself by a good shot, in which, however, I fear that the element of luck played a considerable part. We had started as usual by sunrise, to be gone all day; for we never counted upon returning to camp before sunset. For an hour or two we threaded our way, first along an indistinct trail, and then on an old disused road, the hardy woods horses keeping on a running walk without much regard to the difficulties of the ground. The disused road lay right across a great canebrake, and while some of the party went around the cane with the dogs, the rest of us strung out along the road so as to get a shot at any bear that might come across it. I was following Harley Metcalf, with John McIlhenny and Doctor Rixey behind on the way to their posts, when we heard in the far-off distance two of the younger hounds, evidently on the trail of a deer. Almost immediately afterward a crash in the bushes at our right hand and behind us made me turn around, and I saw a deer running across the few feet of open space; and as I leaped from my horse it disappeared in the cane. I am a rather deliberate shot, and under any circumstances a rifle is not the best weapon for snap shooting, while there is no kind of shooting more difficult than on running game in a canebrake. Luck favored me in this instance, however, for there was a spot a little ahead of where the deer entered in which the cane was thinner, and I kept my rifle on its indistinct, shadowy outline until it reached this spot; it then ran quartering away from me, which made my shot much easier, although I could only catch its general outline through the cane. But the 45-70 which I was using is a powerful gun and shoots right through cane or bushes; and as soon as I pulled the trigger the deer, with a bleat, turned a tremendous somersault and was dead when we reached it. I was not a little pleased that my bullet should have sped so true when I was making my first shot in company with my hard-riding, straight-shooting planter friends.

But no bear were to be found. We waited long hours on likely stands. We rode around the canebrakes through the swampy jungle, or threaded our way across them on trails cut by the heavy wood-knives of my companions; but we found nothing. Until the trails were cut the canebrakes were impenetrable to a horse and were difficult enough to a man on foot. On going through them it seemed as if we must be in the tropics; the silence, the stillness, the heat, and the obscurity, all combining to give a certain eeriness to the task, as we chopped our winding way slowly through the dense mass of close-growing, feather-fronded stalks. Each of the hunters prided himself on his skill with the horn, which was an essential adjunct of the hunt, used both to summon and control the hounds, and for signalling among the hunters themselves. The tones of many of the horns were full and musical; and it was pleasant to hear them as they wailed to one another, backward and forward, across the great stretches of lonely swamp and forest.

A few days convinced us that it was a waste of time to stay longer where we were. Accordingly, early one morning we hunters started for a new camp fifteen or twenty miles to the southward, on Bear Lake. We took the hounds with us, and each man carried what he chose or could in his saddle-pockets, while his slicker was on his horse's back behind him. Otherwise we took absolutely nothing in the way of supplies, and the negroes with the tents and camp equipage were three days before they overtook us. On our way down we were joined by Major Amacker and Doctor Miller, with a small pack of cathounds. These were good deer dogs and they ran down and killed on the ground a goodsized bob-cat--a wildcat, as it is called in the South. It was a male and weighed twenty-three and a half pounds. It had just killed and eaten a large rabbit. The stomachs of the deer we killed, by the way, contained acorns and leaves. Our new camp was beautifully situated on the bold, steep bank of Bear Lake--a tranquil stretch of water, part of an old river-bed, a couple of hundred yards broad, with a winding length of several miles. Giant cypress grew at the edge of the water, the singular cypress knees rising in every direction round about, while at the bottoms of the trunks themselves were often cavernous hollows opening beneath the surface of the water, some of them serving as dens for alligators. There was a waxing moon, so that the nights were as beautiful as the days.

From our new camp we hunted as steadily as from the old. We saw bear sign, but not much of it, and only one or two fresh tracks. One day the hounds jumped a bear, probably a yearling from the way it ran; for at this season a yearling or a two-year-old will run almost like a deer, keeping to the thick cane as long as it can and then bolting across through the bushes of the ordinary swamp land until it can reach another canebrake. After a three hours' run this particular animal managed to get clear away without one of the hunters ever seeing it, and it ran until all the dogs were tired out. A day or two afterward one of the other members of the party shot a small yearling--that is, a bear which would have been two years old in the following February. It was very lean, weighing but fifty-five pounds. The finely-chewed acorns in its stomach showed that it was already beginning to find mast. We had seen the tracks of an old she in the neighborhood, and the next morning we started to hunt her out. I went with Clive Metcalf. We had been joined overnight by Mr. Ichabod Osborn and his son Tom, two Louisiana planters, with six or eight hounds--or rather bear dogs, for in these packs most of the animals are of mixed blood, and, as with all packs that are used in the genuine hunting of the wilderness, pedigree counts for nothing as compared with steadiness, courage, and intelligence.

There were only two of the new dogs that were really stanch bear dogs. The father of Ichabod Osborn had taken up the plantation upon which they were living in 1811, only a few years after Louisiana became part of the United States, and young Osborn was now the third in line from father to son who had steadily hunted bears in this immediate neighborhood.

On reaching the cypress slough near which the tracks of the old she had been seen the day before, Clive Metcalf and I separated from the others and rode off at a lively pace between two of the canebrakes. After an hour or two's wait we heard, very far off, the notes of one of the loudest-mouthed hounds, and instantly rode toward it, until we could make out the babel of the pack. Some hard galloping brought us opposite the point toward which they were heading--for experienced hunters can often tell the probable line of a bear's flight, and the spots at which it will break cover. But on this occasion the bear shied off from leaving the thick cane and doubled back; and soon the hounds were once more out of hearing, while we galloped desperately around the edge of the cane. The tough woods-horses kept their feet like cats as they leaped logs, plunged through bushes, and dodged in and out among the tree trunks; and we had all we could do to prevent the vines from lifting us out of the saddle, while the thorns tore our hands and faces. Hither and thither we went, now at a trot, now at a run, now stopping to listen for the pack. Occasionally we could hear the hounds, and then off we would go racing through the forest toward the point for which we thought they were heading. Finally, after a couple of hours of this, we came up on one side of a canebrake on the other side of which we could hear not only the pack but the yelling and cheering of Harley Metcalf and Tom Osborn and one or two of the negro hunters, all of whom were trying to keep the dogs up to their work in the thick cane. Again we rode ahead, and now in a few minutes were rewarded by hearing the leading dogs come to bay in the thickest of the cover. Having galloped as near to the spot as we could, we threw ourselves off the horses and plunged into the cane, trying to cause as little disturbance as possible, but of course utterly unable to avoid making some noise. Before we were within gunshot, however, we could tell by the sounds that the bear had once again started, making what is called a "walking bay." Clive Metcalf, a finished bear hunter, was speedily able to determine what the bear's probable course would be, and we stole through the cane until we came to a spot near which he thought the quarry would pass. Then we crouched down, I with my rifle at the ready. Nor did we have long to wait. Peering through the thick-growing stalks I suddenly made out the dim outline of the bear coming straight toward us; and noiselessly I cocked and half-raised my rifle, waiting for a clearer chance. In a few seconds it came; the bear turned almost broadside to me, and walked forward very stiff-legged, almost as if on tiptoe, now and then looking back at the nearest dogs. These were two in number--Rowdy, a very deep-voiced hound, in the lead, and Queen, a shrill-tongued brindled bitch, a little behind. Once or twice the bear paused as she looked back at them, evidently hoping that they would come so near that by a sudden race she could catch one of them. But they were too wary.

All of this took but a few moments, and as I saw the bear quite distinctly some twenty yards off, I fired for behind the shoulder. Although I could see her outline, yet the cane was so thick that my sight was on it and not on the bear itself. But I knew my bullet would go true; and, sure enough, at the crack of the rifle the bear stumbled and fell forward, the bullet having passed through both lungs and out at the opposite side. Immediately the dogs came running forward at full speed, and we raced forward likewise lest the pack should receive damage. The bear had but a minute or two to live, yet even in that time more than one valuable hound might lose its life; so when within half a dozen steps of the black, angered beast, I fired again, breaking the spine at the root of the neck; and down went the bear stark dead, slain in the canebrake in true hunter fashion. One by one the hounds struggled up and fell on their dead quarry, the noise of the worry filling the air. Then we dragged the bear out to the edge of the cane, and my companion wound his horn to summon the other hunters. This was a big she-bear, very lean, and weighing two hundred and two pounds. In her stomach were palmetto berries, beetles, and a little mutton cane, but chiefly acorns chewed up in a fine brown mass. John McIlhenny had killed a she-bear about the size of this on his plantation at Avery's Island the previous June. Several bear had been raiding his corn-fields, and one evening he determined to try to waylay them. After dinner he left the ladies of his party on the gallery of his house while he rode down in a hollow and concealed himself on the lower side of the corn-field. Before he had waited ten minutes a she-bear and her cub came into the field. The she rose on her hind legs, tearing down an armful of ears of corn which she seemingly gave to the cub, and then rose for another armful. McIlhenny shot her; tried in vain to catch the cub; and rejoined the party on the veranda, having been absent but one hour.

After the death of my bear I had only a couple of days left. We spent them a long distance from camp, having to cross two bayous before we got to the hunting grounds. I missed a shot at a deer, seeing little more than the flicker of its white tail through the dense bushes; and the pack caught and killed a very lean two-year-old bear weighing eighty pounds. Near a beautiful pond called Panther Lake we found a deer-lick, the ground not merely bare, but furrowed into hollows by the tongues of the countless generations of deer that had frequented the place. We also passed a huge mound, the only hillock in the entire district; it was the work of man, for it had been built in the unknown past by those unknown people whom we call mound-builders. On the trip, all told, we killed and brought into camp three bear, six deer, a wild-cat, a turkey, a possum, and a dozen squirrels; and we ate everything except the wild-cat. In the evenings we sat around the blazing camp-fires, and, as always on such occasions, each hunter told tales of his adventures and of the strange feats and habits of the beasts of the wilderness. There had been beaver all through this delta in the old days, and a very few are still left in out-of-the-way places.

One Sunday morning we saw two wolves, I think young of the year, appear for a moment on the opposite side of the bayou, but they vanished before we could shoot. All of our party had had a good deal of experience with wolves. The Metcalfs had had many sheep killed by them, the method of killing being invariably by a single bite which tore open the throat while the wolf ran beside his victim. The wolves also killed young hogs, but were very cautious about meddling with an old sow; while one of the big half-wild boars that ranged free through the woods had no fear of any number of wolves. Their endurance and the extremely difficult nature of the country made it difficult to hunt them, and the hunters all bore them a grudge, because if a hound got lost in a region where wolves were at all plentiful they were almost sure to find and kill him before he got home. They were fond of preying on dogs, and at times would boldly kill the hounds right ahead of the hunters. In one instance, while the dogs were following a bear and were but a couple of hundred yards in front of the horsemen, a small party of wolves got in on them and killed two. One of the Osborns, having a valuable hound which was addicted to wandering in the woods, saved him from the wolves by putting a bell on him. The wolves evidently suspected a trap and would never go near the dog.

On one occasion another of his hounds got loose with a chain on, and they found him a day or two afterward unharmed, his chain having become entangled in the branches of a bush. One or two wolves had evidently walked around and around the imprisoned dog, but the chain had awakened their suspicions and they had not pounced on him. They had killed a yearling heifer a short time before, on Osborn's plantation, biting her in the hams. It has been my experience that foxhounds as a rule are afraid of attacking a wolf; but all of my friends assured me that their dogs, if a sufficient number of them were together, would tackle a wolf without hesitation; the packs, however, were always composed, to the extent of at least half, of dogs which, though part hound, were part shepherd or bull or some other breed. Doctor Miller had hunted in Arkansas with a pack specially trained after the wolf. There were twenty-eight of them all told, and on this hunt they ran down and killed unassisted four full-grown wolves, although some of the hounds were badly cut. None of my companions had ever known of wolves actually molesting men, but Mr. Ichabod Osborn's son-in-law had a queer adventure with wolves while riding alone through the woods one late afternoon. His horse acting nervously, he looked about and saw that five wolves were coming toward him. One was a bitch, the other four were males. They seemed to pay little heed to him, and he shot one of the males, which crawled off. The next minute the bitch ran straight toward him and was almost at his stirrup when he killed her. The other three wolves, instead of running away, jumped to and fro, growling, with their hair bristling, and he killed two of them; whereupon the survivor at last made off. He brought the scalps of the three dead wolves home with him.

Near our first camp was the carcass of a deer, a yearling buck, which had been killed by a cougar. When first found, the wounds on the carcass showed that the deer had been killed by a bite in the neck at the back of the head; but there were scratches on the rump as if the panther had landed on its back. One of the negro hunters, Brutus Jackson, evidently a trustworthy man, told me that he had twice seen cougars, each time under unexpected conditions. Once he saw a bob-cat race up a tree, and riding toward it saw a panther reared up against the trunk. The panther looked around at him quite calmly, and then retired in leisurely fashion. Jackson went off to get some hounds and when he returned two hours afterward the bob-cat was still up the tree, evidently so badly scared that he did not wish to come down. The hounds were unable to follow the cougar. On another occasion he heard a tremendous scuffle and immediately afterward saw a big doe racing along with a small cougar literally riding it. The cougar was biting the neck, but low down near the shoulders; he was hanging on with his front paws, but was tearing away with his hind claws, so that the deer's hair appeared to fill the air. As soon as Jackson appeared the panther left the deer. He shot it, and the doe galloped off, apparently without serious injury.

**More about American Black Bears
from Bear Trust International**
Bear Trust is solely responsible for the information in this section. Opinions about this information may vary.

American Black Bear – *Ursus Americanus*

Other names: Kermode, glacier, and cinnamon bear all refer to particular color phases of the American black bear.

Appearance:
The American Black Bear is a medium-sized bear with a brown muzzle. It often has a white patch or "V" on the chest. Although black is the predominant color, chocolate and cinnamon brown color phases are also common. Black bears have strong curved claws for climbing, digging, and tearing logs. Their facial profile is relatively straight to slightly convex.

Size:
Adult males usually weigh from 150 to 650 pounds (68 to 295 kg), and females from 100 to 400 pounds (45 to 181 kg). Adults will grow to an average of 45 – 75 inches in length (114 cm to 191 cm), from nose to tail. Black bears in many eastern populations are larger than their western counterparts due to their access to fruiting trees like beechnut and oak. Longevity in the wild can be over 30 years old, though females stop reproducing in their mid-to-late 20s.

Reproduction:
Females typically produce their first cubs at 3 to 7 years of age, depending
on their general level of nutrition. Males reach sexual maturity at 3 to 5
years old. Litter size ranges from one to five, with two to three as average.
Cubs are born in the den in January and remain with their mothers until
they are 16 to 17 months old.

Social Life:
American black bears are solitary except for females with cubs. However,
bears will feed in close proximity to each other, sometimes in large
numbers, if food is abundant and concentrated in a small area.

Food:
American black bears are omnivorous, and feed on a wide range of foods,
depending upon availability. The bulk of their diet consists of emergent
green vegetation in the spring and a variety of berries and nuts in the
summer. In some places, predation on insects, deer fawns, elk and moose
calves, and salmon, provides an important part of the diet.

Habitat:
American black bears are highly adaptable in forested habitats, living in
both arid areas (such as the Chihuahuan Desert) and moist forests, from
sea level to 6,560 feet (1,981 meters). Current range includes northern
Mexico, over 40 states in the USA, and all provinces and territories of
Canada except Prince Edward Island.

Wild Population:
Between 600,000 and 800,000 and growing.

FYI:
Black bears with white coats are called Kermode bears, and are found
along the north-central coast of British Columbia and the Yukon Territory.

Glacier bears are black bears with pale-blue coats.

BEAR TALE FROM THE BIG THICKET
Gilbert T. Adams

Beaumont, Texas attorney Gilbert Adams is a fifth-generation Texan, a rancher, and a wildlife enthusiast. He is a member of the East Texas Black Bear Task Force, and is on the board of directors of Bear Trust International.

Author's Note: This East Texas tale has been passed down generation to generation in our family. As a child on my father's knee, I gleaned that I should be prepared to stand up courageously in the face of overwhelming odds to use whatever one has at hand, but most of all to reach down inside oneself and muster up the great inner spirit that we all possess but are sometimes unaware of its existence.

On a crisp January evening, just after sunset, a father and son were making their way through the rugged Big Thicket wilderness of East Texas. The 11-year-old boy struggled under the weight and size of his father's 12-gauge shotgun. The boy was determined to keep pace with his father, whose broad frame carried the whitetail buck they had patiently stalked. It was the boy's first buck.

They were both eager to reach their log cabin home on the Adams Branch of Pine Island Bayou. The father was relieved to replenish the family's supply of winter meat. His son could not wait to recount to his mother and sister the adventures of his first successful deer hunt in the Big Thicket. After a long, cold day in the "big woods," they were both looking forward to a warm fire and mother's home-cooking.

But there remained a maze of sloughs, cypress knees and tangled undergrowth between them and home. What little starlight was able to penetrate the canopy of the forest seemed to dim with each passing step. It was the dark of the moon.

The boy's father was slowly busting through the dense underbrush that was sometimes shoulder high palmetto and other times just the plain old dense thicket undergrowth that is so typical of this country: briar, poison ivy, muscadine, ty-vine, myrtle and yaupon.

He knew his mother would be increasingly concerned. Whenever Dad was late there was a certain anxiousness at home. He remembered times when his father wouldn't get home at all from a hunt and had to stay in the woods overnight. This was worrisome for Mother but she never let it show much to the young'ns. At least she never thought it showed.

Yes, there were many things that could happen in the big woods. There were panthers, bears, boar hogs with tusks like daggers that could rip at you from ankle to appetite, snakes, each of the four deadliest, bobcats, and wolves. But there was no time to think about all that.

They had almost reached the wagon road running between Thicket and Batson in the very heart of the Texas Big Thicket. It would be easier going then. "Just put one foot in front of the other and don't trip," the boy thought to himself. He repeated the mantra to himself over and over in his head. Any minute now they should see the cut-off.

Suddenly, there was an unmistakable grunt of a bear. His dad instinctively dropped the gutted buck and in a hushed but firm demand instructed his son to give him the gun. The boy involuntarily went on full alert and almost threw the ol' Double to his father.

His dad shouldered the shotgun, took aim and pulled the trigger. Click. Nothing happened. Then, his father remembered that he had unloaded the shotgun before handing it to his son, who was following closely behind.

The huge black bear had turned sideways and was moving in and out of the undergrowth as he began to circle the pair. The boy knew a hungry bear has no fear. Just before attacking, a bear will often circle. The boy realized the bear smelled the fresh deer or what's more, the three squirrels in his coat pockets. Worse yet, the boy thought, he may have a hungering for a three-course meal.

With the bear on the move and only the dimmest of light, the boy and his father froze, hoping to detect the bear's movements. They listened and waited, but heard nothing. Nothing for a full 30 seconds… or 1 minute… or maybe just 5 seconds. The boy couldn't be sure. Time seemed to stand still and an eternity passed as they listened and waited.

The father quietly told the boy to toss him two shotgun shells. The boy reached into his ammo bag. The pouch was brown denim made from his father's old work pants. He had always liked the warm, soft feel of the fabric. But as his fingers frantically traveled the circumference of the bag searching for a shell, he experienced a completely different sensation…

Cold air. A hole. The bag must have ripped on the rugged underbrush!

Suddenly, there was the bear, mouth wide open. Ol' Double was of no use. Father cast aside the empty gun and squared off against the beast. The bear released a ferocious roar and lunged toward Father. Facing a bear, bare handed, what would he do? What could he do?

As the bear charged toward them, his father crammed his fist into the mouth of the bear and continued to push until he grabbed the bear's tail and with all of his strength jerked the bear inside out.

Bear Baiting
Robin Rigg
European Brown Bear

Robin Rigg is with The BEARS Project: Bear Education, Awareness and Research, launched in 2003 by the Slovak Wildlife Society. This is an account of an all-night vigil to see "container bears" in Slovakia's Demänovská Valley. Then Robin describes the current bear situation in Slovakia, and discusses issues related to the management of brown bears. More information about Slovakia's brown bears can be found at www.medvede.org.

The cheeky triangle face of a pine marten reappeared from the refuse bin, morsel in mouth, followed by the rest of its sinewy body. It slipped down onto the asphalt of the parking area and skittered off into the darkness beneath the spruce trees; not quite a bear, but a carnivore, at least. The three of us watching leant back into the thread-bare seats of my Škoda car, a relic from 1989, the year that the Velvet Revolution ended communism in Czechoslovakia. We each resumed our various musings and snoozing as rain drizzled steadily across the dull yellow light of the street lamps.

We were parked in the limestone crucible of central Slovakia's Demänovská Valley, which had been a bustling ski resort a few weeks earlier but now, at the end of April, was relatively deserted except for gatherings of sausage-roasting Poles and, apparently, a number of rather bold bears also interested in tourist fare. Although carnivore conservation can sometimes be depressingly unrewarding work, European brown bears, wolves and lynx have made promising natural and human-assisted recoveries in some parts of Europe in recent decades.

Slovakia now has more bears than at any other time in the past 150 years; local people still have some catching up to do in learning how to live with their now more numerous, omnivorous neighbours. Our present location, in the driveway at the back of a communist-era block of flats, perhaps wasn't very glamorous. But the volunteers with me wanted to see some large carnivores, and Demänovská's "container bears" that occasionally feed on carelessly stored waste, seemed to present as good a chance of a sighting as any.

I snuggled further under my blanket, feet wedged awkwardly between the pedals. At a little after half past four in the morning, it was beginning to look like the rest of the group, sleeping soundly back at our mountain chalets, had made the wise choice tonight. Although the refuse bins we had chosen to stake out were covered with old muddy paw prints, six hours of sitting cramped up in a two-door Rapidka had still to be compensated by more than a glimpse of a "container" marten; I was also wondering if any of the suspicious residents in the flats behind us had called the police yet.

"Wake up, they're here!" Eric's hushed but excited voice dragged me back to consciousness. "There're two of them!"

Richard was awake now, as well, and as we all peered intently through the streams of water on the windscreen, first one and then a second huge bulk drifted ghost-like among the trees just a few metres away from us. The only sounds were the patter of rain and low, mooing contact calls between the bears. They disappeared from sight, and for a moment we thought they had already gone (or had never really been there?). Then, suddenly, Eric pointed in awe down the road to where the larger of the two bears had stepped out into the light from the street lamps.

Bracing itself on its hind legs, it placed both front paws on the refuse container and gave a mighty shove; the bolts held. Nonchalantly, the bear dropped back onto all fours and shuffled off, following its companion, and its nose, round a regular inspection route of likely dining spots. Once they had definitely left, we broke out in excited babbling as we drove back to our accommodation in triumph, on the way casting smug glances at two local hunters slumped, asleep, over the dashboard of their 4x4. No doubt they had been snoring while we observed the "problem bears" they had come to shoot.

The effects of a long vigil caught up with us, and we needed to get some rest before making our slumbering cohorts envious in the morning. We climbed stiffly out of the car and sleepily stumbled up to the chalet, but stopped before going in: something was different about the external decor. Gouged into the woodwork under the windows were the fresh traces of a large set of claws. A more detailed inspection in the light of day revealed further tell-tale scratches. A muddy paw print on the bathroom window confirmed that the bears had indeed been visiting our larder just as we sat watching theirs.

After that night, we took more care about where we left our food. It is hoped that local residents and tourists will learn to do the same without the need for such a sharp lesson!

Summary of Current Bear Situation in Slovakia (2007)

For a variety of reasons, detailed information from Slovakia has not been included in many case studies of the conservation management of the European brown bear (*Ursus arctos*). While Slovakia has not so far been a place of leading scientific research on bears and other large mammals, it offers a wealth of practical experience in the hands-on management of problematic species. Slovakia is an instructive example of early carnivore conservation measures, including attempts at population augmentation 100 years ago and a damage compensation scheme that has been running since the 1960s, of ongoing consequences decades after population recovery and of the outcomes of different ploys to reconcile trophy hunting with conservation of a protected species.

Excessive sport hunting and persecution in the 19th and early 20th centuries almost eradicated bears from Slovakia. By the 1930s, contemporary estimates of the number surviving ranged from about 20 to not less than 60. Sometime between 1908 and 1930 the occupied range became fragmented, leaving an isolated population in the Western Carpathian Mountains of central Slovakia and southern Poland.

A ban on hunting from 1932 protected the few remaining bears and allowed a natural population recovery. Although stopping sport hunting was the only broad-scale conservation measure taken with the specific intention of maintaining bears in Slovakia, several other concurrent factors probably helped, including the expansion of forest cover, recovery of large ungulate populations, a marked decline in livestock grazing, abandonment of fields and orchards in mountain areas and, possibly, supplementary feeding by hunters.

The number and range of bears in the Western Carpathians increased rapidly in the second half of the 20th century. Brown bears had reoccupied all central mountain ranges of Slovakia by 1950 and during the 1970s spread into some peripheral ranges. Contact between bears isolated in the

Western Carpathians and the Eastern Carpathian sub-population became re-established during the 1970-80s, initially in Poland.

The brown bear population in the Carpathians, which includes bears in Slovakia, Poland, Ukraine and Romania, is now the second largest in Europe after that of the northeast. There are probably c.700-850 individuals in Slovakia, which is likely to be c.6% of all brown bears living in the wild in Europe. Population size and distribution have continued to increase in the Western Carpathians in recent years. A few individuals have been regularly present in neighbouring Czech Republic since the 1970s and there have been occasional occurrences in Hungary.

The rapid recovery and ongoing expansion of the sub-population of bears in Slovakia has not escaped the attention of either experts or the public. Hundreds of articles in the popular press have been written about bears in Slovak, in hunting magazines and wildlife management journals. And yet the number of good quality scientific papers published is small. Very little robust research has been done using modern methods, and the participation of Slovak wildlife researchers and managers in the leading international initiatives, networks and events has been irregular. As a result, relatively little is known about Slovakia's bears.

The bear population in Slovakia is now large enough, and hunting pressure low enough, for it to be in no short-term danger of extinction. However, there are clearly deeply divided opinions on how it should be managed. Much of the debate has focussed on how many bears there are and to what extent they can or should be hunted. From a conservation perspective, however, there are issues of more pressing concern. Fragmentation, degradation and loss of habitat, especially by the continued development of mountain areas and the construction of highways, could lead to greater problems for bears in some parts of Slovakia in the not-too-distant future. If bear-human conflicts are not sufficiently mitigated, they might undermine public support for bear conservation.

More about Brown Bears
from Bear Trust International
Bear Trust is solely responsible for the information in this section. Opinions about this information may vary.

Brown Bear: *Ursus Arctos*

Appearance:
The brown bear's coloration varies from dull brown, to almost black, to a yellowish white, and all variations of brown and red. The mixture of its fur coloration gives the fur a "grizzled" appearance, hence the name Grizzly.

Size:
Brown bear size varies depending upon population and diet. Adult males may weigh 300 to 860 pounds 136 to 390 kg). In the lower 48 states of the USA, the average weight is 600 pounds (272 kg). In Alaska and Canada, the average weight is 900 pounds (408 kg). Adult females weigh from 205 to 455 pounds (93 to 206 kg); in the lower 48 states, the average weight is 300 pounds 136 kg); in Alaska and Canada, the average weight is 500 pounds 227 kg). Birth weight averages 11 ounces to 1 pound 6 ounces 312 to 624 grams). Longevity in the wild can be as high as 30 years, but typically 25 years is an old bear.

Reproduction:
Females reach sexual maturity at four-and-a-half to seven years of age. Males enter the breeding population at eight to ten years old, later than other species, due to size and competition with other males. Breeding occurs from early May to mid July. Delayed implantation results in cubs being born in January. The common litter size is two. Typically, cubs remain with their mothers for two-and-a-half years.

Social Life:
Adult brown bears live alone, except for females with cubs. Sub-adult siblings sometimes travel together. Large groups gather where food is abundant, but respect other bears' "personal space." Adult males are the most dominant individuals in group situations. They communicate through complex forms of body language and vocalizations.

Food:
Approximately 85-95 per cent of the brown bear's diet is from vegetation such as grasses, sedges, bulbs, and roots. Insects, fish (salmon being a favorite), small mammals, and carrion are also included in their diet. In some areas, brown bears will predate on moose, caribou, and elk.

Habitat:
The male's home range is larger than the female's. Grizzly bear habitat includes those areas that provide food, cover, and space necessary for survival and reproduction. Use of habitat typically shifts seasonally based on the changing availability of seasonally abundant foods (for example, grasses in spring, berries in late summer). Localized populations are found in Eastern and Western Europe, northern Asia and Japan, Western Canada, and the states of Alaska, Wyoming, Montana, Idaho, and Washington.

FYI:
The largest brown bears are found on the west coast of British Columbia and Alaska, and on Alaskan islands such as Kodiak and Admiralty. Access to fish protein affects their size.

Grizzlies can sprint as fast as 35 to 40 miles per hour (56 to 64 kilometers per hour), and climb trees.

Many cultures have alternative names for the bear to show respect for the power of the animal: "Apple of the Forest" in Finland, "The old man with a fur coat" in Lapland, and "honey eater" in Russia.

Both bears and humans are plantigrade; bears, like humans, walk on their entire foot rather than up on their toes.

Visiting with the Ancestors
Monte Dolack

Monte Dolack's painting Bears of the World *reflects the influence of the Paleolithic paintings in the famous Lascaux caves in southwestern France. Down through the ages, the Bear has been a common subject for artists, who are able to convey the power and magic of the iconic animal through their art and imagination. The Bear motif is frequently used as both symbol and adornment by cultures living in the presence of bears. Toward the middle of the book you will find the full-color rendition of the painting.*

Prior to my visit to the caves at Lascaux, my work had been influenced by ancient art, myth and cultural symbols. Afterward, however, the influence was far more pronounced. This magnified influence has found its way into many of my more recent paintings, including *Bears of the World* created for Bear Trust International and published as a fundraising and conservation awareness poster for Bear Trust. The painting is rich in visual information, including a world map providing a backdrop for the powerful central image of a mythic cave bear. Each of the world's eight bear species is portrayed, along with symbols and pictographs buried beneath layers of translucent paint that lend a sense of texture and unity. Besides being decorative and informational, I tried to make a painting with a visual dynamic that would be modern, historic and mythic. The following is an account of my visit to the Lascaux caves.

In the year 2000, at a time that coincided with my fiftieth birthday, I received permission from the French Ministry of Culture to visit the famous Lascaux caves and view some of the oldest and most celebrated Paleolithic paintings in the world. I had been informed that a limited number of official visits to the caves were granted each year, and that these official visitors included scholars and artists. The opportunity to visit the caves represented an important personal quest for me to go back in time, to the very beginning of painting.

I live in Missoula, Montana, where I have my gallery. I was fortunate to have a neighbor who is a native of France and a professor of French language at the University of Montana. With his help, I was able to write a proper letter requesting permission for a visit to Lascaux for my wife Mary Beth Percival and me. We planned a trip to France around the possibility of a visit to the caves, and hoped our request would be granted. Months went by and we had almost given up. Then, just days before our departure, we received an official document informing us that we had been granted a *visiter exceptionnellement* and that we were to present ourselves at the gate to the Lascaux caves at 4 PM on the appointed day in May.

We arrived at Lascaux early on a beautiful spring day. We located the gate to the caves and waited for the line up of the other people who would join us. We had heard that as many as five or six individuals were allowed in at one time. (In contrast, at Lascaux II, a nearby reproduction of the cave constructed in 1983, hundreds of people visit on any given day.) As 4 PM approached and no others arrived at the gate, we grew increasingly nervous as we stood there alone. Had we misunderstood the instructions? At last, a man and his dog walked over to the gate and asked us for our papers. As it turned out, we were the only two people scheduled for that particular day. Along with our French guide Bruno Desplat, we would have the caves to ourselves.

For me, just the experience of spending nearly an hour in the Lascaux caves was life changing. Bruno, who was also the caretaker, was more than happy to be taking artists into his cave, and he shared our enthusiasm and wonder. The direct bond I felt with the artists who had made these cave pictures far in the past was extraordinarily personal, both intellectually and spiritually. As an American with emigrant ancestors from both Western and Central Europe, I felt an unusually deep connection to my own cultural and spiritual roots that I had never experienced before.

After visiting the caves, it hit me that these were not "primitive" works, but very sophisticated, beautiful and skillfully crafted paintings. There were dozens of pigments used in the creation of the paintings, including rich blacks and blues, a range of yellow ochre, delicate pinks and many reds. As we had learned from our guide, an array of tools had been used to make these pictures, including paint brushes, animal hide sponges and "crayons" of pigment held together with binders of animal fat. Some of the colors were from the cave itself and others from up to 25 miles away. As many as 30 different pigments were used by the artists, and hand-held flint tools found at the site had been used to incise the limestone walls. The paintings were rich with under-laid incised marks that Bruno helped us to see when he turned off the lights in the cave and held his flashlight at an angle that illuminated hundreds of minute figures and engraved symbols. Bruno's favorite adjective for what we all beheld was "Fantastique!" We couldn't agree more. It was fantastic.

The Lascaux caves have an interesting recent history. Located in the Dordogne area of southwestern France, the caves had been discovered by four boys and their dog in 1940. It was a stroke of luck that one of the first people the boys told was a professor of anthropology. After World War II, Lascaux was opened to throngs of enthusiastic visitors, and became an international sensation. However, this popularity was proving fatal to the caves: the thousands of daily visitors had brought in contamination, including an alarming combination of humidity and carbon dioxide exhaled from visitors, as well as the introduction of mold and lichen. The paintings were in grave danger of being loved to death. The caves were closed to the public in 1963.

After the installation of an air conditioning system in 1968, and other precautions, the caves were reopened to very limited visits. This went on quite well until a new, updated air conditioning system was installed weeks before our visit in the spring of 2000. Then in August of 2001, the caves were again closed after Bruno discovered a return of a white mold growing on the paintings. The new high-tech air conditioning system proved to be a complete failure, and in fact actually promoted the growth of mold. It is unclear at this time whether the caves will ever be reopened.

Curiously, the image of the Bear appears only once in Lascaux. There is a predominance of aurochs, bison, horses, red deer and felines. In nearby southeastern France, at the recently discovered and even older Chauvet Cave, there are a great many bear paintings. Because I was interested in working with bears, I began collecting ancient bear images from all of the sources I could find. The bear images in Chauvet Cave are among the oldest and most compelling. Although the Chauvet Cave is closed to visitation, the published photographs of the Chauvet bear painting proved most inspirational to me. It was my life-changing experience at Lascaux that gave me the insight to understand how the Chauvet bears appear, and to use that in my painting.

In Nearness to the Nothing:
Revelations from a Dying Bear
Leon Chartrand
An Essay on the Grizzly

Leon Chartrand is a Ph.D. candidate in environmental phenomenology at the University of Toronto. He is also the State Bear Wise Community Planner for the Wyoming Game & Fish Department and a bear management specialist in the Jackson Hole Region. This essay is an excerpt from a book he is writing.

In fullness of the emptying-of-life event, as the old boar crossed that indeterminate threshold having already faded-into-darkness yet still faintly standing-in-the-light, it occurred to me that I had silenced a voice that had something left to *say*.

Only then, in being open to the otherness of a dying bear, did the teachings of a hundred thousand year old wisdom arise and, in that arising, bring-to-light a world pregnant with meaning. It was a transformative moment, a moment for me to gather a renewed sense of clarity and hope; and, it came at a time of personal desperation. It would be my vocation thereafter to understand the self-emerging truths of this dying event. Certainly no easy task, but I am already on-the-way…

~

Bear came silently into the world. He trod the land so softly that by the time man first caught sight of him he was already king of the land. His palace was the mountain, which was the *axis mundi*, the center of the cosmic world. The mountain's base was founded upon a hallowed ancestral realm; its summit was the meeting place of the gods, the place nearest to the heavens. As numenon of the mountain, the bear was messenger to the underworld and spirit guardian of the supernatural; and, he spent his entire life as a boundless traveler crossing the thresholds between the three regions of the ancient world.

His very being was a unique expression of the cosmogonic *myth* of eternal return, and by myth I do not mean fairytale but rather the *true creation story* of *every* given culture. In winter, when nearly all life had faded, the bear returned to the lower region to reside alongside the Ancient Ones. On the advent of spring, he emerged from the den and brought forth dreams. At the height of summer, he made his home in the alpine meadows along the way to the heavens; and he guarded this route from the profane. In fall, as darkness loomed over Earth, the bear grew restless and retreated deep into the forest in preparation for his eventual return to the underworld. In this way he thrived at the threshold of life and death; his life reflected the cosmogonic symbol of birth and rebirth.

So, too, was the bear synonymous with the holiest times of the diurnal cycle. As a being most active at dusk and dawn, he foraged within the ghostliness of the Between during the most intimate moments of transition. He roamed among the shadows of the forest, amidst rising daylight and falling darkness. His was a life immersed within the concealedness of the lived world at the edge of the dream world. At the height of his reign, the bear became a vision of archetypal proportions. That is why indigenous man fittingly named him as *belonging*-together with the sacred.

This naming of the bear as *belonging*-together with the sacred was not something whimsical, for encountering the bear was a profound event. Often, the bear would overwhelm indigenous man with both fear and fascination. During such events, man confronted a wondrous and awe-inspiring mystery. This was no trivial revelation, for wonder and terror have long been two qualities closely associated with the sacred. In fact, these two qualities—characterized later as *mysterium fascinans et mysterium tremendum*—have reflected man's encounter with the sacred in a way that has transcended culture and religion. Even today the terrible and the wondrous are intimately related to what we now identify as divine, holy, poetic or incomprehensible and they reflect the depths of possibility for confronting mystery within the world.

That being said, it is no mere coincidence that fear and fascination are attributed to even the most recent memoirs of bear encounters. This includes those accounts depicted in the pages of this book. Granted, while many of these explanations may not express these qualities of the sacred outright, they are nonetheless *there* lingering just beneath the surface of explanation. Their presence is either subtly conveyed through the author's deliberate or unintentional use of expression or else prophetically announced not by what the author says but by what the author *does not* say in the saying.

For instance, it is not so much the words of a poem that bring forth truths; rather, it is the truths that come forth on their own from "behind" the words of the poem—for that is really what makes a poem a classic, that is really what makes a poem's greatness surpass cultures and survive even the most tumultuous of historical periods. In any great poem, the truths revealed are always more profound than what the words literally convey.

In this sense, the same is true for memoirs of bear encounters in this book. The most profound revelations of any account of a bear confrontation will not likely be found in what the author writes but in what lies behind the writing, in what the words themselves do not literally express, but say nonetheless. Closer examination will show that this is where references to the awe-inspiring and fascinating mystery are to be found. They are to be found in what is left unexpressed, for what is left unsaid embraces mystery within the world and preserves the integrity of revelations of the actual encounter itself.

But, such pronouncements of fascination and fear—whether deliberately subtle or unconscious—are usually glazed over since what is *right here* staring us in the face is often the most difficult for us to see let alone express. For this reason, most reflections on the significance of the bear encounter only capture a fleeting glimpse of what was profoundly revealed to the human during such an event. This is because the most intense manifestations only self-emerge long enough to leave the human awestruck and speechless for a moment, but then withdraw back into the depths of the world. In this withdrawal, they refuse to be fully grasped and are inadequately recreated by man's use of finite speech, which is finite because man inescapably has a finite understanding of the world. As such, the best explanation of these manifestations cannot be expressed by the written word, since what is most pervasively meaningful reveals itself to us from some unsayable, veiled realm that is always prior to our ability to express literally.

Yet, it has not always been this way—for expressions of the deeply profound were almost always celebrated in ritual and it was the shamanic ritual itself that most fully re-created that profound moment. Shamanic rituals celebrated the spontaneities of life and they acknowledged the human's situatedness within the world. In ritual, the human would give itself over to being-*there* with-in a *more-than*-human world and so become open to the mystery of that world. In that sense, revelations were not best recreated through the use of the written word, but rather through song, dance, art, medicine and oral storytelling. Each of these modes of language bore a distinct revelatory quality and in some cases still do today. Their revelatory quality enabled man to momentarily return to that manifesting moment—to that bear encounter—to see the face of the Other, which enabled him to once again immerse himself in the holy.

Eventually, as previously noted, man tried to recreate these revelations through writing but he met this task to no avail. With his preference for the static nature of the written word, man sought to permanently capture revelations through writing and, in turn, gradually lost his ability to express the sacred in its authenticity. In fact, the loss of his ability to express the sacred dimension of the bear encounter actually began when a different kind of man arrived on the mountain. This man brought reason to expression.

With reason came a gradual death of the gods and an eventual disconnectedness of modern man from the Ancient Ones. This culminated in a desacralization of the mountain and the eventual dethroning of the mountain's last great monarch. Of course, the bear was still admired and dreaded by modern man, but the primary source of his fascination and fear was obscured by his preference for an objective, mathematical and written explanation for everything. As for the revelation of the wondrous and the terrible mystery, it soon became perceived as that which is *not yet* known and something to be conquered rather than as that which can *never be completely known* nor *overcome*; and, as for those interpretations that reflected the presence of a fascinating and awe-inspiring mystery in the bear, these became shelved in the archives of mere opinionatedness.

Indeed, modern man sought tirelessly to gain more and more empirical knowledge about bears, but only within a subjective line-of-sight that was directed and shaped by centuries of traditional thinking that culminated in a fundamentalist view of the world as a collection of objects made constantly available to the human observer. This stood in contrast to the primordial view of the world as *sheer relation* and *pervading difference*. Instead of seeing the world as a *more-than-human*-world and the human as a being always already immersed within that world, modern man perceived himself as an outsider, as a distant observer, and *his* world as a totality and as a collection of objects. He argued that this position enabled him to make value-free, objective assessments.

In turn, no era in human history ever became more "objectively" knowledgeable about bears and no other culture ever demonstrated more complete dominance over them.   The quantity of knowledge amassed barely fit into the archives; and still it kept coming—research study after research study, old facts replaced by new facts, old models revised to include new theories.   What's more, technology became so sophisticated that man could observe bears as if he was, in some cases, actually riding on the bear's back as it moved through the forest. Now exposed by the so-called "correctness" of objective knowledge, no longer would the bear live in the shadows of rising light and falling darkness.

Yet, despite all the knowledge gained during this era, in no way was modern man closer to understanding the bear.   In fact, he thought that understanding involved the meshing and recitation of facts.   Every time he got the chance, he would rattle off a litany of empirically derived characteristics about the bear—its reproductive rate, estimated population size, mortality threshold, etc.—and he would call this "understanding." After a while, he began to justify new facts on the basis of old facts and he would defend them as more correct.   Yet, his mind eventually became so saturated with calculative facts that it grew increasingly more difficult to keep the facts straight or to distinguish between degrees of correctness— for some facts were deemed more correct than others and some facts disproved by other facts. And this says nothing about the disagreements and ambiguities created by competing scientists in defense of their own egos.

In turn, his knowledge was from its very beginning destined to be replaced by the most recent knowledge and so eventually doomed to perish in the wasteland of correctness.   It was a wasteland because this kind of extractive knowledge itself does not give forth life.   This is because knowledge is not the same as understanding.   While it is certainly one aspect of understanding, it is not the only aspect. Indeed, we must ask ourselves, "Is it the bear in the painting or the bear in the thicket that makes us feel most alive?" "Is it bear distribution data or the intense presence of the bear pervading the dark timber nearby that brings-to-light the deeper mysteries of life?"

To be sure, man *understands* the bear in a primordial sense when he sees it emerge from the thicket. He sees a being standing there, whom he may at that moment of intensified self-emergence gather as fearsome or magnificent. He encounters and gathers the bear, who at the same time is encountering and gathering him. This "gathering" or understanding happens *before* man acknowledges the bear as *Ursus arctos horribilis*; *before* he thinks of the bear's reproductive status or physical attributes. Indeed, understanding in this sense is our prereflective grasping of things.

Understanding first arrives in us when we are open to the world and shoots through our entire being; knowledge, on the other hand, is only acquired later when we attack the world with our frameworks of preconceived ideas and patterns of thinking. That is why understanding, not knowledge, has always been the primary source of wisdom. It starts from our situatedness within the world and from our immediate involvement within the encounter itself.

In fact, the arising-gathering moment of the face-to-face meeting is arguably where all our knowledge about bears *begins*. For us to have ever uttered the word "bear" or to have formed an idea of it, for us to have ever grappled with its reproductive rate or to have identified its range distribution, for us to have ever specifically debated its intrinsic or instrumental value or to have sculpted it as a totemic image or to have incorporated it into our cosmogonic myth or even to have named constellations after it, the bear first had to emerge into the clearing and we, of course, had to be there to meet it and gather its thingliness as worthy of being uttered or named. Indeed, the roots of this knowledge, regardless of how overwhelmingly calculative it has become, remains indebted to our having first endured meeting the bear and our having been situated within a bear-occupied landscape.

The name "bear" and the cultural variations therein, did not exist until there was a living being who revealed itself to us and enabled us to utter such a worthy name. Surely, for the Kootenai to have uttered "ni-ta-kyai-o" or "real bear," for the Shoshone to have considered the bear as *puha* or guardian spirit, for the *Männerbunde* or real men society of the ancient Germanic civilization to have ever proclaimed themselves as "berserkers" or, literally, as "warriors in shirts of bears," each culture would have first had to witness the bear as a significant presence in relation to their respective worlds. The *Männerbunde*, for instance, would have had to hunt the bear and see its strength as something that only the greatest warriors of their society possessed; the Kootenai would have had to witness the grizzly or *nitakyaio* as a presence that was somehow "more real" than the black bear or *kyaio*.

Even the taxonomic classification *Ursus arctos* must be traced back to the Latin and Greek names for bear, *ursus* and *arktos*, respectively. These two words were not uttered out of thin air but emerged when the people of antiquity encountered a presence in northern Italy and Greece that was worthy of being named. Indeed, while the stars have peppered the night sky since long before there were eyes to gaze at them, we might say that the constellations did not exist until consciousness gave them notice. So too can it be said for *Ursa Major* and *Ursa Minor*. These constellations never existed until an image of the bear's presence entered the minds of men and brought itself to language.

Likewise, for the Ojibwa to have attributed "everlasting life" to the bear, they first had to see the bear as most "alive" during the transitional moments of dusk and dawn, see its emergence from the den in the springtime and its return to the underworld with the onset of winter. Their long history of being situated within bear habitat as well as their frequent encounters with bears enabled the Ojibwa to see a close relation between bears and the ever-renewing sequence of sunrise and sunset and of seasonal succession. It is therefore not surprising that these people adopted the bear as an archetype of their myth of eternal return. In any of these cases, whether intra-culturally or inter-culturally spread, the wealth of knowledge held fast about bears and the significant roles they served in each society's worldview can be attributed to the facts that these societies lived on the same landscape as bears and routinely endured face-to-face meetings with them.

The same can be said for specialized knowledge possessed by certain individuals in these societies. The bear shaman, for instance, could not attain his or her power simply by studying the cosmogonic origins and medicinal uses of the various minerals, herbs and living beings within his or her world. He could not surpass his status as shaman-initiate through preparation alone, for the initiate did not fully wield the power of a bear shaman simply by learning what his elders taught him. While these teachings were necessary, they were given only as a means to prepare the initiate for his or her openness to the wisdom of the eventual confrontation. The threshold to fully receiving the bear's wisdom and of harnessing this wisdom into beneficial and or detrimental powers necessarily involved meeting and surviving the encounter, being open to receiving these powers manifested by the bear, and giving oneself over to them so as to be transformed into the shamanic identity. Indeed, becoming a shaman, wielding the bear's medicinal powers, possessing its knowledge, was not realized until the initiate underwent some "kind" of face-to-face meeting.

Furthermore, the same is true today for the bear biologist today. Like the bear shaman, the biologist's credibility is entirely wrapped up in his or her having actually encountered a bear. In point of fact, even the most "detached" biologists must acknowledge that his or her study begins and ends in the indeterminate field of experience, for it is precisely from our experience in this preconceptual realm that individuals are first drawn to work with bears. To be sure, the biologist or management officer typically does not choose this discipline randomly but is instead drawn to it by a complex of lived experiences and encounters that "unfold far from the laboratory" in forests and meadows, along stream bottoms and mountain trails.

Still, the essential meaning that we may gather during the encountering-event which drew us to study and conserve bears in the first place is now considered "biased" and therefore not credibly factual by the very discipline we have taken up. Indeed, despite the fact that a biologist's credibility, like the shaman's, is wrapped up in his or her having endured face-to-face meetings with the bear, the very discipline that we pursue considers the meaning we have gathered from these meetings to be "subjective." And, while the body of scientific knowledge has largely been acquired from "objective" types of observations, we must not forget that this kind of knowledge has always been the second-order expression of the encountering-event itself, for the event itself is what grants a clearing for the bear to arise before us and for us to gather it as a "thing" that is significant in a manner preceding scientific analysis or philosophical reasoning.

We must remember that we never come to our thoughts about bears, rather, they come to us. We did not first come to know the bear by pursuing it and taking hold of it, for we did not even know what "it" was. He first came to us from within the world of our spontaneous lived experience and he still fundamentally resides there; and, whether we as individuals have ever actually encountered a bear or not, we only know of them today because others before us have. Ultimately, the knowledge we have today never began in the documentary nor in the genetic laboratory nor even in an ontological debate over the bear's nature, origin or value; it did not begin in the crosshairs of a camera lens nor even in ancient ritual or myth; nor did it begin with the unearthing of old bones or with creating mythical beasts that the bear would later resemble.

Real knowledge—what we may call understanding—begins with our encountering a living, breathing thing who still wanders about in the forest. This is not a thing that only exists in the imagination nor is it something that only reveals itself in ways that science validates as real and correct. Insofar as correctness is mistaken for truth, we need to recall that "truth," in its most primordial form of *alêtheia,* really means "revelation." Likewise, "untruth" should not be mistaken for "error" or "falseness" but rather with "concealment." In this way, what reveals and conceals itself to us always does so first in the preconceptual realm of lived experience. That said, even science must admit that it derives its authority to pronounce what it considers "valid reality" or "correct" from the pre-scientific realm of our being always already situated within a more-than-human world—a world where, at any given moment, the bear moves about undetected in the nearby thicket.

We must therefore be more rigorous in our thinking by reminding ourselves that what we consider knowledge about bears today is really an abstract, derivative or "second-order" kind of knowledge. It is the kind of knowledge that "speaks", for instance, of the ecological relation between the bear, the spawning trout, and the mountain but, in so doing, fails to see that the research study itself remains indebted from the start to the very landscape in which we are already embedded and from which we have already learnt beforehand what a bear, a trout, a stream or a mountain *is.*

That being said, the primary source of fascination and fear of the bear was gradually concealed by the modern pursuit of knowledge—by modern man's obsession with correctness, with his attempt to bring the idea of the bear into accordance the actual bear. And, so this source was quickly forgotten, buried deep within the psyche of modern, rational man.

It would not resurface until decades later, when the environmental movement underwent its own kind of death. This death was exemplified by the de-listing of the Yellowstone bear, which inevitably became a kind of devaluing event since nearly every effort to study the bear and assign value to it had been driven by its threatened identity. But, once the bear was recovered, the bear no longer needed saving and this immediately became a problem—a sort of intellectual crisis—for man had put all of his energy into justifying the bear on the basis of its vulnerability and on its need for man's saving grace.

But, even with recovery success and sufficient protective measures in place, something did not seem right. Still, there was an undying anxiety in man, an unavoidable restlessness to uncover something more meaningful about the bear that all past conservation endeavors had failed to do. Disappointed with the *sterile* results that science and rationality brought forth, he conjured up new ways to protect the bear and he fabricated conspiracies and threats that did not exist. He tried desperately to find a new niche for saving the bear but came up empty. He came up empty because he saw the problem as external to him and he, in turn, assumed that the source of the intense meaning*less*ness that permeated bear conservation was outside of him. But, fortunately, in his finite understanding of the world, there is always something *more* to be seen and the problem itself, he would soon realize, was fundamentally a problem of seeing. In seeing he would find his saving power not just to save the bear, but himself as well.

After a while, it became instantly clear to him that no amount of empirical research would quench his thirst for understanding the deeper meaning of the bear; no amount of knowledge amassed from philosophy would shed light on why the bear's presence mattered so much to him; no amount of finger-pointing would cure his yearning for a deeper meaning that he somehow prereflectively grasped but could not put into words. He looked to others, but they only offered trivial explanations because they too were lost. He looked to the bear itself and to all the empirical facts acquired over the years, but he found only a remnant of the bear's former self, situated in front of the wildlife-viewing platform as a commodity for eco-tourism. He turned to other's personal explorations of the deeper meaning of a bear encounter, but found them unsatisfying, for none of them went far enough, none of them crossed the threshold. Wherever he looked he found no comprehensive answer and grew more and more anxious.

If he was to satisfy his restlessness, he would have to discover a new way to see the world on his own and, in that new way of seeing, he would have to uncover new significances surrounding the bear—significances independent of whether or not the bear was threatened or valuable to the health of the ecosystem; significances independent of the latest research findings; significances more basic than rationality or irrationality. To discover this new way, he would undeniably have to look elsewhere, beyond science and philosophy, beyond the concrete and abstract, to a more rigorous kind of thinking. He would have to think the unthought, but to do this, he would need to leap out of his traditional way of seeing the world. And, where would he "land" after he leapt? No where else but right where he already stood, face-to-face with a dying bear.

~

With my left palm pressed against the bear's thick bristled chest, I stretched my fingers through his silvery coat, marking his heartbeat just below the third rib. With the other hand, I angled the 22-guage-needle towards the pulse and eased it deep into the boar's chest cavity. Pulling on the plunger, a thick droplet of blood made its way into the vacuous hub—a sign that the tip had penetrated the heart. I knew I was about to end his life, that this old boar, all 455 lbs of him, was about to be silenced forever; only his decisive moment now culminated in the bending-action of my thumb, which I placed uneasily at the bottom of the syringe full of a fluorescent pink serum called *Beuthanasia*. Injecting the plunger with steady, slow pressure, the thick solution vacated the chamber and emptied into his heart. Anxious about the irreversibility of my decision, dispirited over his preventable death, I kneeled over the boar and waited. I was at a loss for words, for even then I could not grasp the finality of the moment…

~

During this putting-forth-into-death, I found myself at a loss for words because death itself warrants such speechlessness. Death reminds us time and time again of our situatedness within a world that is always already *more-than*-human. Upon confronting my own finiteness with this dying bear, I stood before him struck, paralyzed, silent. As I watched him fade, my ability to speak profoundly failed me and rightfully so, for the power of speech has never been a secure possession for any of us. In speechlessness, I had actually confronted my own limitation of knowing. This is because our ability to know has always been determined by, or at least profoundly limited by, our ability to speak. And, so I stood silent before him in this unspeakable event.

Silence often reveals a pervasive restlessness in us and for good reason. Idle talk conceals the incomprehensibility that pervades all of life. Silence, by contrast, is a way to genuinely listen to the Others and to let things be; and, in letting be, silence embraces and preserves mystery. In that sense, silence is a *way*. Here, a *way* allows us to reach something; it is a path to understanding. Thus, silence brings things to light in that it allows for the Others to emerge and to announce their arrival on their own accord. In that sense, silence allows for an openness to the mystery, which is a way to reach the Others.

Idle talk is, instead, preoccupied with the trivialities of everyday things and it perceives the Others as objects for human needs and desires. In this way, it is a kind of shrouding over of things and it attempts to conquer rather than preserve mystery, which is not really a way to reach anything at all. In this way, science and philosophy have become idle talk in that they do not let things be but rather attack or impose their frameworks of knowledge upon things. Of course, we may claim that objectivity is a kind of silent observation, but it is not, for it already has a preconceived idea about the Others and it judges and interprets on the basis of a predetermined framework of observation rather than on a genuine openness to the world. It is invasive and conquering, which is not openness at all.

On the other hand, when we are at a loss of words, when we are speechless, we let things be and, as such, we allow the Others to emerge into the open to unveil themselves as themselves to us.   When we are silent, we welcome, embrace and preserve incomprehensibility. Here, my speechlessness during this dying moment was not necessarily a fault or a limitation, but a gift. It was a gift because it prepared the way for this dying bear to manifest itself in an originative way from out of the unsayable realm—from the realm that we have for years tried to conceal in our preoccupations with entities.

In that self-unfolding emergence, the dying bear stood before me in the *arising-gathering* moment of the encounter event. He *arose* into the open and, in that self-unfolding, incited within me a prereflective discovery of myself as a disoriented, lost being—as a being who has endlessly wandered-in-need of a meaningful way to dwell in this world. As a result of this arising, I *gathered* myself as undeniably homeless. I was homeless because I had been so preoccupied with reason that I had fooled myself into thinking that the path home required us to objectify, entrap, quantify, and control everything that we came across so as to make this world more predictable, secure and constantly available. As such, I saw home as some idea *out there* to be shaped, rather than as a place *here* and *now* on this mountain at the center of the world. And, though I stood alone, I was not the only one homeless, for that, it seemed, includes the lot of us.

Grappling to make sense of it all, I found myself at a loss for words in the midst of this dying bear. Only then, after having lost my ability to speak, was I fully prepared to see the bear in an originative kind of way, in a way *prior* to scientific analysis and philosophical reflection, in a way more rigorous than all my past thinking. Only then had I been silent long enough to enable the closedness of this world to open up around me and, in its self-blossoming emergence, overwhelm me. In this sense, it was my fall to silence in the face of death that prepared the *way* for new manifestations to self-emerge.

~

...As a few enduring minutes passed, the bear, lying on his side, expelled a series of deep, lamenting sighs. His tongue extended from open jaw into a pool of saliva; and, though sedated with *Telazol*, he gently licked at this pool as if thirsting for clemency. His sighs were infrequent; his pulse, faint; and the fiercely intense wisdom of a hundred thousand years, manifested by those disproportionately small, beady eyes, surrendered quietly to the blackness of pupil dilation. Fixed in an endless stare, his eyes darkened, gazing inescapably into the Nothing...

~

In the waning moments of this bear's life, I stood in nearness to the Nothing, which revealed a stark reality—that the most certain of all my possibilities is *non*-being. Clearly, death is a public occurrence in the world. This is undeniable. But, while I could acknowledge this fact by saying that "death is part of life," that "all things will and indeed must die," and while I acknowledged my own mortality at that moment, I still found myself caught up in our culture's massive turning away from the fact that death is the most *extreme, absolute* and *intimate* of all *possibilities*. Death is without issue for us.

Death is *extreme* because it is the possibility of *not* being, which inevitably snuffs out all other possibilities. It is *absolute* because, while I can overcome or endure losses, my death is the one loss that ends all my enduring, all my striving, all wandering-in-need. What's more, death is *intimate* in that I must go it alone. Like this dying bear, death is radically personal. Just as no one else can die for this bear, which is distinct from the sacrifice of martyrdom and the killing of others, no one else can die for me. That is, this bear crosses the threshold alone, just as I must do. Lastly, death is a *possibility* not in the sense of something that we may experience in the future some time at the end of life's road, for this suggests that death is an event that is external to us occurring at some point in the future. Rather, death is a possibility *here* and *now*, at this very moment. In short, I know *not when* I will die, but I know that I am *in* death—that, like this bear, I too stare into the Nothing, which always pervades the world *right here* and *right now*.

Indeed, all too often, we see death as something that happens outside of us and we see the Nothing as some onto-theological notion. But, it is not; it is much more basic to lived-experience; it is something always already in the midst of the world and it is the grounds for all thinking and being. We do not explore it because, as stated earlier, we have a finite understanding of the world and what we are talking about here is always *more-than* and *other-than* what is finite. In this way, I purposefully prefer to avoid saying "infinite" because that itself is a trivial temporal description of what the Nothing really "is." It is, in fact, better to say that the Nothing "is not" and, while at the same time, say that the Nothing "is" grounds for the *really* real. What's more, even when we refer to the Nothing as an "it" we are already trying to grasp it as a kind of entity or totality, as a *no*-thing that is opposite of things. But it is not at all just a negative concept.

At the same time, we may also say that it is sheer emptiness, but that would imply that it is sheer meaning*less*ness which is the opposite of the meaning*ful*ness of the supernatural. As such, metaphorically speaking, we might intellectually associate the Nothing with the pessimistic, with the underworld, with meaning*less*ness, with Hell, and we might therefore think of it as the opposite of meaning*ful*ness, of beauty, truth and goodness, as the opposite of the heavens and the realm of the gods. But, none of this is true, for it is all of this and *more;* and, it is our attempts to express it in a dichotomous manner that only limits what the Nothing really "is."

The Nothing, instead and in addition to, is the source of all meaning*ful*ness and meaning*less*ness, it is the source of the divine and the underworld and it underlies all human experience. It is the source of the sacred, for out of the Nothing arise the wondrous mystery and the terrible mystery; the *mysterium fascinans et mysterium tremendum.* From the Nothing arises an overwhelming meaning*less*ness and an intensified meaning*ful*ness. But, still, there is a danger here of oversimplification, which only delimits the Nothing and, in that delimiting, trivializes what it really "is." That said, one expression of the Nothing might be the unsayable, though this by itself is still admittedly inadequate. Nevertheless, this is what I meant when I said that the bear arose from the unsayable realm.

Thus, it is the unsayable realm that brings-to-light the sacred. To look at the sacred aspects of the bear encounter itself, we first need to acknowledge that the Nothing underlies all things sacred and profane. The awe-inspiring mystery and the fascinating mystery associated with the bear arise out of the Nothing. Additionally, we must therefore recognize that the possibility of *non*-being underlies all beings, which includes this bear and me. Every being is the extreme, absolute and intimate possibility of non-being. Only when we confront the Nothing in this way, only when we confront the possibility of not being, do we truly begin to see what is essentially mysterious about the bear and the bear encounter.

Yet, we do not want to face the Nothing. We choose most often to turn away from it and to keep our distance from it. We try to keep our distance from it as a way to take control of the anxiety that nothingness brings forth. Keeping this distance makes us feel powerful and in charge of the most profound of forces. Even with this dead bear before me, death is something I do not or choose not to try to fully grasp. But, I have fooled myself into thinking that my power lies in this denial. By consuming myself with the trivialities and the prattle of everyday dealings, I feel momentarily in control, I feel that I have power over the world, but this is no power in any real sense. It is, instead, an unconscious conspiracy to cover up a deep restlessness within us in the face of an all-pervasive nothingness. And, despite all our preoccupations with the thingliness of the world, we prereflectively know that the Nothing is always already right here. And, it is moments like this—when a dying bear reveals death as the most extreme, absolute and intimate of our possibilities—that we become overwhelmed by nothingness.   Thus, attempting to turn away from the Nothing, trying to keep our distance from it, is like trying to avoid water while swimming in the middle of the ocean.   Certainly, I can tread water, but I cannot tread it for very long. Eventually, the ocean will outlast me.

Be that as it may, I still turn away in denial as we so often do. But, every turning away is at the same time a turning towards. This is what is so convenient about the human's finite understanding of the world. We come to know one thing at the expense of not knowing something else. In the same way, we can turn towards one thing while at the same time turn away from something else. We can be drawn into one revelation while being repulsed by another.

In this case, I can presumably turn away from the overwhelming presence of the Nothing and turn towards everyday preoccupations. But, this is not really a turning away in any real sense. In treading ocean water, I cannot turn away from the horizon that surrounds me. Indeed, the Nothing is the *only* phenomenon that cannot be completely turned away from because it is always right here and right now pervading all things and it makes its presence known at the most uncanniest of times. One such moment is in this dead bear encounter. Perhaps this is why I stood at a loss for words. I was speechless because I could not turn away from the unsayable realm overwhelming me.

~

...At a moment when his carcass seems to be all that remains, the bear's nearness is felt and perhaps even more so. Just as a grizzly sow can incite more anxiety amidst the shrouding blackness of a moonless night, when she may or may not be stealthily moving about outside our warm tent but makes her presence felt nonetheless—this time in the creaking of a lodgepole bending in the wind or in the busyness of a vole scampering across our camp, always keeping just a glance ahead of our spotting it. Indeed, the sow's presence, felt more so in her absence, manifested in the precipitous sounds of a vole or the swaying tree, can be more intense than any confrontation with a huge boar on a dimly lit forested trail. So too is it the case with this dead bear. I feel his presence now more so than when he was alive.

~

Just as darkness makes us feel the reality of light, it is *absence* that makes us feel the reality of presence—and this is not solely attributed to the dying moment, but is something that pervades all of life and is notably manifest in the bear encounter. In fact, it is presence felt through absence that has long influenced the moods of our wanderings through bear-occupied forests and, it is these encounters that have always been the more fundamental grounds for our thinking about them—something Muir knew, something Leopold tried to express, something most depictions of bear encounters fail to grasp. Whether we encounter the bear's presence face-to-face or we encounter its presence hidden amidst the shadows cast behind encircling fir trees—enthralling us and terrifying us all at the same time—we realize in a prereflective sort of way, that the bear's presence has always been here, indifferent to scientific analysis or philosophical reflection.

The dead bear, first and foremost, even in death always remains something *more*, something wholly *other*-than itself. And, despite all our calculative efforts to understand him or his kind or to assign value to him, his presence, felt more now in this dying moment, eludes the capabilities of traditional thinking—for we are venturing into the more primordial realm of the incomprehensible. This realm, the realm of the unsayable, is always and already ontologically prior to science and reason and does not speak the language of common sense. It is the realm that sees the beauty of the sunset first, before seeing the sun through a Copernican lens.   The truths revealed by the former give way to meaning more so than the correctness established by the latter.   It is the sunrise and not the earth's orbital path that gives us life and something meaningful to live for. Similarly, it is the pervading presence of the bear deep in the forest and not the collared bear at the wildlife-viewing platform that stirs something deep within us and calls us home.

To be sure, we always grasp the meaningfulness of the bear in a prereflective way during the encounter.   This I cannot express more emphatically and confidently. We encounter him in the forest, emerging from the grassy meadow to stand before us in the clearing. In that emergence we stand fascinated and or fearful. And, if we have not been too corrupted by traditional thinking, we see the bear in all its wonder and awesomeness rather than as an object for empirical analysis or philosophical reflection. To get a sense of what I mean here, we need to consider, once again, the phenomenon of fear and fascination as they relate specifically to the sacred and to the bear encounter itself.

Fear is a relational involvement of "the fearsome," "the fearful" and "fearing." Each *belongs* together in a threefold sense in that we cannot think of one without at the same time be thinking of the other two. For instance, the bear *arises* before the human as "the fearsome" only when the human somehow discovers beforehand the harmful character of the bear and, in this discovery, becomes afraid. The human, considered in this case as "the fearful," discovers the fearsomeness of the bear in a way that is ontologically prior. That is, the human *gathers* the bear as harmful only because the bear somehow shows itself in a prereflective way as detrimental to the human. This *arising-gathering* event—wherein the fearful human prereflectively discovers the harmfulness of the bear arising before him and so becomes afraid—is what we call "fearing."

Thus, fearing as such is both a fear *of* what arises as threatening—the bear as the fearsome—and a fear *for* what discovers itself as threatened—the human as the fearful. In this case, fearing as such is a *belonging*-together of the fearsome and the fearful. The fearsome *belongs* to the fearful insofar as it "needs" the fearful to discover it in its fearsomeness. The fearful, on the other hand, *belongs* to the fearsome insofar as it must grasp the fearsome in its detrimentality in order for it to be afraid—that is, in order for the human to be fearful, it "needs" the bear to arise before it as fearsome. From this standpoint, the *togetherness* of the fearful and the fearsome is determined by the *belongingness* of the two. This belongingness is the arising-gathering event we call fearing as such; it is nothing less than the relation itself of the fearsome and the fearful.

As with any encountering event, this relation is not an "either or" kind of relation. Surely, we can be the fearful because we are thrown into a more-than-human world where things like bears can arise before us and so threaten us. Yet, we can also be the fearsome because we are already immersed in a worldly relation with things that can always gather us as harmful to them. In this way, just as we can hear and be heard, touch and be touched, see and be seen, so too can we threaten and be threatened—so too can we be fearsome and fearful all at the same time. Though we may be afraid of the bear and so choose to turn away from him, that same bear may also be very much afraid of us and, as a result, turn to flee as well. In any case, the fearsome and the fearful determine each other by their belongingness to the arising-gathering of the encounter. In this threefold sense, the fearsome, the fearful and fearing as such comprise the phenomenon of fear.

Yet, fear of the bear is not the same as fear of death or fear of the Nothing that arises as a result of our encounters with the bear. There is a key distinction between the two. Fear of death and the Nothing is a realization of being homeless, of being nowhere and swallowed up by the Nothing which is always here and now. Fear of the bear, on the other hand, is a fear of something real and definite in the world—the bear itself. In this way, fear of the Nothing reflects an overwhelming awareness of ourselves as immersed up to our necks in a world that is *more-than* and *other-than* human and, in that awareness, we see ourselves as on-the-way towards death and not at home in the world. In this sense, we become all the more anxious and it is during these moments we become overwhelmed by a fear of the Nothing. This dead bear encounter is one such example, for it revealed an awe-inspiring mystery—a *mysterium tremendum*—and I stood silent. Here, it was not the bear itself that emerged as threatening but rather the Nothing that came forth as a result of this bear's death.

And, yet, at the same time, the dead bear encounter also brought forth a wondrous mystery, a *mysterium fascinans*. Here, wonder can also be understood in a threefold sense as involving that which is wonderful, the wonderer, and wondering as such. As with the phenomenon of fear, all three belong-together in that we cannot think of one without at the same time be thinking of the other two. Only, as opposed to the overwhelming meaning*less*ness that can be brought forth by the terrible mystery of the Nothing, it is an overwhelming euphoria, an ecstatic sense of intense meaning*ful*ness that can be brought forth by the wondrous mystery of the Nothing. In any case, my encounter with the dead bear also revealed the wondrous mystery of the Nothing and in that revelation, I was overwhelmed by the sheer terror of death as the most extreme, absolute and intimate of all my possibilities; yet, I was equally ecstatic over the intense wonder of a world that was pregnant with meaning.

All this was equiprimordially disclosed to me during the dead bear encounter. It was through the unfolding of mystery, however wonderful or terrible, that I most felt the dead bear's presence. I felt his presence most in his absence because in absence—in hiddenness—resides mystery. That is why we so often feel the bear's presence more in the deep forest or in the darkness of night when he is near but not seen as opposed to when we encounter him foraging in an open meadow at midday. To be sure, in this bear's death, I felt his terrible and magnificent presence through a self-unfolding of the Nothing. And, I could not turn away.

~

...I am now convinced that my encounter with the "hidden" bear is more profound than any working-up-event, when the bear gets baited, trapped and sedated—as close to me as ever—only to be weighed, tattooed and collared. At the very least, this dead bear lying before me, in his crossing over into the Nothing, has brought to light something I have long ignored, even forgotten: that even in death, he is always prior to scientific analysis or ethical reasoning; that despite the tower of ideas we have erected about him, his presence is always fundamentally *more-than* any inquiry. Perhaps, as Muir noted, he really does possess a kind of terrestrial immortality, for there is always something unreachable, something unknowable about him; there is always an imponderable essence that refuses to be unveiled yet makes itself felt nonetheless, reminding me of my endless wandering in need of a place to dwell in nearness to the *mysterium fascinans et mysterium tremendum.*

~

The question of how to viably dwell alongside bears is unquestionably the decline of the sacred. The decline of the sacred means simply that the reality of the awe-inspiring and fascinating mystery is no longer the uncontested center of the world and that striving to dwell in nearness to the sacred is no longer the final and unchallenged place for us to call home, or so it would seem. Of course, the waning of the sacred is much more complex than a mere change in perception; it is something deep within the psyche of rational man. The loss of the sacred is the loss of a whole system of symbols, images, and rites, which have long been immediately validated by human encounters within the daily-lived world.

In losing a sense of the fascinating and awe-inspiring mystery, we have lost our sense of connectedness with an immanent world, with a world that is always pregnant with meaning, bursting forth with numinous presence. Instead, science has allowed us to unleash our logic upon the world; but, in so doing, we have become disconnected and disenchanted with such an objective, empirical world—for this world that we have shaped no longer answers the needs of our soul; it no longer connects us with this dying bear. Instead, we wander-in-need, we are cast adrift, striving aimlessly for a dwelling place, even though that place has always been right here. Still, our sense of homelessness does not always make its presence fully felt because we remain captivated by technology's powerful promise to make us masters of the entire earth.

This vision has enthralled us so much so that we have spent the last century stripping the bear and its world of their mysteriousness and turning them into objects to be studied, controlled and made constantly available for our wants and needs. Thus, it is hardly expected that the bear rug, the bear photograph or the marble sculpture on sale in the streets of Jackson Hole could ever have the same sacred significance that the carvings would have had for the totemic societies or the images would have had for the shamanic journey. This is simply a psychic fact, for these earlier symbols sprang from the depths of the human soul. Unlike the art and images of bears today, these earlier images revealed a numinous presence, a more profound reality that nourished us.

That being said, the best hope for the bear's long-term viability must be in its ability to continue to inspire religious imagination, in its ability to uniquely express the more-than-human elements of a sacred reality. More so than its own genetically and culturally acquired *bear-ness*, more so than its forty million year trek of selective adaptations, more so than its *ursocentric* consciousness, more so than what we can acquire through science or rationality, the most valuable asset to the great bear's viability lies in its ability to bring-to-light the unsayable and to, once again, reveal a world so pregnant with meaning that we gain a renewed sense of clarity and hope.

Of course, if we are talking about bear conservation that lasts a hundred years, then certainly it is management strategies and tactics, scientific research and technological innovations that will sustain the bear. But, if we are talking about conservation that lasts for ten thousand years, then the key to the bear's long-term viability lies in its revelatory power, in its ability to bring-to-light a sacred reality.

Now more than ever, it seems clear that our greatest task of learning to viably dwell alongside and within bear-occupied habitat is no longer just a socio-political problem nor is it a problem that can be saved at its most fundamental level by science, technology or philosophy. It is really more of a spiritual problem of modern man—one whose greatest danger is oversimplification. It is not a problem whose solution calls for mutual isolation, where we either conquer or remove ourselves from all that is wild and volatile or else keep what is wild at a safe distance. This is no solution because mutual isolation is both an attack and a fleeing from our situatedness within a more-than-human world. Nor is it a problem whose solution calls for adopting a paradigm of peaceful coexistence. Peace is an unrealizable notion that underlies our traditional ways of thinking. In fact, neither of these paradigms—mutual isolation nor peaceful coexistence—can be realized in the end. Succinctly put, mutual isolation never existed, for man has never been an island; and, peaceful coexistence will never exist, for the island has never been nor will it ever be without some degree of violence. We are instead dealing with sheer relation, which is awe-inspiringly and wonderfully mysterious.

Thus, the solution fundamentally begins with being open to the mystery of this world and to releasing oneself to the revelations of that world. In that openness and releasement, we can embrace and preserve incomprehensibility. But, this is not something to be taken lightly or to be trivialized. It must be done with critical, poetic reflection, with an originative thinking that is far more rigorous than any thinking we have adopted thus far. It is the kind of thinking that goes forward by taking a step back. It is not, however, a call to return to the past in any full sense. Our homelessness cannot be resolved by regressing to a past state any more than it can be resolved by progressing towards some ideal state. It is, instead, a problem that is to be resolved here and now, in the present moment, in our way of seeing of the world. It is a problem of genuine seeing.

To see or to perish, that is no doubt the very condition laid upon us. It is, in fact, the very condition laid upon every living being in the world. What we are now was shaped by our perceptions of the past. What we are in the future will be shaped by our perceptions of today. Thus, our future and the bear's future are directly dependent on our ability to see here and now. And, so, we must begin to ask ourselves, "See what?"

~

This dead bear's presence still moves undetected beneath the surface of everyday dealings, always foraging along the talus slopes of the mountain, concerning himself solely with rolling over boulders to feast on moths. Thus, while his presence may now be physically absent, he is nevertheless near, hidden in the darkness of the surrounding forest, veiled by the far side of the ridge, *foraging in the undergrowth of our ideas*. In death, it seems most certainly clear, that there is still life. What gives life—what nourishes us, what calls us home—always springs forth from the unsayable and the bear has always been a unique manifestation of that realm.

~

In the beginning, there was a mountain. That mountain was at the center of the world.

Deep within the minds of men, the mountain remains. We are still drawn to it by the crowds, by the millions, though we seem to have forgotten why. We go for the scenic beauty, for the photograph, but we fail to see this as revealing a deeper yearning in us to be at the center of the world, to reside at the most holy of all places.

There still resides an underworld deep within us upon which the mountain is still founded. From this lower psychic region, a thousand voices ring out. These voices are those of the Ancient Ones and their calls are the echo of our conscience. We need only listen to what they are saying, for they are the *really real* voices of "reason."

The summit remains a place for the divine; we need only see the mystery that resides there and the hope that shines forth from the heavens. To this day, we yearn to go to the top of the world to be amongst the supernatural, the most holy. At the top is where the light shines brightest, and so we too hope to stand in the light of wisdom. The way to get there, then, is the new vision quest, the new shamanic journey, of our times.

The mountain is still home to the bear and the bear still crosses the threshold of life and death. So too does he roam amidst the shadows of rising light and falling darkness; so too does he bring forth life during the spring. To this day, the old boar remains for us, as he did for ancient man, a being of archetypal proportions. His identity still *belongs* together with the unsayable; and, when we look to the mountain, when we travel its slopes, we still think of the bear. Deep within us, he still roams at the center of the world.

All this was revealed equiprimordially to me as I stood before a dying bear. With the renewal of metaphor, we can once again evoke these self-emerging truths, for we have the power to call forth the mystery that pervades our world. In that evocation, we can preserve the awe-inspiring and fascinating mystery and find our way to the center of the world amidst a sacred reality, which has always been right here and right now but the farthest and most difficult for us to reach.

The Day Mei Xiang Disappeared
Brenda Morgan
Giant Panda

Brenda Morgan is a zookeeper at the National Zoo in Washington, D.C.

One of the fondest memories that I have of the Giant Pandas that currently live at the National Zoo in Washington, D.C. is what happened the day Mei Xiang disappeared. Whenever I think of that day, I can't help but chuckle to myself.

Tian Tian and Mei Xiang had only been here at the National Zoo for about two weeks, and at that time they did not have access to the outside yards, only to the inside enclosures and an area that is partly outside that looks out into the yards that we call the "patio." Two of the four walls of the patio are made of mesh, which is in the shape of a regular chain-link backyard fence.

In one of the two patios, there is a large scale where we weigh both of the Giant Pandas every morning while we stand in the adjoining area that we call the keeper cage. Both Mei Xiang and Tian Tian love the scale: they love to sit on it, hide behind it, and climb up on it. And when they sit on the scale to be weighed, they are rewarded with their biscuits, or sometimes pieces of apple and pear.

On this particular day, the day Mei Xiang disappeared, I saw her walk from one of the inside enclosures out into the patio where the scale is kept. So I went out to the keeper cage to look into the patio to talk to her, and see if she was ready to be fed. However, when I walked out into the keeper cage, I did not see Mei Xiang in the patio. Thinking that she must have gone back inside, I went back into the building to look into the inside enclosures and see where she had gone. Again, no Mei Xiang! How could this be possible? I'd just seen her walk outside.

Back into the keeper cage I went, thinking that maybe Mei Xiang had hidden behind the scale. I called her name to see if she would appear. She was not behind the scale, not in the patio and not in any of the inside enclosures. But then where could she be, since she did not have access to the outside? She had to be somewhere. I was beginning to feel very nervous; why could I not find her?

At this point, all of us who work with the giant pandas started looking and calling for Mei Xiang. We could see where Tian Tian was, but still no Mei Xiang. It made no sense that the giant panda could just disappear into thin air. Finally, I went back into the keeper cage, where I just happened to look up.

And there was Mei Xiang, hanging upside down, looking for all the world like a black and white Panda bat. She was gazing down at me as if she were saying, "What do you want? I have been here all along. I heard you calling me. People are so silly. Why in the world did you not look up?"

Mei Xiang had climbed up the mesh, about 12 feet high, to the very top of the patio, and hung herself upside down from a single piece of conduit pipe that ran from one

Mei Xiang and Tian Tian in patio with scale side of the patio to the other.

She was very comfortable up there, and loved to hang there from that day on. The only difference, of course, was that she had taught all of us to look up!

Visiting Giant Pandas at the National Zoo

Come visit Mei Xiang and Tian Tian. One of the most popular exhibits at the National Zoo in Washington, D.C. is the giant panda exhibit. Who doesn't love to see a giant panda? The zoo also has a real-time camera on its website (www.nationalzoo.si.edu), as well as a wealth of information about Mei Xiang and Tian Tian, and about the giant panda.

Mei Xiang and Tian Tian are a breeding pair. Because female pandas have an ovulatory period during only a two-day peak, once a year, a lot of planning on the part of the zoo's staff is involved. Because giant panda populations in the wild are declining, zoos play an important role through their captive breeding programs.

More about the Giant Panda
from Bear Trust International
Bear Trust is solely responsible for the information in this section. Opinions about this information may vary.

Giant Panda - *Ailuropoda Melanoleuca*

Other Names: Xiongmao (giant bear cat)

Appearance:
Giant pandas have sharply contrasting black and white coloration. The front paw has six digits and functions like an opposable thumb

Size:
Male pandas in the wild weigh from 190 to 275 pounds (86 to 125 kg).
Female pandas range between 155 to 220 pounds 70 to 91 kg). At birth,
cubs weigh about 3 to 5 ounces 85 to 142 grams). In captivity, giant
pandas can live longer than 25 years.

Reproduction:
Pandas reach sexual maturity from four-and-a-half to six-and-a half years
of age. Mating season is in the spring from March to May. Cubs are born
in August or September. Dens are found in hollow trees or caves, where
one cub is raised at a time. Cubs are weaned at nine months, and remain
with their mothers for up to a year and a half.

Social Life:
Pandas live alone except for females accompanied by cubs. Home ranges
for males average 3.3 square miles (8.55 km), and 1.8 square miles (4.66
km) for females. Home ranges for females are usually mutually exclusive,
while male pandas may overlap those of several females.

Food:
Pandas eat branches, stems, and leaves of at least 30 species of bamboo.
Bamboo comprises 99per cent of the food consumed by giant pandas in
the wild. They must eat 25 to 40 pounds (11 to 18 kg) of bamboo daily to
maintain the required nutritional state.

Habitat:
Giant panda inhabit mountain forests at altitudes of 4,000 to 11,500 feet,
characterized by dense stands of bamboo (see Diet, above). Pandas are
found in southwestern China, along the eastern edge of the Tibetan plateau
in six small areas in Sichuan, Gansu, and Shaanzi provinces.

Wild Population:
Estimate between 700 and 1000 in the wild, and declining.

FYI:
Pandas are considered one of the rarest species in the world.

Pandas are active mainly at twilight and at night.

Their eyes are adapted for night vision.

They were considered the domestic animal of the Chinese emperors.

Eleven distinct calls have been identified for Pandas in the wild.

Typically, pandas don't hibernate, even when living in higher elevations.

A Cautionary Tale
Sterling Miller, Ph.D.
An Essay Regarding Self-Proclaimed Bear Experts

Sterling Miller is Senior Wildlife Biologist for the National Wildlife Federation, a conservation organization whose mission is to inspire Americans to protect wildlife for our children's future. He shares some tips on how to distinguish a real bear expert in an era of Timothy Treadwell, junk science, and publicity seeking.

Like most biologists who have spent a career doing field studies on wildlife, I have my share of interesting stories. These include immobilization attempts that had their scary moments, bears awakening prematurely from immobilizing drugs, black bears that have frightened me when I entered their dens to replace radio-collars, bears mating and fighting other bears, stupid things that people do around bears, bears found in strange places, etc., etc.

Rather than recounting these anecdotes, most of which have little instructive value to them, I instead offer a cautionary tale about self-proclaimed bear 'experts' and how to tell them from real experts. I'm motivated to do this not because I want to discredit any individuals, but rather because of what I see as a disturbing trend toward putting undue credence in those who do not merit it.

Probably the most extreme example of one who does not merit credence is the late Timothy Treadwell. Tim and his girlfriend Amie Huguenard were killed by a bear on the Alaska Peninsula in the fall of 2003. His life and death were widely publicized, and became the topic of at least two books and a widely distributed movie.

Here are some guidelines that will help when trying to sort out whether to believe one of these folks.

1. Does the person work for a university, or federal, state, provincial, or tribal natural resource agency? If so, it is likely that he or she is credible because universities and agencies will quickly get rid of people who are not reliable, truthful and who make judgments based on evidence rather than on beliefs or anecdotes. If you have doubts about the credibility of someone outside these organizations, ask someone within a university or agency about them.

2. Does the person have a record of publishing in peer-reviewed literature? Scientific journals use the peer-review process to weed out articles that are not well-supported by the evidence presented. People who self-publish books or popular articles have not had the judgments expressed therein exposed to critical review by their peers, and these judgments should be viewed with skepticism. Additionally, it is worthwhile to find out whether the person has published in peer-reviewed journals *recently*. A few papers published a decade or more ago may not be enough to indicate that someone is current about bears any more than your doctor would be if he or she stopped reading medical journals after leaving medical school.

3. Is the person a member of a professional society? There are many professional societies to which people can belong, and most of these do not require credentials. The Wildlife Society, however, has a certification procedure, and if a person is a Certified Wildlife Biologist, this designation indicates that he or she has achieved a certain level of professional competence and credibility. Even if

uncertified, the fact that he or she cares enough to be a member of a professional society and receive their publications indicates a level of professional responsibility.

4.   Does the person have academic qualifications?   If so, this demonstrates that he or she has at least been exposed to the process of critical thinking and analysis.

None of these criteria is sufficient by itself, of course. Many excellent biologists work outside the university and civil service systems. At the same time, not everyone working within these systems is excellent at what they do. Furthermore, some biologists who know a lot about bears never bother to take the time, nor assume the responsibility, to publish; they spend their lives collecting data, which then die when they do. Additionally, many excellent biologists do not bother to become professionally certified; keep in mind, anyone can become a member of a professional society.

Yet again, I am also acquainted with a number of people who have few if any of the characteristics listed above, but who can claim significant accomplishments, and who are owed a high level of credibility, including some lawyers, photographers, and conservation activists. But however imperfect, the above considerations will weed out a high proportion of those who do not merit anyone's confidence when they talk about bears. Specifically, each of the listed considerations would have winnowed out Timothy Treadwell.

It is unfortunate that the talk shows and other media outlets too often gravitate toward false and self-anointed experts when they need a quote or opinion. They are often seeking something colorful to draw an audience, rather than good, solid, objective facts.   This tends to reinforce inappropriate behaviors in the minds of the media consumer.   It is worthwhile, therefore, that everyone apply a yardstick, such as the list above, in judging whether an "expert" in truth has any legitimate expertise, or if the expertise instead refers to an expert ability at self promotion.

How I Learned About Bears
Chuck Bartlebaugh
Grizzly Bear

Chuck Bartlebaugh is with the Center for Wildlife Information. In Mike Lapinski's book Grizzlies and Grizzled Old Men—A Tribute to Those who Fought to Save the Great Bear—*there is a chapter devoted to Chuck. Below, Chuck shares a few vignettes from his early days photographing bears, revealing that he hasn't always known how to behave properly in grizzly country. Today, he can hardly believe what a greenhorn he was back then, and how lucky he is to have survived his indiscretions unscathed.*

Admiralty Island, Alaska. I go to visit Stan Rice, and I take ice cream. Stan, who used to work for the government, has retired to the island, lives in a small cabin, and doesn't have anyplace to store ice cream. As I approach the cabin, I hear Stan inside talking. I assume he has another visitor.

"Stan, you in there? It's Chuck Bartlebaugh," I shout.

Stan opens the door, and out runs Belinda. Belinda is a big, fat brown bear. Stan has raised her since she was a cub. She ignores me and heads off somewhere.

Stan and I visit, and enjoy the ice cream. Then I decide to do a little exploring, take some photographs, take in some of the island. Stan says he's got some work to do in his garden, and heads outside too.

I putter around a bit with my cameras, and then I see Belinda near the garden, where Stan is busy working the soil. She then slowly heads off in the direction of the water, and I decide to follow right behind. I think this might be a good opportunity for some photographs. And I think I'd enjoy the company, too.

Stan put down his spade and said, "I wouldn't do that if I were you, Chuck. I wouldn't get so close to that bear"

"Why not? You had her in your cabin. She hangs around here all the time," I said.

"Oh, you mean Belinda. Well, that bear's not Belinda. I've never seen that bear before in my whole life."

* * * * * *

McNeil River, Alaska. There's a lot of bears on the river. Bears and salmon. For a wildlife photographer, the McNeil is hard to beat.

Patricia and her three cubs

I made the acquaintance of Patricia on the River. Patricia and her three cubs. Who could resist photographing such a charming family? And Patricia apparently found me charming, as well. She'd sit right next to me. As long as I held still, she'd even roll over on her back to nurse her cubs.

I got some amazing photographs, some of my best, I used to think. It was so easy to get on the wrong track like this, forgetting that bears are wild animals, and not subjects happy to pose for the photographer. Of course, I look back now on my experience with Patricia and shake my head. I look at the photographs. Was I out of my mind? If 100 yards, at minimum, is considered a safe distance for photographing bears, what was I doing sitting with Patricia practically in my lap?

So, yes, I've made some big mistakes around bears. And I've been lucky. Bears are unpredictable. Now, I would never consider getting close to a bear. I take my photographs from a safe distance, and I still get high quality shots.

I just needed to get educated.

* * * * * *

Back on the McNeil River. One last reminiscence. Of Patches, a dominant grizzly bear. He was out on the river, fishing. I was watching from up on the bank (I guess I wasn't completely crazy even back then). He's concentrating hard. Then he strikes.

Up he comes with a king salmon. It must be 60 pounds. It's huge, yet he is able to hold onto it with his mouth. What a prize catch.

Then he does what any male would do. He begins to prance up and down along the shoreline, back and forth, showing off his fish. Back and forth. I still wonder if he was doing that for my benefit, so I could capture him in this photograph. So you wouldn't think this was just another tall tale about a big fish.

Patches and his prize catch

Tom Mangelsen Photos

Fish for Dinner—The Grizzly
At the Polar Bear Dance—The Polar Bear

Wildlife photographer Tom Mangelsen travels the world, capturing images that amaze us with their beauty and wonder. And in the way a picture is worth a thousand words, his photos also instruct us about our natural world. Bears are among his favorite subjects. Tom has generously contributed the following photographs to this book. While we know that anthropomorphizing bears is not scientific, we could not resist adding captions to tell these stories.

FISH FOR DINNER

Now for the fish course.

Hold still, will ya?

Couldn't be fresher.

Maybe some berries for dessert.

Wow, I guess my eyes were bigger than my stomach.

I sure miss the old fishing hole.

AT THE POLAR BEAR DANCE

"And remember, stay away from those bad boys."

The Bad Boys scope out the dance.

"I didn't know you could polka."

One, two, cha cha cha.

"Whew, I think I'll sit this one out."

The Wallflowers

Visiting with the Ancestors

BEAR TRUST INTERNATIONAL

Bears of the World by Monte Dolack

Trail Crew Days
Bob Lange, Jr.
Grizzly Bear, Black Bear

Bob Lange recently retired from the USDA Forest Service. Back during his college days, Bob spent the summers of 1965 through 1969 in Glacier National Park building, maintaining, and improving trails, and performing other tasks, as a member of a trail crew. This was real backbreaking, back-country work, where bear encounters were not unexpected events. A few of these encounters he never forgot.

It was mid-September on a warm afternoon above tree line. We had just closed up a fire lookout tower for the year. I was leading on the trail, headed down the eight miles back to the ranger station. In truth, I was thinking more about a cold beer than a bear.

The trail was steep and switch-backed. I rounded a steep hill, and ran smack into a grizzly bear. I didn't hit him, because he was on his hind feet with his paws out. I could see every detail in those paws. He let out a roar.

This happened so fast that the three guys behind me walked right into me, and as a consequence pushed me forward, even closer to the big bear. I was paralyzed. I couldn't have picked up a stick or a rock to defend myself even if they were right at hand. Maybe that's what saved me, my paralysis.

That day, the bear just stood there, roaring and staring me down. Then, just like that, he jumped off the trail and ran down the steep mountain into the brush 100 yards away. I stood still, breathed deeply for a while, and then we proceeded down the mountain. I can report that that night, I had several beers. Today, the memory of those big bear paws is as fresh as the moment it happened.

* * * * * *

It was late spring, the beginning of the season in the Park. We were a small trail crew. On our first day, going up to Trout Lake, we bumped into a grizzly bear in the afternoon. He was at the foot of the lake, and he made it clear that he didn't want us there.

We made camp for the night. We figured we were safe, with the three mules and horse. We tied the animals up to some fir trees, in a circle around the camp. We figured they'd let us know if the bear decided it wanted to pay us a visit.

It had been a long day. We ate and went to bed. But we couldn't get any sleep.

The bear spent the whole night growling, tearing up rotten logs, digging in the dark. What a racket.

The mules and the horse spent the whole night bucking, snorting, circling on their leads. But at least their leads held.

And the members of the trail crew? We spent the whole night revving our chainsaw and feeding the fire.

We left at first light, and went back over the ridge to Lake MacDonald. The bear probably settled in for a nap, happy to be rid of us.

* * * * * *

It was the middle of the summer. We were camped up Park Creek. This is a long way from the ranger station, and a long way from good sense. We were staying at an old campsite by a patrol cabin.

We had this black bear that was tearing everything up when we left camp each day to clear or build trail. We got tired of the mess pretty quick and decided to do something about it. We had an old, worn out, sheet metal camp stove. We also had twelve-inch nails, the kind we used to build bridges.

We pounded a bunch of the nails through the bottom of the stove. We filled the stove with rocks, and hoisted it up into a spruce tree with a rope. Then we baited the ground underneath and waited.

Here she came. She was under the tree, working at the bait, when I dropped the spikes and rocks. But she was quicker. She leapt out of the way. I expected her to take off into the woods, but instead she ran right up the tree, up about 15 feet.

The only solution was to fire up the chain saw and cut down the tree. But as soon as that tree started to go, she charged down it, walked right off my back, and headed into the woods. I guess she was smarter than me. But at least she didn't come back.

In the Market for Bears
Sy Montgomery
Asiatic Black Bear

Writer and National Public Radio commentator Sy Montgomery
shares this chapter from her book Search for the Golden Moon
Bear, Science and Adventure in Pursuit of a New Species (Simon
and Schuster, 2002). *Traveling to Cambodia with Gary J.*
Galbreath, Ph.D., professor of evolutionary biology at Northwestern
University, the two embark on a remarkable journey looking for
Cambodia's elusive golden moon bear.

As we pull over at the market at Kampong Som—a street fragrant with
French bread and roasting swallows, crammed with wedding dresses, live
lobsters, chain saws, flyswatters, cooking pots—our Toyota is thronged
with children trying to sell us snails and clams. Our companion, Sun
Hean, chats in Khmer with a pregnant woman in a blue pantsuit. Does she
know where we might find a moon bear?

The name of the animal evokes the luminous night. Its original Latin
moniker—Selenarctos thibetanus—honors Selene, the Greek goddess of
the moon, because of the white crescent mark on the animal's chest.
Otherwise, the moon bear, big and shaggy, with prominent, round, upright
ears, and often, a thick mane like a lion's, is black as the tropical night—
and as mysterious.

Rudyard Kipling called it "the most bizarre of the ursine species." It
doesn't look like it belongs in the tropics. In fact, the first specimen
described by science came from the foothills of the snowy Himalayas.
Though moon bears are found from northeastern Russian and China to

Afghanistan, they are little studied. Not until the 1960s did scientists realize these dark, heavy beasts, panting beneath their thick coats, padded through the heated, steamy stillness of Cambodia's jungles.

Yet in the same forest where grasses grow into trees one hundred feet high and banyons spill curtains of hair-fine aerial roots from treetops, the moon bears of the Himalayas scratch and snuffle. At dawn and dusk, they shift like shadows among gingers and bamboos. Their imprint is unmistakable. On the straight-boled, spotted trunks of bee trees, they carve their five-fingered signatures with black, recurved claws. In the crotches of tropical oaks, they break tree limbs to create springy resting platforms for their up to 325-pound bulk. In glossy monsoon soils, they leave their footprints. With five rounded toes and a long heel pad on the back foot, their footsteps look like those of giant humans.

But you could spend years exploring these tangled rain forests and never see a moon bear. Instead, you would find them, as we did, caged in back of tourist hotels, chained outside of city pharmacies—and at markets like this one.

The pregnant woman doesn't ask what two young, well-dressed Cambodians, a sunburned blonde, and an American professor might want with a moon bear. She is an animal dealer. She knows that here in Cambodia, people buy bears for many reasons. They are treasured as household pets and kept as roadside attractions. They are sold for their meat and for their teeth. People eat their paws in soup and use their gall for medicine.

What *we* want from a moon bear, though, is stranger than the woman could possibly imagine. We want only to pluck out, with my eyebrow tweezers, a few of its hairs.

We already have a small zoo of hairs tucked in vials inside the professor's camera case. Each vial holds the genetic information of a bear captured from a different, known site. It is not the hair, per se, but its base, the living cells of the bulb, that contains the information we seek.

After we return to the States, a laboratory in Idaho will extract from these specks of flesh the genetic information contained in each bear's DNA, and compare them.

In this way, we hope to document what could be the first new bear species to be reported in over a century.

But in order to do so, we need the hair of a black moon bear who has been captured in this province, a bear from the fragrant, misty forests of the Elephant Mountains.

The animal dealer says she *had* a moon bear for sale—but just that morning she'd sent it to Phnom Penh. For what? I ask Sun Hean. "For pet. For restaurant. I don't know," he answers. But the dealer does confirm that the bear had come from the rain-forested slopes of the Elephant Mountains. And there will be more where it came from.

Two mountain systems comprise most of the wilderness left in mainland Southeast Asia: with the adjoining Elephant Mountains and Cambodia's highest peak, Phnom Oral, the Cardamom range, occupying much of western Cambodia, huddles in the shape of a Q beneath a cloak of monsoon clouds. The rainfall here is the highest in Cambodia, and the jungles the most dense. The spice-scented forests harbor creatures beautiful, deadly, and ancient: clouded leopards, with spotted coats soft and thick as mist; tiny primitive deer called muntjacks, their upper jaws curiously spiked with fangs. There are more tigers here than anywhere else in the country, and possibly, more wild elephants than anywhere else in Indochina. In similar habitat in neighboring Vietnam, scientists discovered in 1989 fresh tracks of the Javan rhinoceros species thought extinct on the mainland for nearly half a century; some think it might yet survive here, too.

The other, wildest mountains are the Annamites. In a great igneous spine, they run for more than six hundred miles from the northeastern corner of Cambodia up along the border of Vietnam and Laos. A mosaic of rain forest, dry evergreen woods, cypress and old-growth pine, the

Annamites preserve, in the words of the great American wildlife conservationist George Schaller, "a living lost world." Four hundred species of birds have been cataloged here, a count only cursory. Of the roughly dozen large mammal species discovered in the world since 1900, nearly half of them—including a two hundred-pound antelope with spear-like horns, a giant, barking deer, and a zebra-striped rabbit—have been found, since 1992, in the Annamites.

Eventually our quest will lead us into both these mountain jungles. But before we would step into that wild and leafy realm, we would need to search its looking-glass opposites: private zoos, hotel menageries, and noisy, crowded streetside markets.

In Kampong Som, it appears that most of the wildlife is destined for the dinner plate. Along the street, where dentists advertise their services with large paintings of white, extracted teeth, a beautiful young woman, her hair tied up neatly beneath a conical hat, tends a charcoal fire over which skewered bats are roasting. In a pink plastic bowl beneath a dome of woven rattan, live frogs, tortoises, and cobras await the soup pot. In the palm oil of a neighboring vendor's wok, three-inch grasshoppers sizzle.

"Is there any animal that people don't eat here?" I asked Sun Hean.

He thought for a moment. "The vulture," he answered solemnly.

The scent of pigs' blood mingles with the fragrance of temple marigolds. To be looking for a new species here seems irreconcilably absurd.

But it is no more unlikely, really, than the way our expedition had begun.

* * *

The route that led to the market in Kampong Som was circuitous, winding from China to the Amazon, from Hancock, New Hampshire, to Bangkok, Thailand. I had come to Cambodia thanks to extraordinary coincidences and extraordinary people.

Dr. Gary J. Galbreath was one of them. A professor of evolutionary biology at Northwestern University and a research associate of the famous Field Museum, Gary had been president of the Chicago-based Rainforest Conservation Fund when it took on funding the Tamshiyacu-Tahuayo Community Reserve in Peru in 1991. We met there in 1997 when I was researching a book on the Amazon's pink river dolphins.

"Did you know," Gary asked me as our boat chugged up the tea-colored river, "this place used to be full of giant, carnivorous Terror Birds?"

No, I did not. This he quickly remedied.

"They were feathered dinosaurs, essentially, long after the dinosaurs went extinct," he began. "It's possible a human being even saw one. They were the dominant predators in South America during the Age of Mammals. The Terror Birds even made it to Florida—to Daytona Beach! They found some fossils there. But only twenty months ago their *arms* were found—and it turns out they weren't winged like we thought."

This modest, green-eyed, middle-aged professor had me mesmerized.

"They had evolved tearing arms, with two fingerlike projections to grab their prey," he continued. "The fingers are fused bones, like the panda's thumb. Terror Birds began to decline when dogs, cats, and bears came down from North America, three million years ago or so. And if that didn't do them in, then people came eleven to thirteen thousand years ago and killed off their prey, the giant ground sloths and zebras . . ."

I was next surprised to learn that zebras arose in North America; that horses are more closely related to dogs than pigs; that a friend of his had shot for dinner, and thus discovered, a new species of pig, the sweet-smelling Chacoan peccary, and that, as a graduate student, Gary had acquired a pair of armadillos who liked to sleep with him in his bed. But I was not surprised to learn—much later and from another biologist—that at Gary's last lecture of the year, his students gave him a standing ovation.

After each day's fieldwork, when the others' talk often turned to jobs or family, photography or politics, Gary and I would take a canoe out on the dark waters of the Tahuayo and talk about animals and evolution.

It was on one of those starry, timeless nights that he told me about the golden moon bear.

Gary had been a delegate of the American Society of Mammalogists for the group's first official meeting with its Chinese counterpart in Beijing, back in 1988. Afterward, he had traveled south, to explore the tropical rain forest of Yunnan Province with a small contingent of other biologists.

"We were in this little town in Yunnan called Simao. My friend, Penny, called me over. She said there was something I should see. And there, in this little cage—it was sort of like a town mascot, and taking peanuts, very gently, from people's hands—was this young male bear, maybe ninety kilos, with tall, round ears and a white V on the chest. But what was remarkable was, its coat was golden. I had never seen anything like it."

In fact, Gary was stunned. The biologist was facing a creature he could not identify.

Quickly, he sorted through his encyclopedic zoological memory. There were only eight know species of bear on Earth. Obviously this was not a polar bear, or a panda. Nor was it an American black bear—although "black bears" can be brown, cinnamon, blond, or even white, the ears on this animal were too big for an American black bear. It couldn't be a spectacled bear, a native of South America's Andean highlands. It looked nothing like one, having a longer snout than this short-faced bear, and lacked the circular white markings around the eyes that make the spectacled bear look like it is wearing glasses.

Besides the panda, four other bear species are known in Asia. Sun bears—named for the patch, often sunrise orange, on the chest—barely range into tropical Yunnan. But this clearly wasn't one. Sun bears, the smallest and most tree-loving of bears, have inconspicuous ears, short, jet

fur, long claws, and huge, stout canines. Nor was this a sloth bear, also
known from Asia's tropics—it has masses of fluffy, messy, black hair,
unusually mobile lips, with which it sucks termites out of their hills like a
vacuum hose, and nostrils it can slam shut to keep termites from crawling
in. The only Asian bear with a coat that ever comes close to blond is the
brown bear, the same species (although a different subspecies) as the
American grizzly. But it is unknown from the tropics. The only Asian
bear with big ears like this was a moon bear—but Gary had never heard of
one with a golden coat.

He took photos, and so did his friend and colleague, physician Penny
Walker. "I was photographing it in case it wasn't known," he said. "But
what were the chances of my discovering a new bear? For all I knew,
someone in the literature long ago described a blond bear like this."

The next day, at the Kunming natural history museum, Gary looked
through the collection of moon bear skins. All of them were black. But
during China's Cultural Revolution, all the specimens' tags were
destroyed, so he had no idea where they came from—or even whether
moon bears had ever before been recorded living in Yunnan.

"It was enough to excite interest," he said. "This was of potentially
significant biological import." Variation in coat color is important to
document, Gary explained; one of the biologist's principal tasks, after all,
is to describe the natural world. An unreported color phase in an existing
species is an exciting finding, akin to making the first reports of a black
panther (which is a dark form of the normally black-and-gold spotted
leopard) or a white tiger (a pale-coated from of the Royal Bengal tiger).
But the golden bear could be a discovery far more spectacular. Gary knew
from his postdoctoral work on New World owl monkeys that, in the
absence of genetic analysis, coat color alone can serve as a way—
sometimes the only way—to tell different species apart. If the golden bear
represented a new species, it would be the scientific finding of a lifetime—
the first new bear reported since the panda more than a hundred years

before. "This could be a major biological discovery," Gary realized. "But I was telling myself, I'm sure these things were known . . ."

When he returned from China, Gary made an exhaustive search of the scientific literature. He checked explorers' accounts of zoological expeditions throughout Asia. He laboriously translated manuscripts from French and German. He discovered only one account of a bear from Southeast Asia that wasn't black—a 1906 report of a young male bear with brown hair tipped with gray. Secured from an animal dealer, it was said to have come from the Shan States of upper Burma and thought to be a kind of grizzly. It was tentatively given the subspecies name *Ursus arctos shanorum*. There was no mention of a blond bear. Anywhere.

Gary had always wanted to go back to Simao and find out more, he told me. But his demanding teaching load at Northwestern was compounded by his administrative duties as associate director of the undergraduate biology department. Besides, what were the chances that bear was still there? Several times, he had started to write up an account of the golden bear for scientific publication, then abandoned the idea. "This was just one specimen. It could have been a mutant individual—not a new color phase, not a new species, not anything."

Still, the image of that bear stayed with him for nine years. Like a siren, it beckoned him, nagged him, teased. He could not forget it—but he did not see how to pursue it, either: "There was only one," he said, "just one, weird bear."

Or so we thought—until one year later, when I met Sun Hean.

At a birthday party in the small New Hampshire town where I live, a friend brought a guest whose power and importance went largely unappreciated by the others. Shy and unsure of his English, with a round, boyish face, Sun Hean looked like a foreign graduate student, which he was. But he was also, although still in his twenties, the deputy director for the Wildlife Protection Office of Cambodia—the equivalent of the second in command of the United States' Fish and Wildlife Service.

I asked him about bears. Had he ever heard of a bear in his country that wasn't black?

His dark eyes widened. Yes—in fact, a member of his staff had just sent him photographs of a strange bear. It was the color of gold.

It was living in a cage just east of Kampong Som, the captive of a wealthy palm oil plantation owner. Sun Hean was fascinated by it; he didn't know what it was. Cambodia had two known species of bear, the sun and the moon bear. This one, with its mysterious golden coat, looked to him like neither.

I arranged for Sun Hean and Gary to meet. I, too, flew to meet Sun Hean at the University of Minnesota, where he was next sent for graduate studies as part of the Fulbright scholarship that had brought him to the United States. The two men compared their photographs of different animals, taken a thousand kilometers and eleven years apart. They were virtually identical.

We began to plan our expedition.

* * *

Few travel guides were available for Cambodia. The country was usually included in larger volumes mostly devoted to the safer and more alluring Thailand, or sometimes with Vietnam and Laos. The sections on Cambodia did not begin on a hopeful note. *Travelers' Companion* noted that the Phnom Penh English-language newspaper, *Bayon Pearnick*, carried helpful articles for visitors, such as "Keeping Your Head While Losing Your Wallet," and a story on the latest public safety effort, the designation of Feburary 24 as National Mine Awareness Day. (In the 1980s, the government had also declared a National Hate Day, setting aside May 20 as a day for everyone to reaffirm his hatred of former Khmer Rouge leader Pol Pot.)

Cambodia is the most heavily mined country on earth, with four to eight million land mines, according to one estimate—at least one land mine for every man, woman, and child still left alive when the Khmer

Rouge were overthrown in 1979. The Communist forces had seeded fields and forests with explosives, fashioned from 60-mm and 82-mm mortar shells and from sections of iron water pipes stuffed with TNT, sugar, fertilizer, and shrapnel. These were supplemented with Chinese pressure mines, small as a lady's compact but capable of blowing off a leg. They were hung from bushes, buried along paths, placed near wells, at riverbanks and around fruit trees—anywhere people would go. As a result, 1 in 236 Cambodians is an amputee. An Australian Red Cross doctor called the one-legged man "the most obvious characteristic of national identity." Some thirty-five thousand of Cambodia's citizens have lost a limb to a land mine, and according to the reports we read, another three hundred to seven hundred more injuries were being added to the list each month.

Compounding the injuries from land mines was the fact that doctors could do little to help. Cambodia had no decent medical care, we read. Foreigners who get hurt or sick in Cambodia are advised to evacuate to Bangkok. Most of Cambodia's doctors were killed by the Khmer Rouge, who also destroyed most of the hospitals. Those who remain have no pharmaceuticals. The local life expectancy listed in our guide was 40. "According to this, we should both be dead already!" Gary noted when he read the statistic.

In his thorough manner, Gary had searched for travel information before we departed that summer. He had printed out, among other things, a report on Cambodia by the Control Risk Group Ltd., which prepared what it touts as up-to-the-minute online advisories for business travelers. In June 1999, it rated Cambodia thus:

> Political Risk Rating: *high*
> Security Risk Rating: *high*
> Travel Risk Rating: *high*

In the mid-nineties, the Khmer Rouge had been the main safety concern for foreigners in Cambodia, as the infrequent Western visitor was an easy target for terrorists. In 1994, the Communist rebels had kidnapped, in two separate incidents, four Britons, an Australian, and a Frenchman, three of whom were tourists. All were later murdered.

But by the time we were planning our travels, Sun Hean had assured us the Khmer Rouge were "no problem." When we had met in Minnesota, he had mapped out our route: from Phnom Penh, we would drive west, through the Elephant Mountains, to Kampong Som. We would then take a ferry to Koh Kong, and further explore the Cardamom range.

"Road travel outside cities is not recommended," Gary read to me from his risk report—not only because of land mines, but also because of antigovernment guerrillas. The Communist guerrillas' field forces had swelled to eighteen thousand in the early 1990s, and supplied with Chinese weapons, were said to be concentrated at our destination—the Cardamom Mountains. And the road to the port of Kampong Som, the report said, was potholed and thronged with bandits.

I had heard about the bandits. "Government soldiers, as well as Khmer Rouge rebels, sometimes resort to highway robbery," I read to Gary from a 1996 travel guide. "Bandits regularly hold travelers at gunpoint as they point torches into the eyes of long-distance taxi drivers—who now build the extortion money into the cost of a trip."

"The bandits might take our money," Gary resolved, "but they're not getting our bear hairs!"

Later, we found Cambodia listed in the 2000 edition of *The World's Most Dangerous Places*. "Don't be fooled," wrote its author, Robert Young. "With the demise of the Khmer Rouge, the violence simply doesn't make as many headlines." A pamphlet that the United Nations-sponsored peacekeeping unit had issued its soldiers and workers in 1992 contained Khmer phrases Young felt would be still useful to travelers today:

"That's a very nice gun, sir. I'd be honored to give you the gift of my truck."

* * *

We got a good deal on air ticket from Korean Air Lines—no doubt
because we would fly roughly the same route that the ill-fated KAL Flight
007 had plotted before it was shot down over Kamchatka in the 1980s.
Surely every passenger on board had the same thought as we watched the
map on our personal video screens showing our plane skirting Russian
airspace—all except Gary. "Look," he said cheerfully. "We're flying
over Kamchatka—where the really giant bears live!"

For thirteen hours, on our flight from Chicago to Seoul, and then on the
five-hour flight from Seoul to Bangkok, we talked bears.

"According to Ognev," he said, citing the great Russian zoologist,
"there are two kinds of grizzlies on the Kamchatka Peninsula: one the size
of the American grizzly, the other the size of a Kodiak." These bears were
giant enough—an American grizzly can weigh 700 pounds, and a male
Kodiak, 1,800 pounds. But there could be a third, even larger. Siberian
hunters claim that Arctodus-like bears may also survive there—bears
twice the size of a Kodiak.

Arctodus simus, the giant short-faced bear, was the largest terrestrial
carnivore that ever lived. On long legs, it raced after zebras, camels, and
bison and brought them down with a bite from canines larger than a
leopard's It would have been far swifter than a grizzly (who can, for short
periods, run forty miles an hour) and more ferocious than a cave lion. For
the first humans who invaded North America, Arctodus would have been a
horrifying predator. "No kill by hunters would have been defensible
against this beast, no hut would have been safe at night; no human would
have been able to outrun this bear; and few trees would have been present
or tall enough to climb for safety in the open country where it roamed,"
the wildlife biologist Valerius Geist wrote of the creature. In fact, the
Canadian scientist suggests that it was this bear that slowed the
immigration of humans from Asia to the New World. So agile and
predatory a beast, he writes, would have "made human life in North

America impossible. Only when this fauna collapsed did humans make inroads."

Arctodus was believed extinct by the late Pleistocene, twelve thousand years ago. Might it still survive? "Occasionally a hunter shows a TV crew what he claims is a skin of one, "Gary said. He doubted it; but we both savored the thought. We wanted more bears.

Bears were special animals to both of us, for a variety of reasons. Gary had always been impressed by their size and ferocity. "They're big, and even as a youngster I liked that about them," he said, his green eyes glowing with childhood daydreams. "You think of them as being, in the temperate zone, at the top of the heap, like the lion in Africa or the tiger in Asia."

Besides, for Gary—whose passion for mysteries extended to devouring whodunits and even to loving algebra (since it required solving for the unknown)—the bear clan offered a fascinating taxonomic puzzle. "Nearly everywhere there have been bears, there have been arguments about how many different types there are," he said.

The varied appearance of grizzlies shows the common name for the species, brown bear, is a misnomer. He prefers to call them all grizzlies. For instance, the so-called red bear or Himalayan grizzly, also knows as the Isabelline bear, *Ursus arctos isabellinus*, can be reddish, brown, yellow, or even white. There's a blue bear, also considered a grizzly, *Ursus arctos pruinosus*, who lives on the Tibetan plateau, whose coat is grayish-black with a blond face. In Turkey, Iran and Iraq survive the last of a lighter-coated grizzly, *Ursus arctos syriacus*. And there are grizzlies of all different shapes, sizes and habits in between. A dwarf grizzly survives in the Gobi Desert of Mongolia; ten-foot-long grizzlies patrol the taiga of Russia's Vladivostok area. On Admiralty Island live huge, coal-black grizzlies. They, DNA studies now show, are the closest relatives of the polar bears—who are among nature's more recent inventions. The polar bear is a species less than half a million years old.

"And what about moon bears?" I asked. "Where do they fit in?"

"Ah!" said Gary. This was his favorite sort of question, for it required him to travel back in time. "Moon bears are the least changed of all the Old World bears," he said. "You could even argue they are the lineage from which most other Old World bears evolved." Four million years ago, a small bear now known as *Ursus minimus* ("small bear") appeared in Eurasia—an animal about the size of a modern sun bear, perhaps a hundred pounds. But other than its size, "*Ursus minimus* probably looked much like a moon bear," Gary said. "So much so, in fact, that except for the age of the bones, it would be extremely difficult to distinguish fossils of *Ursus minimus* from the skeleton of a living moon bear."

In the temperate and subtropical forests of Eurasia, this early bear was a generalist, able to thrive in a variety of habitats, Gary explained. It could climb trees but was not restricted to thick forest. It could eat meat, but could survive on plants, too. As the climate continued to cool and the world became seasonal, the descendants of *Ursus minimus* were able to outlast the Eurasian lions and hippos who had been its cohorts in the Pliocene and Pleistocene. It was this moon bearlike creature—not the ferocious, short-faced Arctodus—that gave rise, in the turbulent ice ages of the Pleistocene, to all the modern bears except the South American spectacled bear and the enigmatic panda.

Gary took his greatest delight in exploring the origin of things. By the time he was in second grade, he had already memorized the geologic time scale, as well as the scientific names for most of the major animals in each. He kept an extensive collection of plastic dinosaurs, as well as a scrapbook for clippings about rare and vanishing animals: rhinos and elephants, a living legacy of the Pleistocene—like bears are.

As a child, Gary's deepest wish had been for a time machine. But as a grown-up scientist, his greatest dream was to discover and to name a new species in our own time. The golden bear offered him a shot at every biologist's Holy Grail.

For me, bears held a different fascination. I knew several personally. In New Hampshire, a friend of mine, wildlife rehabilitator Ben Kilham, had rescued several litters of orphaned American black bears when they were so young that their noses were still pink and their eyes still blue. I had held some of these babies in my arms. When they were youngsters, I had watched them gambol in the northern woods, smelling and licking their way through a realm no human can experience. Their world is a symphony of scent, so rich in information, Ben came to understand, that bears may even be able to assess the nutritional and perhaps medicinal properties of plants with nose and tongue. I would return home feeling blessed by another world, redolent with the heady, musky, rich-earth smell of their fur, the caress of their wet, ribbonlike tongues still tingling my skin.

With Ben and with other wildlife biologists, I had also tracked wild, radio-collared black bears through the woods of Massachusetts and Vermont. One of the bears I followed was a ten-year-old female known as Number 125. Bear biologist John McDonald and his colleagues had studied her for eight years, tracking her each winter to her den to tranquilize, weigh, and examine her and her generations of cubs.

One February, we had followed the beep of the telemetry receiver to Number 125's shallow den beneath a slab of granite. Before John had a chance to warn me, and before the veterinarian had tranquilized her, I wedged my face into its opening. I looked directly into the mahogany eyes and tan muzzle of a fully alert mother bear and her two cubs.

My face was inches from her jaws. But I was never for a moment afraid. I knew that American black bears, unlike grizzly bears, almost never attack people. They do not consider us prey and are far more likely to flee than to strike out, even in defense of cubs. I knew that this female was probably more mortified than angry to see me, a hideous human, invading the sanctity of her nursery. But I knew something else as well.

Meeting her eyes, I recognized in her brown gaze an ancient knowing, a cognizance remarkably humanlike, and yet more-than-human.

Humans have known this about bears since the dawn of our kind. For possibly as long as fifty thousand years, festivals of the bear ceremonies have celebrated the bear as a sacred messenger and mediator, a teacher, a traveler between worlds. Throughout human history, people have claimed kinship with them. Bears are strikingly humanlike: when they stand on their hind legs, when they sit, back against a tree, their postures look like ours, their front legs hanging down like arms. Their hands are dexterous enough to peel a peach. (The Blackfoot Indian word for the human hand is the same as the word for bear paw.) They are so intelligent that skilled trackers like Pennsylvania-based bear biologist Gary Alt has documented them outwitting people by causing their own tracks to vanish—by carefully backtracking. Ben Kilham considers bears at least as smart as chimps, though the animals are very different. In so many ways, bears mirror, then exceed us: in strength, in size, in sensory acuity. So we have made them our teachers, our mentors, our inspiration. The Khanty and Mansi people of Siberia say they received fire and weapons from the world's first bear. Many Native American tribes say the bear taught them the use of medicinal herbs. (And bears may in fact number among the animals documented to use plants as medicine. Just one example: an Alaskan hunting guide watched, puzzled, as a grizzly methodically stripped the bark from a willow shrub, which bears don't normally eat. He shot the bear and noticed the bear had an abscessed tooth—around which was packed willow bark, the source of salicylic acid, the active ingredient in aspirin.) The fierce Germanic warriors, the Berserks, took their name from the beast, and wore its skin in an effort to take on bear magic.

These northern peoples saw bears perform the impossible each spring. Emerging from the deathly still of hibernation out of gravelike dens, bears rise, Christlike, from the dead. The wise female bear, like the grandmother I had met in her den, brings forth her young from the earth itself, a netherworld Genetrix. Perhaps it was the bear who taught us to expect miracles. Some researchers suggest this is why humans bury their dead, trusting the bear's promise of transformation.

The Ostyaks, of western Siberia, say the bear began as a heavenly force, born of a union between the sun and moon. The bear still dwells in the sky. Ursa Major dominates the northern night, making its passage around the Pole Star in Ursa Minor, the star that has guided our kind for millennia, and given us our aptly named "bearings." At both ends of the universe, from the underworld den to the sky, the bear helps us find our place in the renewing cycle of the cosmos.

So, for our different reasons, Gary and I both saw, in this bear, opportunities as golden as its mysterious and intriguing coat. Whether we would describe a new species or an unknown color phase; whether we would witness miracles or achieve transformation; whether our story would lead to renewal or frustration—of course we could not know. But we were willing to follow a bear into a mine field to find out.

* * *

If he had anything like a totem animal, Gary mused on the plane, it would be the bear. The sole emblem on the Galbreath family crest, he said, is the head of a bear in a muzzle.

The symbol suggests controlled power. The Montgomery family crest, on the other hand, suggests unbridled rage: it shows a woman holding up the severed head of her enemy. This might have alarmed another traveler about to spend six weeks with a member of such a clan. But Gary, ever generous and optimistic, took this as a good sign. He noted that Galbreath means "foreign mercenary" and Gary means "spear-carrier." On paper, at least, we made a ferocious combination. "Considering where we're going," Gary had told me, "we should make an exceptionally successful team."

But in the fever-dream jumble of the market at Kampong Son, I have my doubts.

In the migrainous heat, an old woman spits blood on the dirt. No; she is chewing betel, the nutmeg-sized fruit of the graceful *Areca* palm. It produces a mild narcotic that reddens the saliva and stains the teeth black. The woman looks up at me and, parting bloodied lips, offers me a shocking, generous, grandmotherly smile—and then returns to tending a brace of skewered songbirds on the grill. Their eyes have melted, their beaks burned black.

We drive on to seek another bear.

More about Asiatic Black Bears
from Bear Trust International

Bear Trust is solely responsible for the information in this section. Opinions about this information may vary.

Asiatic Black Bear - *Ursus Thibetanus*

Other Names: Himalayan Black Bear, Tibetan Black Bear, Moon Bear

Appearance:
The Asiatic black bear is medium-sized, with a black coat and a lightish muzzle, with white on the chin. There is a distinct white patch on the chest which is sometimes in the shape of a "V." The "golden moon bear" represents a color phase.

Size:
Adult males range from 220 to 440 pounds (100 to 200 kg), while adult females weight from 110 to 275 pounds (50 to 125 kg). Birth weight is 10.5 ounces (298 grams).

Reproduction:
Female Asiatic black bears mature at three to four years of age. Mating practices and birthing seasons are different between populations. Cubs are weaned at less than six months, but may stay with their mothers for two to three years.

Social Life:
Little is known of the social organization in the wild.

Food:
Asiatic black bears eat fruits, nests of bees, insects, invertebrates, small vertebrates, and carrion.

Habitat:
Asiatic black bears inhabit forested areas, especially hills and mountainous areas. They are distributed through Southern Asia, Northeast China, Japan and Far Eastern Russia. Their habitat varies by seasons; they spend their summer at higher elevations and descend to lower elevations during the winter.

Wild Population:
The population of Asiatic black bears is unknown. They are threatened by habitat destruction and the harvesting of forests.

FYI:
Asiatic black bears and American black bears are sister taxa; they are more closely related to each other than to the six other living bear species.

In northern parts of their range, Asiatic black bears den to hibernate, but in the in the southern limits of their range they probably do not.

Bibi and the Python
Gabriella Fredriksson
Sun Bear

Gabriella Fredriksson has worked in Indonesia since 1994, initially on orangutans but later on Malayan sun bears. She is co-chair of the Sun Bear Expert Team, Bear Specialist Group, for the International Association for Bear Research and Management (IBA). Here, she shares some details on doing research in Indonesian Borneo, then tells the amazing story of Bibi and the phython.

Beep…beep…beep…beep. The stable signal is reassuring, telling me the sound from the radio collar (literally, a radio transmitter attached to a collar) indicates that the female sun bear and her cub are still sleeping. After more than one year of trying to trap these elusive and shy bears, we have finally managed to get a radio collar on three female sun bears.

I'm sitting on a ridge in the forest, and it is 3:45 A.M. Male Bornean gibbons have started their eerie morning calls—very different from the loud, female, bubbly territorial songs which start around 5 A.M. It is still cold in the forest, and occasional rustlings nearby from invisible nocturnal mammals in the leaf litter are keeping me awake.

Once a week we follow each of the radio-collared sun bears for 24 hours to get a picture of their activity patterns. We check the signal of the radio collar. This tells us whether the bears are active or resting, every ten minutes. The bears seem to have a pattern much like humans here in East Kalimantan (Indonesian Borneo): they wake up at around 5:00 AM, spend the whole morning foraging for food, have a short siesta during the midday heat, and then it's back to foraging until early evening, after which they usually sleep peacefully on a large log or up on a big tree branch until next morning.

In addition to the three wild females, we have also put radio collars on three sun bears we have released in the forest. We received these three bears from the Indonesian Forestry Department when they were small cubs, each of them confiscated from the illegal wildlife trade, which still thrives in Indonesia. Sun bears are occasionally held as pets when they are cubs, but frequently get killed when they are about two years old, when they have grown large and have become destructive or dangerous as pets.

Cubs are typically caught in the forest during logging operations. A female sun bear usually gives birth to one cub, and the baby bear is born as helpless as a newborn cat—blind and with little fur. The mother bear keeps the cub in a safe place, such as a big hollow log, until it is able to walk and climb around a bit. Then it spends most of its time sleeping up in the forks of small trees until the mother comes back from foraging. By the time it is three-to-four-months old, it can follow the mother around and learn how to forage. Sun bears do not have the need to hibernate, as they live in the tropics with food available in some form all year round.

The cubs we have released were initially taken for walks in the forest by me and my assistants until they were about one or two years old. By then, they had learned sufficient forest skills so that they did not need our additional fruit feedings. Once the bears became independent, we radio-collared them and followed them in the forest twice a week to make observations of their behaviour.

The many days of observations in the forest have been the most enjoyable part of the research I carried out on sun bears. As the bears were used to us, they would allow us to follow them around all day whilst they were foraging, playing, resting or whatever they were up to. These observations have given us an invaluable insight into the behaviour of sun bears.

Sun bears are omnivores, and primarily feed on termites, ants, and beetle larvae. A single bear can break into more than 100 termite nests a day! If and when available, they eat a large variety of fruits. The bears love the smelly durian fruits, and will gorge themselves during the fruit season—in fact, sun bears play a key role in Borneo by spreading large seeds around the forest. Honey, although a favourite, is only found occasionally by the bears.

Sun bears have very long, sharp claws that enable them to dig easily into the ground, and break into logs. Their massive jaw muscles make it possible to bite through the bark of hardwood trees in search of insects and honey, and their extremely long tongues help them to extract these foods from crevices. Most of our information on the diet of sun bears comes from scat analysis. We collected more than 1200 scats during my five-year study in the field. From this, we would find out what the bears eat and when.

The sun bear is the smallest of the world's eight living bear species, weighing only about 30 to 65 kilograms (66 to 145 pounds). Sun bears occur throughout Southeast Asia, from the eastern edge of India, northern Burma to Laos, Cambodia, Vietnam, and Thailand, and farther south to peninsular Malaysia and on the islands of Sumatra and Borneo.

Bornean sun bears are the smallest of all sun bears, separating them currently into a subspecies, *Helarctos malayanus euryspilus*

Almost every sun bear has an individually distinct chest patch which is typically yellow and can range from circular to a more usual 'V' or 'U' shape. The name 'sun bear' probably originates from the colour and shape of the chest patch. The sun bear has front feet which are slightly turned inward, large naked paws, and long curved claws, so it is well adapted for climbing trees and breaking into the nests of stingless bees.

* * * * * *

Bibi and the Python

One sunny morning, about a month after we caught the first wild female sun bear, I came across one of my assistants on a ridge in the forest. He made me listen to the radio signal of the female we called 'Bibi.' It seemed that the collar had switched to "mortality mode," which happens if a collar has not moved for more than four hours. My thoughts were that the sun bear had probably dropped the radio collar, as it had been put loosely around her neck because she was rather skinny when we caught her.

I went off in search of the collar, which led me to a swamp not far from our campsite. Swamps in the forest here are not great fun, as they are full of spiny rattans and other prickly climbers. I finally pinpointed the signal, which was coming from a dense rattan thicket, but I needed to climb over a log to enter it. I noticed something with a white colour lying there.

My first thoughts were that it was a large rice bag, and that someone had killed the bear and stashed it in the bag under the thicket. But after a closer look, I noticed that the white colour was in fact the distended scales of the underside of a huge snake—and only then did I see that it was actually a giant python lying there curled up! It took a couple of seconds before I realized that the radio collar must be inside the python, meaning that the adult sun bear female was swallowed whole by the snake!

The python had a huge bulge in its middle, and when I put my radio antenna next to the bulge in the snake, it became clear that indeed the radio collar/bear were inside the snake. I called my assistants on the radio to come and have a look. In hindsight, calling them was a bad idea. After seeing the size of the snake and realizing that it could obviously easily swallow one of them—the snake was more than 7 meters long—my assistants refused to enter the forest alone at night for our frequent bear activity studies. So I was left to do all the night work alone.

* * * * * *

Fortunately no more bears were swallowed by pythons during my study. But the truth is, the main threat to sun bears comes from people. The tropical hardwood rainforests that are the sun bear's habitat are highly valued by humans for timber production, and they are rapidly being converted to second-growth forest, cash-crop plantations, or other human uses. Huge areas have also been devastated in recent years by fire. Malaysia and Indonesia are the world's leading exporters of tropical hardwoods, and most of these exports originate from the sun bear's shrinking habitat. In other parts of their range, like Vietnam, Cambodia and Laos, sun bears are also seriously threatened by hunters harvesting their body parts and gall bladders, which are highly valued in traditional Chinese medicine.

Obviously if these clever and attractive bears are to survive in the wild, more serious conservation efforts are needed both to stop hunting and to protect the habitat in which the sun bear plays such an important role.

More about the Sun Bear
from Bear Trust International
Bear Trust is solely responsible for the information in this section. Opinions about this information may vary

Sun Bear - *Helarctos Malayanus*

Other Names: Malaysian, Honey Bear, Dog Bear

Appearance:
The sun bear has a short, sleek, black coat, with a muzzle that ranges from a gray color to a faint orange. The crescent-shaped chest patch is white/yellowish/orange. The paws are large, and have huge claws suitable for climbing, digging and breaking into rotten logs. Sun bears have the longest tongues of all bear species in order to extract insects from crevices.

Size:
Adult male sun bears weigh 60 to 145 pounds (27 to 66 lg); female sun bears are somewhat smaller. The average length of the sun bear is 51-74 inches (130 to 188 cm). At birth, cubs weigh about 10 ounces (284 grams).

Reproduction:
Little is known about the reproductive behavior of the sun bear in the wild. Cubs remain with their mothers until they are fully grown, at about 2 years of age.

Social Life:
Sun bears seem to be solitary, but little is known of their social organization in the wild.

Food:
The sun bear's diet is omnivorous, and includes termites, fruits and nuts, ants, beetle grubs, occasional scavenging, and some vegetative matter.

Habitat:
Sun bears inhabit evergreen tropical forests, from sea-level to lower montane areas. Sun bears are known in Southeast Asia from northern Burma, Bangladesh, Eastern India, southern China, Laos, Cambodia, Vietnam, and Thailand, Malaysia and the islands of Sumatra and Borneo.

Wild Population:
Unknown. Sun bears are threatened due to habitat conversion, development and poaching.

FYI:
The sun bear is the smallest species of bear.

Up in trees, the sun bear is the most agile of all bear species.

How Sun Bear Sent His Greetings to Moon Bear
A Fable

*Fables appear throughout world literature, in oral and written form,
to illustrate a moral lesson, to explain events, or to instruct. Fables
typically feature animals, which are given human qualities. Bears
are common elements in fables. The following story uses the fable
form to briefly familiarize the reader with the Sun Bear and the
Moon Bear (Asiatic Black Bear).*

In the Kingdom of Animalia, in the Phylum of Chordata, Class of
Mammalia, Order of Carnivora, Family of Ursidae, live the Sun Bear and
the Moon Bear. Since the beginning, Sun Bear had heard about Moon
Bear, but had never seen him. Moon Bear, too, had heard about Sun Bear,
had looked high and low, but could not find him. And so, to discover if
the other bear really existed, Sun Bear and Moon Bear set out on a journey
to seek the other out.

Sun Bear, whose sisters and brothers called him Helarctos malayanus,
left his home deep in the tropical rainforest, where the tall trees reach into
the sky, and heavy honeycombs hang off the branches. Although he was
the smallest of all the bear species in the Kingdom of Animalia, Family of
Ursidae, Sun Bear was just as brave as all of the others. And while he
loved his home deep inside the lowland rainforest, he had a curious streak,
which matched the mango-colored crescent of sun on his chest.

Moon Bear, whose sisters and brothers called him Ursus thibetanus, left
his mountain home in the temperate forest, where there were acorns and
chestnuts to feast on in autumn, and bamboo and hydrangea in the spring.

Although he was big and plump, as most bears in the Family of Ursidae tend to be, Moon Bear had strong forelimbs and claws to help haul himself up into trees. And while he loved his home, he had a curious streak, which matched the cream-colored V on his chest.

◆ ◆ ◆

One late afternoon, after sleeping much of the day, as nocturnal animals are inclined to do, Sun Bear ran into three humans coming along the path: Jake, Haley, and Max. Sun Bear was very shy, but he took a deep breath for courage and said, "Pardon me. I am Sun Bear, and I am looking for Moon Bear. You look like travelers who know the world, the way all humans do. Can you help me?"

"Sun Bear? You look more like a dog. Surely you're too small to be a bear," said Jake, leaning on his hiking pole.

"I am indeed a bear," said Sun Bear, standing up on his hind legs and sticking out his long tongue to make himself more imposing.

"Well, I'm going to call you Dog Bear. But please do not take that as an insult. I love dogs, and so do my brother Max and my sister Haley," said Jake.

"Yes, we all love dogs. Maybe you would like to come home with us and meet our dog Sydney," said Max

"I am much too busy looking for Moon Bear," said Sun Bear. "Have you seen him on your travels?"

"We saw Giant Panda and Brown Bear, but no Moon Bear," said Max.

"Maybe you can never find him," Jake said. "Think of it this way. When the sun is out, it outshines the moon, which hides. When the moon is out, the sun has gone to bed. They never meet up. Maybe it's the same with the Sun Bear and the Moon Bear."

"Jake," laughed Haley, "that just doesn't make any sense. Sun Bear, don't pay any attention to my brother. He has his head in the clouds."

"Well, if you do see Moon Bear, please be so kind as to give him my greetings. Please be so kind as to tell him that I am looking for him," said Sun Bear.

"We will," said Haley, Jake and Max, and waved goodbye to Sun Bear.

◆ ◆ ◆

Meanwhile, far, far down the path, Moon Bear was looking for a good spot to go to get some rest. He had spent another long day looking for Sun Bear and was bone tired. Then down the path came three humans: Jordan, Gary, and Jeff. Moon Bear usually avoided humans, but he brushed off his fur to make himself more presentable and said, "Pardon me. I am Moon Bear, and I am looking for Sun Bear. You look like travelers who have been to many places, as is the way of all humans. Can you help me?"

"Moon Bear? You look like Black Bear. What makes you Moon Bear?" asked Jordan, leaning on her hiking pole.

"I do not know this Black Bear. I know Giant Panda and Brown Bear, but I have never heard of Black Bear," said Moon Bear.

"Black Bear lives where we come from, which is far away," said Gary. "But I've never heard of Moon Bear, and I don't think I've heard of Sun Bear either."

"I think Sun Bear is Honey Bear, and I think Brown Bear is Grizzly Bear," said Jeff. "But I don't think Moon Bear is Black Bear. Black Bear does not have a V on his chest."

Jordan laughed. "All of these bears. No wonder why you can't find Sun Bear, Moon Bear."

"Or maybe Sun Bear is Moon Bear at night, when the moon is out, and Moon Bear is Sun Bear during the day, when the sun is out. And that is why you will never find Sun Bear, no matter how hard you look, Moon Bear," said Gary.

"Well, if you do see Sun Bear, please be so kind as to give him my greetings. Please be so kind as to tell him that I am looking for him," said Moon Bear.

"We will," said Jordan, Jeff, and Gary, and waved goodbye to Moon Bear.

◆ ◆ ◆

Many days later, Haley, Jake, and Max were sitting by a splashing waterfall, resting their weary feet. They heard familiar voices in the distance. Then, into view, came their cousins Jordan, Jeff, and Gary. "Sit down with us and rest your weary feet," said Haley. And they did.

"We met the most curious little bear some time back. We called him Dog Bear, because he was only as big as our dog Sydney," said Jake.

"He was looking for Moon Bear," said Max. "But we couldn't help him out."

"That is amazing," said Jordan. "We met Moon Bear some time back."

"We thought he was Black Bear at first," said Jeff. "You know, Grizzly Bear's friend."

"But he had a V on his chest," said Gary. "He was looking for Sun Bear."

"That is amazing," said Haley. "Dog Bear is the same bear as Sun Bear."

The cousins looked at each other in astonishment, and laughed. The waterfall splashed a merry tune. Nutcracker squawked overhead in a tree, and Yellow-Throated Marten scampered up the trunk to visit.

"Do you suppose they ever met up?" asked Max.

"Well, if our cousins met Moon Bear before they met us, and we met Sun Bear before we met our cousins, and then we all met here, then I think we can say that Sun Bear and Moon Bear might be meeting each other right now, just like we are," said Jake.

"I agree with Jake," said Gary. "Their paths must have crossed, just as ours have."

"Jake and Gary," chimed Haley and Jordan, "you've got your heads in the clouds."

Hunting the Russian Bear
Downs Matthews
Polar Bear

Downs Matthews, writer and editor, has published extensively about his experiences with polar bears. This is an account of the polar bears on Wrangel Island in Siberia's Chukchi Sea. In 1992, Matthews joined with wildlife photographer Dr. Dan Guravich to found Polar Bears International, a nonprofit conservation group seeking to improve conservation through education.

Had Commodore Robert Peary first spent ten days here hiding in a snow blind in subzero temperatures in the hope of seeing a mother polar bear bring her newborn cubs out of their birth den, he would never have gone looking for the North Pole. But that is what wildlife photographer Dan Guravich and I are doing. Air at 20 degrees below zero F. pushed by a 15-knot east wind chills us as if it were 60 below. Our tea has frozen in its thermos. Icicles hang from Dan's moustache. Muscles cramp. Patience dwindles.

We remind ourselves that there are more than 500 polar bear den sites on the flanks of this frozen rock in Siberia's Chukchi Sea. We know the deep snow on this slope of Thomas Mountain shelters a mother and her cubs. But she is clearly in no hurry to bring her babies, now just eight weeks old, out of a warm safe den into a frigid and hostile world.

Now and then we peer through a peep hole at the den site some 150 yards up the gentle slope of this hillside. Except for a small air hole at the base for ventilation, nothing reveals its presence. Yet generations of polar bear females have come here in the fall to fashion a chamber beneath the snow where they may give birth in late December or early January.

Now it is late March, and time for this family to break out as scores of other bear families are doing elsewhere in this arctic maternity ward. The new mother hasn't eaten for five months. Her fat reserves are depleted. Her weight is down to half what it was when she entered her den at the beginning of winter. She needs to move out on the sea ice of Long Strait to feed on seals. Yet she is anxious about the safety of her little ones. Predation by adult male bears and wolves, accidental injury, and starvation kill half of all polar bear cubs born each year.

Does she know we are here? Hard to say. Will she and her cubs ever make their debut? Yes. But on her terms. Is her patience greater than ours? Infinitely so.

Hold on! Something moves! Black nostrils on the end of a Roman nose poke up through the snow. A slender white head follows. Can she be coming out at last? With nostrils flaring, the adult female sniffs deeply of the cold dry air. Her olfactory powers are among the best in nature, but we are downwind of the den. She turns her head, looking around, checking for danger. Then her small brown eyes fix on our igloo, a small excrescence in the vast wind-sculptured smoothness of the snow cover.

We crouch and wait, hearts thumping, cold forgotten. She stares, unmoving. The seconds tick by. Minutes pass. A quarter of an hour. She ducks back into the hole, waits, and pops out again. More watching, waiting. Finally, she widens the opening with her shoulders. With the slender curved claws of her in-turned front paws, she pushes away the snow and crawls into the open for the first time in months. She watches our blind steadily.

Except for an occasional glimpse through our peep holes, we stay hidden and quiet.

The mother turns and calls to her cubs, a soft chuffing sound. Then out they come, one, two, three, little white teddy bears bouncing out of bed, shoe-button eyes blinking in the bright light, wet black tongues tasting the keen air, small round ears alert for mother's orders.

Dan removes a small plug of snow to open a window in the igloo. Taking his camera from the heated bag that holds it, he puts the lens through the opening and takes aim. With a sound no louder than a whisper, the camera's shutter opens and closes. Its tiny motor advances the film to the next frame and a second exposure.

One hundred and fifty yards away, the mother bear hears the almost imperceptible, but alien, sound. She snorts a command and the cubs plunge into the den like three marshmallows into a cup. Their mother turns for a last accusing look at the treacherous igloo and then dives in after them.

We wait another hour before leaving, even though we know the show is over. Grateful for the chance to move, we trudge three miles back to the small hut we occupy at Point Blossom on Cape Thomas with Russian zoologist Dr. Nikita Ovsyanikov and two rangers of the Wrangel Island Nature Reserve, Leonid Bove and Grisha Kaurzin.

Just short of six feet, strongly built, and at 40, tough as a walrus tusk, Nikita is deputy director of science for the Nature Reserve, in charge of all things ecological on the island. Leonya (the familiar form of Leonid) could model as the quintessential Russian. Tall, wide-shouldered, narrow-hipped, and ectomorphically lean, he has a wide, chiseled face, large, soulful gray eyes, dark brown hair and beard, and slender hands. Grisha, in contrast, is a short, wiry Chukcha. With his knowledge of native wildlife and cold-weather survival skills, he is a Siberian Leatherstocking.

During the long night, as a south wind brings rising temperatures, the mother bear escapes the den with her youngsters. Tracks show the family has struck out down the valley of Thomas Creek for the shoreline four miles away. There, the trail disappears amid a wilderness of broken ice and pressure ridges where seals lie sleeping.

For centuries, Wrangel Island has served as a haven for polar bears. Researchers believe many, perhaps most, of the polar bears that hunt the ice of Alaska's Bering Sea, Arctic Ocean, and Beaufort Sea, actually were born on Wrangel Island and its small satellite, Herald Island.

With a surface area of 3,069 square miles (795,000 hectares) Wrangel approximates the combined size of Delaware and Rhode Island. Tiny Herald Island adds just three square miles to the total. You'll find Wrangel at 71.25 degrees north latitude by 173.38 degrees east longitude.

Prior to 1926, Wrangel had no permanent inhabitants. Russian scientists arrived in 1976 to create the Wrangel Island Nature Reserve. Known to polar bear zoologists throughout the world, Wrangel has become a laboratory for the study of *Ursus maritimus*. That's why we are determined to go there.

From Nome, at a cost of $10 a mile, Bering Air flies us and our 1,300 pounds of food and gear 200 miles across the Bering Strait to the small Russian port of Provideniya. There, with the help of local officials, we charter a huge Mikoyan jet helicopter to haul us 380 miles to Mys Schmidta. The price is $2.00 a mile. The negotiation takes four days.

Shmidta, built in the Cold War days to support a major military airfield, now serves air traffic along Siberia's eastern coast. After a night in the airport's hotel (for the two of us, about thirty-five cents U.S.) we board an elderly Antonov 2. Built in 1940 with fabric-covered wings and tail and powered by a nine-cylinder radial engine, the AN 2 is the workhorse of the Siberian Arctic. Lacking both creature comforts and safety gear, kept in the air with wire and ingenuity, untroubled by fussy regulators, the old airplane easily accommodates the two of us, our mound of luggage, and four other passengers also bound for the tiny village of Ushakovskoe on Wrangel Island.

Nikita meets the plane with his snow machine. Red- haired, red-bearded, he seems as big as a polar bear in caribou parka and sealskin mukluks. He takes us to his house, one of 60 here. As second in command at the Reserve, Nikita rates four small rooms and an adjoining storage shed. Foot-thick walls of wood and plaster insulate against the pervasive cold. An iron stove burns scrap wood or coal for heat. Water comes from snow melt stored in the town's reservoir and delivered weekly by truck. There's no sewage system. Waste water gets thrown outside to freeze. No problem until it thaws. The toilet is a hole in the floor of an uninsulated privy.

Next day, robust Russians toss our cargo and Nikita's snow machine into the AN 2, and we climb on top. We stop on the way at Doubtful Village, once an army base, but now a ghost town occupied by a hermit named named Pavlov. There are Pavlovs all over the Circumpolar North, old men living in self-imposed isolation in such remote places as this. Pavlov greets us warmly in Russian. "Da," I answer, "Spasiba," thereby exhausting my vocabulary. A year later Pavlov will be found dead, his body partly eaten by polar bears. Chances are, Nikita will contend, Pavlov died a natural death before bears found his corpse.

At Cape Thomas, the AN 2 slides to a stop on a frozen tidal pond near the cabin. Leonya and Grisha roar up on their snow machines to unload the plane and ferry us to the quarters the five of us will share for the next two weeks.

Nikita's Thomas Camp house consists of two rooms, each with one small window. One room, 8 by 20 feet, contains four bunks made of salvaged doors. The other, 8 by 15 feet, has an all-purpose wooden table and two benches. An oil-burning heater keeps the temperature above freezing. Our toilet is a hole in the snow about 40 feet from the cabin. Blocks of snow give the user some protection from the wind.

Nikita has been studying arctic wildlife here since 1980, employing measures that he describes as "simple and soft." Usually, he adds, biologists do the opposite. "They force the animal into distorted behavior so as to make things easy for themselves. This is why efforts to protect nature fail."

Too often, biologists embrace a consumerist ideology, he says. "They approach nature as something to be used and exploited as a means to earn a living. They claim to do research for knowledge when they are actually doing it for money."

It's dangerous work, not because of the animals, but because of the weather and terrain. Above the Arctic Circle, an injured animal is a dead animal. The same rule applies to people. At temperatures down to 40 degrees below zero, with the nearest human help 50 miles away, even a slight misfortune can lead quickly to death.

Lack of proper food can also have grave consequences. The three Russians have been surviving on boiled caribou meat. Gorging on Dan's spaghetti carbonara, they drink glass after glass of tea sweetened with three or four helpings of our sugar. They have had none for six months.

"If you live in the Arctic without sugar, you die," Nikita says, "but slowly."

The rangers make their rounds daily, driving 20 to 30 miles on Russian-built snow scooters. Each machine tows a komatik, or baggage sled, on which Dan and I recline to ride. Even though the snow looks soft and the terrain smooth, a ride on a komatik has a lot in common with falling down stairs. A thin cotton mattress and layers of heavy clothing help cushion our aging bones.

We head east along the base of Thomas Mountain toward Unexpected Creek. Grisha points out a den, and through binoculars, I can see a mother polar bear watching us. Slowly and quietly, we approach, but at a distance of 300 yards, she retreats inside. So much for the notion that bears are near-sighted.

Turning north up the valley of Unexpected Creek, Nikita spots a mother and her three cubs on a hillside about a thousand feet up. With binoculars, I can just see them. The cubs seem no larger than snow flakes. Two are chasing each other and rolling in the snow. The third has discovered tobogganing. On his stomach, he slides gleefully down hill for a hundred feet or so. Then scampering back to the top, he does it again. Their mother watches benignly. Scraping away the snow, she uncovers a patch of grass and begins to nibble at it. Nikita explains that she has not defecated in five months, and she needs roughage to get her digestion working again. Eskimos used to insist that before going into her birth den, the bear would stuff her rectum with grass to prevent defecation. The plug, they said, would be forced out with her first stool. Another myth dispelled.

"When I first began reading about polar bears, I learned they were supposed to be solitary animals," Nikita recalls, "but they are not solitary. It doesn't mean that bears are solitary just because they travel a lot alone over the ice. They are social animals. They have friendships. They prefer to be with each other. They walk and sleep together."

Neither Nikita nor his rangers carries a gun. When you have a weapon, he says, you tend to rely too much on it and quit using your brains. It is too easy to make a mistake.

"I walk unarmed among the bears," he says. "I can do it because I understand the animal. I do not place the bear in a situation in which he feels he has to defend himself."

On a saddle between two hills at the headwaters of Unexpected Creek, we find a recently vacated den site. Grisha and Leonya thump the snow, listening for the hollow sound that betrays the location of the two chambers and their connecting tunnel. With a snow saw, Grisha enlarges the hole in the lower chamber and then carves an opening in the upper chamber as well. Thirty feet up slope, the larger chamber is a round cave four feet in diameter. The interior surfaces show striations left by the mother's claws as she smoothed and shaped the walls and raked off snow to cover the feces of her infants, small brown clumps about the size of a house cat's stools. A slight odor of ammonia from the cubs' urine permeates the interior. A layer of snow about a foot thick covers the roof. Enough sunlight penetrates the snow pack to illuminate the interior with a dim blue-green glow. To prove you can do it, Grisha enters the top chamber and slides down to the lower chamber, popping out of the snow like a large lemming with a pleased grin.

On the following day, Nikita sets out on foot to look for bears amid the sea ice piled up at the base of Thomas Mountain to a height of 15 feet.

He returns with a souvenir, a hat-sized ring of birch bark separated intact from some tree far to the south and blown ashore.

To relieve the pressure of cabin fever, I place the birch bark crown on my head and announce, "Behold! I am the king of Wrangel Island."

"Not so," says Nikita, the Russian scientist. "The king of Wrangel Island is the polar bear."

More about Polar Bears
from Bear Trust International
Bear Trust is solely responsible for the information in this section. Opinions about this information may vary

Polar Bear - *Ursus Maritimus*

Appearance:
Polar bears have a distinctive white appearance. The neck is longer and the head is narrower than other species of bear. The front paws are large and used like paddles for swimming. Paws are heavily furred. In contrast to their grizzly bear cousins, polar bears only have 4 functional mammae, which is related to their smaller litter size. In contrast to other northern bears, only pregnant females will enter dens for extended periods over winter: all other bears remain active.

Size:
The polar bear is the largest land carnivore alive in the world today. Males weigh from 880 to 1750 pounds (399 to 794 kg), and average about 1200 pounds (544 kg). Females weigh from 440 to 660 pounds (200 to 299), averaging 500 pounds (227 kg). At birth, cubs weigh about one pound (454 grams). Life expectancy in the wild can be as long as 30 years. In captivity, life expectancy can reach 40 years

Reproduction:
Females reach maturity at 4 to 6 years. Polar bears mate from late March to late May, and cubs are born between late November and early January. Litter size ranges from 1 to 3 cubs; two is most common. Cubs remain with their mothers until they are two-and-a-half years of age. (In western Hudson Bay, some females used to wean cubs at 1.5 years).

Social Life:
Polar bears tend to be solitary animals except for females accompanied by cubs. Adult males can be social during the ice-free period and have been observed play-fighting. Their home ranges overlap; polar bears are not territorial.

Food:
Polar bears are the most carnivorous of all the bears, and live almost entirely on ringed seals and bearded seals. They rely on the thick blubber layer of the seals to provide an energy-rich diet. Their diet may include other seal species and young walruses, as well as grass, kelp, and berries. They will also scavenge on the carcasses of terrestrial or marine mammals.

Habitat:
The preferred habitat of polar bears is the annual ice over the continental shelves adjacent to the shorelines of the continents and archipelagoes throughout the circumpolar Arctic. During ice-free periods, males tend to remain along the coast, while family groups and sub-adults move further inland. The furthest south that polar bears live all year round is James Bay in Canada. During the winter, polar bears move as far south as Newfoundland and into the northern Bering Sea. Polar bears are found as far north as the North Pole, but here the densities are low. Dens usually occur on land but are commonly found on the sea ice in Alaska.

Wild Population:
The population of polar bears is estimated between 20,000 and 25,000 in 19 subpopulations with varying status (some stable, some declining, and some unknown). Global warming is affecting some populations, although others are not showing any indication of impact. Pollution is a concern in some areas.

FYI:
Polar bears are classified as marine mammals.

Cubs will ride on their mother's backs to cross open water, or when weak or cold.

Polar bears are excellent swimmers.

The soles of a polar bear's foot have small papillae and vacuoles like suction cups to make the bear less likely to slip on the ice.

While polar bears appear white, their skin is black.

The Great Nanuq
Jean Craighead George
Polar Bear

Jean Craighead George has written over sixty children's books and received numerous awards for her writing, including the Newberry Award for her contributions to American literature for children. "Nanuq" first appeared in a Bear Trust International children's publication, Bears of the World.

Adrenalin stings. We were seven miles from Barrow, Alaska, standing on the blazing sea ice. It was May, the month of Eskimo whaling and the month of counting bowhead whales by Inupiat Eskimo scientists and scientists from the lower 48 states. The all-night, all-day sunlight was thawing the ice. In a few weeks, the spot where we stood would be water. That is fearful enough, but not as fearful as the cry, "Bear in camp!"

My son, Craig George, coordinator of the whale study in Barrow, slipped his rifle from its sheath. No one goes out on the sea ice without a bear rifle. Polar bears do not observe the rules of civilization. Rifles are to warn and, if necessary, to shoot this most dangerous carnivore in North America.

Craig pointed to a strip of open sea. I lifted my binoculars. A regal polar bear was gliding like wind-blown crystals along the edge of the ice. He looked soft and cuddly.

"I could hug him," I cooed.

"Don't even think that!" Craig said. "I took care of an orphaned polar bear named Ursus when I first came to Barrow."

The bear, Craig explained, weighed about 1,000 pounds and had massive shoulders and neck. Like all bears, he liked to play, so Craig would roll a huge airplane tire up against his cage. The bars were four inches (10.1 cm) apart. The tire was more than two feet (.61 m) wide. Ursus would reach out, grab the tire, and pop it into his cage through the narrow slit. Craig would praise him, then effortlessly, the bear would press the tire against the bars and pop it out again. "The polar bear," Craig said slowly, "is not only the strongest animal I've ever seen, but the smartest."

Ursus had watched Craig open the latch on his cage every day at feeding time. Craig gave the bear's interest no thought. "Then one day as I approached his cage," Craig said, "Ursus put his nose and a paw against the latch and, with a single movement, opened the door. He was free. I dove for and slammed the door closed."

"No hugging bears," I agreed.

The camp bear's grace was unimaginable as he glided over rough ice, his black eyes and nose defining him. Craig was worried. The bear was a 2-year-old. Like all in his age group, his mother had abandoned him. She was ready to breed again and had gone off to meet her mate on the ice floes, where most male polar bears spend their entire lives. The 2-year-old knew little about hunting, and he was hungry. Hands on our guns, we watched until he disappeared behind a pressure ridge, a mountain of ice that thunders into existence when the pack ice that endlessly circles the North Pole crashes into the shore ice.

This is a dynamic world. It is always moving and changing, piling up, disappearing. Whale Camp is necessarily easy to pack up. It consists of "the perch," a man-made castle of ice where the scientists stand to look down and count the whales on their way from the Bering Sea to the Beaufort Sea in May and June. There is also an acoustic—sound-enhancing—shed on a movable sled. Hydrophones record the voices of passing whales. Finally, there are the living quarters—a cook tent and two sleeping tents.

When the camp bear was gone, Craig and I climbed up onto the perch and looked out on the otherworldly home of the polar bear. Before us, endless miles of turquoise blue ice floes floated on blue-black sea water. White clouds with dark bottoms hung along the horizon. Geese, ducks, and jaegers—big hunting birds of the northern seas—flew landward by the thousands. In this vast no-man's-land, *Nanuq*, the great polar bear known to scientists as *Ursus maritimus*, hunts seals, narwhales, and beluga whales.

The fur of a polar bear appears white but is actually hollow, air being the best insulation. In addition, the hollowness conducts the sunlight down to and is absorbed by the black skin. The white color is an illusion, but the sense of smell is not. Polar bears can detect the breath of a seal surfacing through an ice hole three miles (4.8 km) away.

These ice-and-sea-dwelling animals live as far south as Newfoundland, Canada, but only where ice floes circulate. Late March through May is the mating season for the polar bear. The fertilized egg remains undeveloped for about four months. It begins developing sometime in late September. Three months later, between November and early January, the tiny, one-pound (.45 kg) cubs are born. The mother is half asleep in her den dug into a snowdrift. Polar bear dens are always near the coast on south-facing slopes that catch the warmth of the spring sun.

I often wondered how the Inuit people felt about sharing their homeland with this magnificent but dangerous predator. Last spring, I found out while visiting a school in Wainwright, Alaska. "Bears in town!" the principal announced at the end of the school day. "Do not walk home. Take the bus."

"Respect," I said to myself. The Eskimos are respectful of the great *Nanuq*.

Then the principal added: "And don't walk under building eaves. Icicles are falling like swords." And they are respectful of their environment.

Views from the Bear Den
David S. Maehr, Ph.D.
American Black Bear

Dr. Maehr is Professor of Conservation Biology at the University of Kentucky, Department of Forestry. In addition to writing over 100 technical papers, he has written three books on wildlife. In the following account, he describes why there's nothing quite as interesting—and athletic—as field work.

After chasing bears for the better part of a decade as an agency biologist, then another decade as an academic researcher, my role evolved increasingly to a conveyor of information and keeper of the bottom line. Trips to the field had become occasional forays to teach a new graduate student the fine points of setting a spring-activated snare or the proper steps in the dance to inject a trapped and angry study animal with an anesthetizing compound. Rarely was I enjoying the buzzing insects, sticks in the eye, bleeding wounds, and long hours in the woods that make this work fun.

With an up-and-running project, field visits were mostly therapeutic escapes from the academic brick house. But when Ph.D. student Dave Unger injured his knee while capturing a large male bear on an eastern Kentucky Pine Mountain hillside in November of 2004, this pattern changed. Going against my advice to take a couple of ibuprofen and start rigorous calisthenics to work out the kinks, Dave sought a second opinion that resulted in surgery, crutches, a handicapped vehicle permit, and the order to stay out of the field until May 2005.

My two Ph.D. associates Jeff Larkin and John Cox may have grumbled about Dave's lapses in balance and proper falling technique, but we were secretly happy to have an excuse to get in some regular field work on Kentucky's most imposing carnivore. Despite busy schedules with teaching, grant-writing, paper-editing, graduate committees, and endless meetings, we cleared our calendars to accommodate the 20 or so trips to the field that would be necessary to examine black bear hibernacula, replace aging radio transmitters, and pick up others that had fallen off.

Weekends were not exempt. Our days typically began at 5 A.M. or earlier, and we often returned to Lexington after 10 P.M. Temperatures ranged from the upper teens to nearly 70 – seemingly all in the same day. When not driving along winding mountain roads through Appalachian hollers, we were usually walking straight up and down the steep, rocky slopes of bear habitat. The following accounts are excerpts from this unplanned field season.

February 18, 2005

When Jeff Larkin makes like a carpet, his success in doing so is hindered by a bulky physique – a fine-tuned musculature designed for racing bobsleds down Olympic ice chutes. With a 250-pound Kentucky bear hurtling downhill through hemlock saplings, mountain laurel, and a tangle of dead branches from fallen trees, he did his best to burrow as the black shape expanded like a stampede with each crashing step (he later called it a looming freight train). I could see a streak of black, the flicker of Jeff's purple fleece jacket through the jungle of dormant twigs, then silence as the bear raced away into a small drainage. Not worrying for a second that Jeff was any worse for the wear, I suggested to him in a matter-of-fact manner that he probably ought to keep an eye on the bear because I had succeeded in administering a 4 cc dose of Telazol with a 1.4 meter-long aluminum syringe pole. In a few minutes, she would be feeling the effects of the drug.

While Jeff unfurled his 3-element Yagi antenna to pinpoint the location of the bear with our digital VHF receiver (only later would he revel in the small bruise on his elbow that was inflicted by F3), I removed my camouflage Gore Tex jacket and covered the three helpless cubs that lay squirming in a shallow nest of dry leaves. The nest was protected from the elements by an eave of sandstone caprock. It was from this shallow slit of a cave that the bear emerged after being poked with the needle.

I had hoped that she would demonstrate the same fidelity to her den as another female bear had done in Florida just a month before. The Florida bear, the target of a winter den invasion to replace a $3500 GPS radio transmitter collar that had been identified as faulty by the manufacturer, had surprised us by having a cub on January 10 (most Florida bears give birth in February). After this bear was injected, she too had exited her den (a tangle of branches under the horizontal trunk of a tree thrown by one of the three hurricanes that had criss-crossed peninsular Florida the previous summer). But perhaps ten meters out of the den, this bear had paused, apparently remembering her single newborn cub, turned to look back at the den, then returned to it. We were then able to change her radio collar in the shadow of her den after the drug had taken effect.

Kentucky female F3 exhibited a similar maternal hesitation that allowed me to use the short jab pole. After I verified her position by flashlight, she crawled to the lip of the den preparing for what I thought would be a bolt downhill. Instead, she turned to look at her cubs, then returned to hover over them. This change in position put me in range of her massive right shoulder.

If anesthetizing agents worked as portrayed in the movies, we would have had the entire bear family together at their rock shelter. Instead, Jeff and I spent the next 20 minutes stalking the signal of F3's radio collar through hat-snagging and flesh-ripping brambles. By the time we spied her motionless on a sunny side slope, her escape route was looping back toward her den. Her breathing was slow and steady as we considered our next steps. We would now succeed in changing her collar, but our challenge was one for which we were unprepared.

After Olympian Larkin attempted a clean and jerk of her hefty rump, with no success in budging her, we realized the futility of getting her back to the original den. This bear was big, fat, and in perfect condition to raise all three cubs. We felt lucky that a dose intended for a 200-pound animal had worked so well for one that was much larger. While I deployed a new collar around the bear's neck, I noticed that the collar's leather spacer, designed to rot and break after several months of wear, was stretched like a piece of taffy and ready to tear. Another few weeks and this valuable bear would have been lost as a study animal.

Only a few paces from F3's collapse was a low-branching American holly – one of only a handful of broadleaf species at this latitude to retain green foliage through the winter. Behind it was a shallow recess in the bank of the hill. Next to this was a pile of trees, bull-dozed downhill from a trail that lead to a nearby reclaimed strip mine. Jeff began scraping and gouging with whatever woody tools he could find among the local debris. I then began the hike back to the original den and the Gore Tex-wrapped cubs. They were silent and warm under the fabric. I gently removed the jacket and inserted it as a liner in a blue nylon field pack. I then stuffed the cubs into the pack (only one protested at the man-handling), zipped it shut, slung it on my shoulders and returned to mama with six pounds of bear on my back. Now, at noon on February 18, it was in the mid-40s as a hairy woodpecker chattered overhead, and Jeff identified the nasal caw of a common raven.

Jeff's construction job was taking shape while F3 lay quietly in the sun and the cubs remained nestled in their synthetic fabric hibernaculum. He had supplemented the wall of fallen trees with a new one positioned at 90 degrees and on the down-slope side of the ersatz den. It was built of American beech, black oak, white oak and everything else that he could break, pry, and lift. We created a lining with dried leaves and hemlock boughs.

Then we dragged F3 into the insipient cubbyhole. This was no easy task. With Jeff pushing (no doubt imagining the bear as a bobsled with Jello-like consistency) and me pulling, we inched her the three agonizing yards into the new den. It took us about ten minutes to get her this short distance. The cubs went in next – two males and a female – placed by their mother's grand belly and the well-used teats that would continue to drive the cubs' rapid growth and the family's den emergence in April. Though defenseless and toothless, the cubs had well-developed white claws that snagged the threads of our shirts. Their pink noses were soft and smooth, their ears had recently unfurled, and one cub's dark, milky eyes peered about as we examined her. This one had salt-and-pepper mottling on her brow, contrasting the solid black of her brothers.

Now we dragged in long branches to form the den's roof, plugging gaps with hemlock and mountain laurel. Local hemlock trees donated the finishing touches as we completely enclosed the structure in terminal branches combed with tiny striped leaves. It was now a green fort, a branchy Appalachian igloo, with four bears quietly adjusting themselves for their continued winter togetherness.

While this was already one of my more memorable bear experiences, it was made surreal by the landscape across which we had hiked to get there. From 10 A.M when we exited my Subaru bristling with antennae, jab pole, and backup dart rifle, until 2 P.M when we limped back, we were constantly bombarded by the sound of semi-tractor trailers jake-breaking and accelerating along dusty roads to and from strip-mined pits. This part of Kentucky is the heart of Appalachian coal country, keeping regional electricity costs down while transforming forests to a patchwork of grassy pastures and woody remnants. F3's original rock shelter den was a mere five yards from the edge of a barren hillside – the result of building a pond to capture the sediments that flow from the roads and reclaimed pastures that were a mere 150 yards away. Soil and rock had been scraped by a dozer to form the dike that would hold the silty slurry until it filled in. Two years earlier we found another female's den at the edge of an active mine with freshly blasted boulders and splintered trees surrounding her excavated hole in the ground. We wondered how bears tolerated such disturbance.

Although our research was funded by a grant from the state wildlife agency, our activities were fully permitted and official, and there was no secret about our project, Jeff and I felt like commandos sneaking in to raid some strategic military target. We wanted to avoid interaction with people in order to reduce the possibility that someone would retrace our steps and add to the disturbance that we were intent on causing in the name of research and conservation. Any additional disturbance might be enough to cause F3 to abandon her den and helpless cubs.

Our cross-country trek covered about a half mile across this once contiguous forest. First, to avoid the dozer operator who was starting his D9 Caterpillar under a cloud of diesel smoke, we crossed a grassy, terraced hillside bordered with artificial drainages piled with body-sized boulders called rip-rap (designed to prevent the erosion and collapse of entire re-contoured, reclaimed escarpments).

Second, we passed over a remnant ridgetop forest and onto the dozer trail with fresh mud and scrapings of the two-ton blade.

Third, we walked under a power line and through the brushy easement leading down to the coal truck haul road. Here, every step kicked up puffs of gray dust, atomized from oily shale and clay then deposited on everything as the trucks rumbled past.

Fourth, we took another trail down a remnant wooded hollow with equal parts strip mine disturbance and woodland island: an abandoned 50-gallon drum here, a rusted paint can there, and an expended yellow plastic shotgun shell underfoot.

Fifth, the radio signal of the bear collar led us to another post-reclamation settling pond, catching the sediment that oozes across new contours and down the valley after each rain.

Sixth, round a bend in the old dozer road and into a wooded glen that was formerly idyllic and inhabited by a human family in a now-abandoned cracker house, with tool shed, satellite dish and plastic hoses that once carried clear mountain water to kitchen and garden.

Seventh, back up to a view of a wooded hillside perforated with a five-acre clearing, and the den-side settling pond filling with more sand, clay and organic matter that washes more quickly now from higher elevation. Jeff says we're darn close – the amplitude of the signal suggests we are a stone's throw from the radio collar (at this point we still didn't know if it was on the bear or on the ground with leather spacer ripped apart). Now it became a matter of snooping under logs and vegetation – looking for a dropped collar, finding a likely hole in a rock, or hearing the puttering gurgle of contented, nursing cubs.

From the air, F3's rock den, nestled under a few scraggly hemlocks, does not stand out. But from 1000 feet her choice seems remarkable in the context of the surroundings. At this height, the denatured landscape is apparent. In addition to a major coal haul-road within a few hundred yards of her den, forest openings are everywhere. Although forest is still plentiful in the region, entire hillsides now support grasslands, the simplified remains of strip mining.

Elsewhere, active mining operations raise a dusty haze with occasional mushroom clouds of dust and rubble thrown into the air by the explosions that loosen the coal's overburden of bedrock. Bears appear to do best in the east when forests are large and contiguous. Despite this, the black bear in Kentucky has recolonized the state even though its remaining forests have become increasingly fragmented.

How could this be? I would suggest that two factors are at play here: the ability of many wildlife species to adapt to human activity, and the ugly factor. The former happens wherever sufficient habitat exists for wildlife, and where human activities are regular and predictable in time and space. Examples of this include waterfowl feeding in roadside ditches, Cooper's hawks nesting in Midwestern suburbs, and black bears living at the edge of urban landscapes in Florida.

The ugly factor relates to the tendency for people to avoid recreating in places that are not aesthetically pleasing. While at least one hunter had recently used the area near F3's den for squirrel or rabbit hunting, an abandoned homestead, sterile settling ponds, and a proliferation of coal trucks likely makes this place unattractive (and perhaps dangerous) to local recreationists.

In the winter when bears are in their dens, human activities are even less likely. This is a place that can get cold, but not nearly snowy enough for traditional winter sports. Further, the slippery, grimy clay of the haul roads are not the ideal setting for the tire-spinning ATV riders who seem to go everywhere else on these 2-cycle demons. By the time hunting seasons are over in the fall, bears have the woods in this ugly place to themselves.

* * * * * *

April 13, 2005

Dave Unger and I returned to F3's artificial den site on a rainy Wednesday. Meetings were missed, classes skipped. The den was empty. Coal trucks were hauling on a different road, so we parked as close to the den as we could. A steady drizzle had soaked the ground, turning the clay road to a gray slick. We walked straight to the nearest tangle of trees and blackberry, across a riprap drainage, then along old logging trails to the base of the American holly.

As we approached, it became clear that F3 would not be there because her radio signal was emanating from the direction of the original den. Larkin's construction job was absent of bear sign – no tracks, no hair, no scats. It was relatively intact, however, with a hole in the top near the base of the hill. She had simply pushed the overhead logs to allow her exit. The pristine appearance of the structure suggested that she did not stay long after awakening from her drug-induced paralysis. I hoped that she had settled into the cap rock den quickly after making the three trips necessary to carry her cubs to the better, original rain-proof shelter. It made me wonder if mother bears could count.

* * * * * *

February 26, 2005

The den of F6, just a scant two miles west across highway 119 from F3's hillside hideout, was centered in a remnant of Kentucky wilderness. F6 was the last of the Kentucky females that needed a collar replaced in 2005. We began our trek to her den from Little Shepherd Trail (named after the fictional Civil War era character in John Fox, Jr.'s 1903 novel, *The Little Shepherd of Kingdom Come*).

The GPS told us that we were only 0.64 mile away, but we could not pick up her radio signal from the top of 2500-foot Pine Mountain. There would be plenty of up-and-down before we reached the coordinate that suggested her whereabouts. Our first challenge was to negotiate a rhododendron thicket that blanketed both sides of a ravine. In front of this nearly impenetrable jungle was an obstacle course of young red maple, cut from the edge of the road and now fallen like matchsticks.

Our heart rates were up before the rhododendrons further slowed our now sweaty approach. Rhododendrons are, for all the world, terrestrial mangroves: low, twisting branches that act like the tangled prop roots of the tropical trees that line many of south Florida's coastlines. There was no walking here. Moving up the ravine was a creeping affair – pulling on a stem here, a vine there, never standing for more than a few seconds to curse and catch our breath. At the top, the rhododendron thinned, a view opened up, and we finally heard the faint beeping of F6's radio transmitter.

The gray, leafless forest now spread before us with chestnut oaks, black oaks, cucumber magnolias, and the eerie shapes of large black gum trees: some supported clumps of mistletoe, others had gigantic burls, the product of successful battles against disease. Back on top, we skirted the exposed spines of cliff lines that led us gradually down through greenbrier vines and the broken branches of Virginia and pitch pines, mostly dead after the southern pine beetle infestation of a few years back.

John Cox operated the receiver and noted that F6's motion-sensitive transmitter was sending the signal of a moving bear. Her signal strengthened as the hillside became steeper and the terrain became once again mountain-like, steep and rugged. Now we were encountering bear scats filled with the mashed remains of chestnut oak acorns, many of which still covered the forest floor, some sending exploratory tap roots into the decaying leaf litter.

As the hill gave way to the start of another cliff line, John suggested that F6 was up and moving away from us – the signal had attenuated dramatically in the last few steps. But the bear's signal was still in the same northward direction, so I suggested that we press on. Perhaps the dramatic topography and boulder-strewn valley were creating a bouncing and erratic signal. It would not have been the first time that a wintering bear evaded us long before our arrival.

The forest had suddenly taken on a distinctly different atmosphere. To me, it seemed as though we had entered one of those mythical valleys, tucked away and intact: an accident of human efforts to extract every last scrap of marketable wood and every root of every ginseng and golden seal for a society with misdirected priorities. Reveling at the scene of second-growth tulip trees mixed with older white oaks and narrow bands of rhododendron along a racing mountain stream – running clear and cold without the threat of contamination from anything but the atmosphere – a ruffed grouse exploded from a hidden nook and sailed downslope before us, its broad terminal tail band of auburn contrasting with the wintry colors of the season.   The beauty of this place rivaled anything in the Appalachian Mountains.

F6's signal was now strong again. Had we merely caught up to a solitary female roaming the woods on a sunny winter day? Soon we forded the shallow stream and began yet another ascent toward the opposite cliff line. Just days before we had stood upon an expansive slickrock formation, peering across this same valley, and listening with frustration to a radio signal that was too remote to warrant a den search. We had decided then that a successful approach would start from the top of the mountain rather than at its base. Little did we realize that our first attempt to find F6's den had ended by misinterpreting a bouncing radio signal – we had been likely no more than a stone's throw from the transmitter.

John led us back uphill toward and beneath the spot where we had stood four days before. Three of us trailed John silently as the signal's strength increased with each step. Finally, examining the signal strength indicator on the receiver, John whispered that F6's signal had lost all directional qualities. We were too close for the antenna to effectively tell us which way to go.

Now we needed to prepare for the possibility of a denning bear, curled in a leaf nest at the base of a rhododendron or perhaps nestled in some rocky crevice under an overhang. The sun reflected off the quartzite pebbles and polished grains of the bleached sandstone cliff as we loaded the pole syringe with Telazol. There might be precious little time to load the proper device if we startled the bear at an open nest.

We held the air-powered dart gun in reserve. With pole in hand, and careful not to lose the $30 syringe contents by accidentally poking a branch, I began a short but steep climb toward a burnt-out tree stump, perhaps ten feet from the cliff line. While thinking that complete silence would be critical to a successful capture, a loud crash, "Umph," and brief thrashing caught my breath. John grasped a rhododendron to keep from falling farther after his misstep, and all was quiet again.

Now at the base of the cliff, I scanned every nook and cranny for a den entrance. There were rhododendron tangles, crevices, downed logs, and overhangs. But the only feature that was directly in line with John's two hours of navigating was a small hole in the ground that disappeared under the cliff.

Unlike our encounter with F3, this time I was prepared with a flashlight in my pocket. I put down the pole syringe and crept to within a few feet of the hole, watching for motion, before kneeling to peer inside. The entrance to the hole sloped down at 45-degrees, a pathway of rich soil covered with dried leaves. Scanning from left to right, I saw scattered leaves on flat, table-like rocks that had fallen from the cave's roof perhaps hundreds of years ago. Pigmentless roots dangled from the dripping ceiling that extended maybe 30 feet in.

Then a bear cub, sitting with partly opened eyes beside a massive black mound. The sound of nursing revealed a second cub as two yellow-green lights suddenly aimed in my direction. The white of her radio collar, ear tags and tawny muzzle contrasted with her black coat. This bear was bigger than F3, but she was much less reactive to my presence. Still, she was too alert to allow anyone to crawl within striking distance of a four-foot pole. I quickly retreated to weigh our options.

The air rifle could easily launch a dart to the bear. However, the angle of the entrance would complicate a balanced shot, and there was plenty of cave behind the bear for her to retreat out of our reach. And then, there was always the possibility that she would barrel out of the cave like F3.

The complications were sufficient to consider aborting the capture attempt altogether. The one thing that seemed to be in our favor was F6's choice of a cave rather than a more exposed den site. The constant sound of the stream below, and even John's crash ten minutes earlier, had likely not even registered on the ears in the cave. I also realized that the grueling march into this valley would be all the worse for its uphill trend and the cloud of a mission unaccomplished.

I then asked research assistants Laura Patton and Joe Guthrie to bring the rest of the gear to the cliff base so we could transfer the drug from pole syringe to rifle. My hands were unsteady as we handled syringes and needles. I had no familiarity with this particular gun as I examined the safety mechanisms and the bolt-action cocking device. It had simple iron sights, a benefit in this low-light situation. As long as the mother bear stayed still I would have no problem hitting the target – she towered over the cubs even in her prone position.

Initially, I thought that I could hold the Surefire flashlight against the barrel to illuminate the bear while squeezing off a shot, but the irregular entrance made that impossible. Handing the light to John, I stretched out for a shot, contorting my body until the gun was upside down and I was nearly on my back. I was half in the cave and half out. F6 was slowly moving her head as the cubs nursed. I twisted John's hand to shine on the target, 20 feet away. As he held the light steady, I positioned the sights on black fur and fired.

A Pneudart projectile contains an impact-activated plunger that flashes through an orange plastic tailpiece when it hits. I waited long enough to see the flash, and a still stationary F6. She seemed oblivious to the impact. John and I then quietly retreated from the cave entrance. After ten minutes without any indication of movement in the cave, I crawled completely into the cave with the pole syringe and a little more Telazol; her continued head movements suggested that she was not nearly ready to handle. Again, the injection of the drug elicited little response, but F6 crawled about four feet farther into the cave. At this point, a third cub was apparent in the nest, a hollowed out earthen bowl lined with leaves raked in from outside.

Again I retreated to wait. A final inspection ten minutes later revealed a motionless mother bear, and a fourth cub, previously hidden among the leaves and a mass of ursine protoplasm.

We now figured to have our hands on F6 in a few minutes, so we prepared the new radio collar, gathered our tools, and readied our measuring tape and data sheet. It was time for the strong hands to get immersed in the operation, because the next tasks were to remove the cubs, change the radio collar on the mother, and reposition her in the nest.

Naturally, John and Joe volunteered. The cubs emerged one by one like a reverse bucket brigade at a barn fire, finding their way to a fleece jacket that was cradled by Laura. They were all silent except for a female that protested when a few hairs were plucked for subsequent genetic analyses. The others were two males and another female. They were somewhat more developed than F3's cubs – about the same weight but each with milky blue eyes open, and about 16 inches in total length (tip of nose to tip of tail).

Soon a series of grunts and curses emerged from the cave entrance as John and Joe jockeyed the bear back into the nest. Joe then handed out the old collar, while I handed him the new one. Within 15 minutes, all that remained was to reunite the cubs with their giant of a mother. The measurement John took of her chest girth, 47 inches, suggested F6 was nearly 300 pounds. Come May, when the family of five emerges from the cave, F6 will likely be closer to 200 pounds, the result of the winter-long fast and the constant nursing of the cubs.

Laura and I returned the cubs to the nest. They were silent save for the protesting female. They quickly became a mass of soft black fur and sharp white claws as they nuzzled into their mother's belly fur. We then exited, leaving F6 to slowly recover in the warm and well-protected hibernaculum.

Outside, we put away our gear, donned our packs, then followed Laura as she blazed a trail up the cliff line toward the top of Pine Mountain and Little Shepherd Trail. It was 4 P.M when we left and after 6 when we emerged on the narrow, bumpy trail. Staying at the edge of cliffs and on the tops of ridges, we were unable to avoid tangles of greenbrier, but at least we avoided the endless rhododendron thickets that hindered our hike to the den.

Laura was effortless in winding through the understory vegetation—at once a steamroller and wood sprite—while the rest of us struggled to keep up. Our hike took us to a cliff that appeared to offer no detour. We ended up dropping 20 feet down a nearly vertical wall, and into a relatively narrow rhododendron hell that ended on the far side of the last ravine before the road. Our vehicle was another half mile away, but we welcomed its obstruction-free flatness. The return completed an approximately five mile circle of near vertical hiking. We left Pine Mountain as twilight settled on the mountain.

* * * * * *

March 3, 2005

Not all of our visits to winter dens resulted in handling bears, although most were intended to do this. At minimum, we tried to come away with a pinpointed location and description of the den. Sometimes the target bear was up and walking long before we neared the immediate area.

A young male – less than 150 pounds at his first capture the previous summer – had established a den near Lily Cornett Woods, a state-owned area with a remnant of old growth forest. Male 27's den, however, was on a recently clear cut hillside, criss-crossed with logging trails and tangles of cut tree tops, blackberry brambles, and greenbrier vines. Larkin, Cox, and I had intended to drive part way up the 1000-foot hill, then walk the rest of the way.

A locked gate announced the now-abandoned Defeated Creek Coal Mine, the gate blocking our way. In a recent flight, John noticed a network of trails leading to the top of the hill, so we donned packs and Gore Tex and began the climb. First we checked on the bear's radio signal. He was still on the hillside, but for the first time this winter the signal was in the fast pulse rate mode that indicated the collar had not moved in at least four hours. This suggested three possibilities: 1) the bear was dead (hence the common name for this electronic device: mortality switch),
2) the collar had fallen off the bear, or 3) the bear was sleeping deeply. The last two days had seen a drop in temperature and a snowfall that now blanketed the ground. Up to 14 inches had fallen on nearby Black Mountain, but here it was minimal.

Defeated Creek Den

Still, it was cold enough that the bear may have entered a deeper hibernation. The sun was shining brightly but the temperature was still in the 20s. Song sparrows, northern cardinals, and Carolina chickadees sang as we headed uphill to solve the mystery of the mortality signal.

The combination of recent mining activity and the ravaged hillsides, scalped of their diverse hardwood tree overstory, made this another place that was seemingly unsuitable for a wintering bear. The difference between this den location and that of F6 was that the male bear had chosen an area devoid of active mining, the logging had ceased long ago, and a locked gate kept vehicle traffic out.

We followed a winding coal truck road for about a mile, passed a pile of discarded hydraulic hoses, then crossed a small grassy drainage and into the zone of cut trees. For several hundred yards we followed the tracks of a lone coyote. The hike soon became a step-by-step exercise in concentration – calculating foot placement to avoid a fall on the slick snow that coated the mud and gravel below. At the top of the ridge we encountered irregular log-skidder trails and plenty of thorny brambles.

The collar's signal was still in mortality as we neared to a dozen or so yards.

Cut tree tops were everywhere. A lone black gum tree towered over a confusion of branches. This is where John thought the dropped collar must be. As Jeff loaded the dart rifle some 30 yards downslope, the pulse rate changed from the fast mortality mode to the more typical and slower head-up pulse rate. The collar was still on the bear, and, clearly, he knew we were there.

Within seconds, we heard the rustling of branches, but never saw black fur. I jockeyed around blackberry shrubs and downed timber while holding the rifle, but to no avail. In what seemed like seconds, the bear suddenly appeared about 200 yards away on the hillside across from the trail we had walked up. He looked very large – nothing like the gangly sub-adult that Dave Unger had captured last summer – as he scrambled over tangles of trees pushed down by bulldozer. He was amazingly silent and fast, but he exhibited a certain unsteadiness that likely was the grogginess of hibernation. He would now start looking for a replacement to his suddenly compromised hiding place.

Jeff retraced the bear's egress by tracking sharp footprints in the snow. The den itself was nothing more than a slightly hollowed saucer of leaves and mud that seemed haphazardly positioned under a felled red maple tree. It also seemed very small, perhaps one yard across. There was no effective protection against the elements, especially from above. However, what this den did not have in overhead protection, it made up for with thick concealing vegetation.

As we had proved, nothing was about to surprise this bear even if he was deeply sleeping in his winter stupor. This site would add another to Dave Unger's winter den sites, a single data point in the painstaking process of gathering enough for statistical analysis. Not much of a pattern had, as yet, emerged. Such a tolerance for a wide array of den sites suggests that there is potential for population expansion to the west.

Perhaps this bear was the colonizing front and would be a part of the specie's retaking of the Daniel Boone National Forest. Only the North Fork of the Kentucky River and a network of highways stood in his way.

* * * * * *

March 12, 2005

Thus far, all of our efforts to re-collar a male black bear this winter had met with frustration. Several dropped collars, likely far from their previous wearers' winter dens, provided no useful information. A December 2004 walk-in on a mature male on Pine Mountain yielded nothing but the confirmation that he was still alive (and remarkably mobile). Within minutes of our closest approach through mountain laurel, Virginia pine, and greenbrier – perhaps 50 yards – he was on the other side of a wide valley.

During our exit on a dry southeast-facing slope, we found a relatively large and fruit-producing American chestnut, battling blight with a multitude of dead stems, yet producing dozens of the spiny pods that contained the future of this disease-decimated, former forest dominant. The young male at Defeated Creek at least allowed us to get close enough to find his winter den (the open ground nest in the snow), before he bolted away.

Male 30 was one of the last on the list, and inhabiting an area in Harlan County with which none of us had previous experience. John had flown over it on a telemetry flight and we had GPS coordinates taken from the air to help us get close, but several hours of reconnaissance would be necessary to find the best approach from the ground. He believed that the bear was denned within a quarter mile of a large power line, and near the top of a ridge (where else?).

Some nearby settlements included Creech, Twila, and Teetersville. Our first try took us to a steep and muddy road that was too slick for our baloney-skin tires to grasp – this one gained us altitude but we were still more than a mile from the den. We returned to the hardtop road to look for alternatives.

A narrow asphalt road parallel to Banner Creek led past a Franciscan friars' retreat and a mountain cottage, and was just close enough to let us pick up a weak radio signal. The strongest signal indicated that we would be making a long climb through second growth hardwoods and along a choice of two mountain drainages. We parked the Bronco in a small clearing used for local campfires and as a staging area for a narrow ATV trail. We donned our gear, including a new aluminum pole syringe, and set off into the brisk 30-degree air. We soon were unaware of the cold as the flat trail turned upward toward Potato Ridge and the summit of Chunklick Spur, a mere stone's throw from Beartree Gap.

At the end of the ATV trail, we noticed a drop-door cage trap, baited with cat food in a small white plastic bowl, apparently set for raccoon. There was no sign of recent human activity beyond this for the rest of the day. Our walk along the stream or on the bed of an old logging road was hindered by blackberry thickets, so we frequently crossed back and forth until we chose to take the high point between the two drainages.

The ascent was generally at a 45-degree angle, sometimes steeper. Most of the large oaks had been cut and removed from the forest within the last ten years as evidenced by the state of decay in their stumps and discarded tops. Here and there a tree-of-heaven (an invasive exotic from China) became a handhold for pulling our way up. Another exotic, multiflora rose, grew where enough light filtered through the canopy.

We flushed a couple of ruffed grouse – always a surprise as they exploded from cryptic hide-a-ways. John stopped occasionally to check on the radio signal which alternated between slightly stronger, then disappearing altogether. This phenomenon was surely the product of signal bounce and attenuation that was exacerbated by rugged topography and the bear's choice of a den site (if the transmitter was even still on the bear).

Soon we encountered flat terraces covered with autumn olive (another non-native), black locust, blackberry and elderberry – apparently we were on the remains of an old contour strip mine. These species are common on the re-vegetated surface mines in the region, thriving where lots of light and little competition allows them to establish. The soils here were a spongy mixture of oily shale (a "waste" product of the mining process), clays, and organic stuff from the nearby forest and volunteering plant life. Water was backed up in shallow recesses against the sloping banks of the upslope grade. We paused to take a new bearing. Now the signal was an unwavering pulse, growing steadily stronger with each yard of hard-fought advance up the mountain.

On one of the benches, John caught up to Joe and me, asking if one of us had the dart rifle. Our quizzical expressions turned him back downslope to retrieve the gun and case that had slipped off his shoulder. He looked especially haggard on his return. The intervening 20 minutes were enough for the cold of inactivity to creep into our feet – at least the sun was out and we were nearing our target. John looked spent, so we waited another few minutes, then climbed to the last mine bench before the summit.

From this point, we walked parallel to the contour looking for where the antenna pointed down to the strongest signal. A pair of wild turkeys appeared overhead and glided silently downhill to a new foraging site. A Carolina wren sang its bubbly call, always a vociferous singer even outside the breeding season, but especially on a sunny, early spring day.

John was again suddenly far behind us. I was worried that he was having a relapse from a strained back and perhaps the flu, but he was confirming that we had passed above and beyond the signal. The backtrack took us down to the next lower mine bench by way of a steel pipeline and logging skid trail, unused for years. In a mere 100 yards of crabbing down and sideways, we were now below the signal, yet we had descended a mere 50 feet. The bench took us to a tangle of grape vine, blackberry, and elderberry – dry and leafless – growing in the shadow of an isolated cliff that was perhaps 20 feet tall and 60 feet wide. Chestnut oaks grew in line along the top edge, with five-foot icicles hanging from rocks and roots.

John now indicated the signal was exceedingly strong, and that it had changed to the head up position. Given our previous experiences with males, there was no point in using the syringe pole, especially if the element of surprise was gone. So we loaded a 5-cc Pneudart with Telazol and slipped it into the breech of the rifle. I was hoping that the den was in a secure nook of rock and that the bear was deep enough inside that he would stay put. I started uphill through the brambles, with thorns tearing fabric and skin alike. I tried to move quickly while keeping the gun in a safe position and my eyes on the base of the cliff. There was no way to be silent.

John was ten yards behind me monitoring the bear's radio and pointing to my left. When I broke free of the brambles, the sandstone cliff stretched equally to the right and left. To the right was an open crack that was well lit and shallow. A few dried leaves underneath were not the stuff of a bear nest. A dim trail, perhaps padded on by broad flat feet, extended to my left. John continued to point in that direction.

I put the gun's safety in the off position as I approached a black hole where the cliff disappeared into the mountainside. I could now approach relatively quietly, but there were only 30 feet between the hole and me. I strained to see into the darkness, and made out what appeared to be the faint grayness of a radio collar. It seemed to move slightly as I squinted to see more.

Without warning, the bear was out of the cave. He was growling and tooth-snapping at me as I held the rifle to my right shoulder, ready to shoot. His appearance was vivid – the lines of his mouth (shark-like when seen from my lower vantage point), nostrils, both brown eyes, and massive blackness were etched against the gray of the sandstone. He pounced toward me along the narrow trail. There would be no safe crossing of paths along this natural alleyway. I did not want to take a shot toward his head and risk hitting an eye or having the dart glance off his side or shoulder. But I told myself that if he came any closer I would fire – perhaps that would deter him from running me over.

I stood still. Perhaps my stubbornness was enough for him to choose a different escape route. Regardless, he abruptly stopped after a few purposeful steps toward me, as if to better analyze the puny obstacle in his way, then turned and headed toward a higher exit. His alternate route likely saved me a good thrashing. The target was clear, and the iron sights were lined up. An orange flash popped into his left hip and the bear took off in the opposite (proper) direction. A full dose would be 8 cc for this bear – easily 450 pounds (a dramatic change from his summer 2004 lankiness). I wondered if the 5 cc under dose would be enough to even slow him down.

I suggested to Joe and John that we wait a few minutes in hopes that the bear would gradually succumb to the drug without feeling as though he was being chased. About five minutes was all we could stand. We stowed all of our gear, donned packs, grabbed receiver and antenna, and took off on his trail – big paw prints were evident in mud and leaves.

Unlike the females we had handled, M30 was solitary; there was no complication with cubs. Should he completely evade our chase, he would simply find a new den and continue his winter lethargy. None of us were lethargic now – the bear escaping the three intruding, diminutive omnivores, the three of us crashing down hillsides and through brambles after what we hoped would soon be a sleepy, giant omnivore.

We ran and skied down the loose tailings of mine refuse, decaying leaves, and rocks. There was no hesitation through brambles. Eventually we reached a dry creek bed with a moss and fern-covered boulder obscuring our view. I peered over hoping M30 would be motionless below. He wasn't. Joe then pointed ahead. Perhaps 100 yards away up a steep slope and across the draw, he was watching the bear with binoculars.

The bear was no longer running, but stationary with his head bobbing up and down. We sat and waited a few more minutes. I then crept to get closer with another dart containing the rest of the needed dose. Due to the steepness, I could not see the bear as I approached him from below, so I depended on Joe to tell me if the bear reacted to me. Soon I could see the black mound of fur, the colored streamers in his ears (he was uniquely coded with orange and green for individual identification), and his massive head as it wobbled like one of those spring mounted bobble-heads in the back window of a sedan. He was head-up on a steep talusy slope, chest down, and with legs that could no longer push him forward. He was not going anywhere, but he was still too alert for us to safely remove his collar and reattach a new one.

I administered the other 3 ccs of Telazol into his meaty right shoulder. Within five minutes he lost his tenuous grip on the loose shale and dirt, and slid a few feet into a dead limb and some thick grape vines that held him from sliding farther. We all then pulled him around and back on his chest, removed the dart from his shoulder (the one in his rump had dropped out during his initial escape) and began our workup.

I had loaned Joe an extra pair of Army surplus, camouflaged, foul-weather pants to keep him dry and protect his jeans from rips and shredding. The pants had pockets where one normally expects them, but they were bottomless. That is, they were designed to allow access to the primary set of pants underneath.

I failed to describe this design attribute to Joe. So it was no wonder that he stowed the ratchet in one of those pockets as we jockeyed M30 into a workable position. This was perhaps our most important tool after the dart gun. It would be needed to remove the nuts from the old collar, and, more importantly, to tighten the nuts on the new collar. It had apparently escaped through the bottom of his pants leg.

We spent the next ten minutes frantically sifting leaves and dirt next to and underneath the now still giant. His girth (a chest circumference measurement that is correlated with body mass, or weight) indicated that he was well over 400 pounds, perhaps pushing 500. We had to work to keep him from slipping farther downhill. His coat was thick and shiny. He seemed the picture of adult male black bear health, complete with handsome scars to the face and impressive paws that could dispatch an elk calf (or researcher) with a single swipe.

This perfection was marred when we discovered a puncture wound beneath his left shoulder. The wet, pinkish area was about an inch across and mostly covered with black hair. It was certainly not caused by the dart – none were fired in that direction and the wound did not look fresh. Upon further examination, we found another wound: a two-inch-wide patch of white, hairless skin directly opposite the first wound and on the inside of the leg beneath the pit of his shoulder. At the center of this patch of skin was a red hole, larger than the one on the outside of the leg, clean but unhealed. It was clear that M30, over the span of weeks and months, had licked this spot free of hair in an effort to keep it clean.

We neither saw nor smelled any sign of infection. Although we could not be sure, and did not have any forensic tools with us to investigate further, this bear had apparently been shot with a high-powered rifle. The hole on the outside was small, the probable exit wound on the inside was perhaps twice as large. Another few inches up and the shoulder would have been shattered, a few more inches back and the heart would have been hit. This was a lucky bear.

Although the healing was not complete, we could not palpate a broken bone, and his sheer size suggested that he was not having any thermo-regulatory or nutrition challenges. After reflecting on some of the massive injuries that bears have been known to make full recoveries from, we deemed his prognosis a very good one. Finding the ratchet under a layer of leaves and twigs, we removed the old collar, and replaced it with a new one.

Because part of our mission involved an examination of the den, Joe and I returned to get photographs, estimate basic dimensions, and deploy an old radio collar so Dave Unger could easily find it in the spring for his inventory for detailed measurements of all known winter den sites. We chose this time of year to simulate the conditions under which many of our bears select their dens, not the leafless conditions that prevail in March.

John remained near M30 to make sure the bear did not roll farther down hill or get tangled in a branch or vine, but also because John had little energy left (later he would confess few memories of the descent, though he distinctly had a vision of his boss about to get flattened and chewed on by an angry bear as it emerged from the dark hole in the cliff). Back at the den site, we were impressed with the large cavernous opening and nest that M30 had built by pulling vines and other debris into the cave. It looked nearly woven, a very large bird nest, perhaps four feet across and two feet deep. If he lifted his head from this spot and looked out (as I suspect he had done from time to time over the last three months), he would see a spectacular landscape of forested, rugged hills.

Jagged sandstone at the cave's opening completed the framing of this pastel painting. The nest was only a few feet from the outside. He had certainly felt the cold as if he was outside, but the rocks had blocked virtually any wind. That openness likely kept M30 in a relative state of awareness, but he was still sufficiently hibernating that we got close enough for a shot. Some of the inside walls of the cave were wet enough to support mosses and lichens. A small tunnel about five feet up and in the right arch of the opening contained a small midden of feces and nut chewings that had been made by a small rodent, perhaps a deer mouse. No other animal sign was evident. A large, greenish bear scat had been deposited about three feet from the edge of the nest. We collected it for future food habits analyses. It appeared to be full of grass and other fibrous material.

After taking a few photographs of the den, we left to collect John and check on the bear. M30 was stirring and had his head up, while John was conscious and rested, so we packed gear and retraced our steps to the Bronco. It was late afternoon as we pulled back onto the highway, listening to the final minutes of regulation play, then overtime of UK's basketball tournament win over LSU. We could only guess what M30 was doing and feeling since we left him to complete the metabolization of the Telazol.

I imagined his sense of the experience following my appearance outside his den, the sting of the dart, his eventual collapse on the mountainside, and our prodding examination of his condition. Such helplessness for such a powerful beast. Was it mostly a foggy memory or a vivid recollection? I thought of Gary Larson cartoons and his humor of talking wildlife and suburban families abducted by aliens. I thought he would remember most of the ordeal – if only he could speak.

* * * * * *

April 2, 2005

Although the wintry forecast included rain with possible snow accumulation on Pine Mountain, time had about run out on checking winter dens. Soon they would be emerging and returning to their never-ending quests for food.

Today was Dave Unger's first day back in the field since his knee surgery last fall. We planned on checking on a radio collar that was emitting the fast pulse rate of a stationary transmitter, and examining a den that had been used by a bear family last year. Forestry graduate student Tara Littlefield and my son Clif were along to help, especially in case Dave's knee was not up to a day of hiking.

The drive to Cumberland was largely through a torrent. During lulls in the rain along State Highway 15 through the Hazard area, mine residue from the tires and trailers of coal-hauling trucks created a gray haze on the windshield that was made worse by having only one functional wiper blade. The streams were swollen and straining the banks of the North Fork of the Kentucky River and the Cumberland River. We commented that one of the benefits of the deluge would be the scouring of the river banks and the partial removal of the trash that would eventually build up again. The Ohio River would soon be receiving a pulse of discarded plastic diapers, garbage bags, and anything else that would float.

We pulled off the road just outside the settlement of Hiram. Dilapidated houses, abandoned vehicles, and kudzu made this stretch of narrow highway like so many others in eastern Kentucky. The rain was steady, but no longer a downpour. Pine Mountain rose abruptly from the west side of the road. The rapid beating of the transmitter was loud and of sufficient strength that it had to be a mere hundreds of yards uphill.

As with so many forest edges, our path took us through tangles of greenbrier and thickets of regenerating tulip poplar. The vegetation under a roadside power line just 30 yards up was a confusion of vines and sprouts that was exacerbated by the regular trimming of all woody plants across a 20 yard swath. Eventually the path to the transmitter took us into a forest dominated by scarlet oak, chestnut oak, and mountain laurel, as highway sounds receded. Rivulets were running full-bore downhill with the rain, now turning to snow.

We paused every few minutes to catch our breath and confirm the direction of our search with the telemetry equipment. In about 20 minutes, the signal was sufficiently loud to make the determination of direction difficult. If the collar was still on the bear, he certainly would have heard us coming and moved his head to triangulate on his intruders. This would jar the internal switch back to the slower pulse rate of an active bear.

The transmitter remained in the mortality mode. We trudged on another 30 yards. I then saw the white radio collar on the ground next to a recently fallen scarlet oak. As Dave caught up, his attention fixed on examining the LCD readout on the receiver, I shielded the collar from his sight, then jostled it with my foot while watching his expression change. As the 100 beats-per-minute pulsing instantly changed to 60 bpm, Dave's eyes grew large and his body tensed. He called for our silence with wildly gesturing arms because we had apparently awakened the wearer of the collar.

Unable to maintain the charade (and not wanting to prolong our exposure to the slushy snowfall), I flipped the collar to Dave's feet before he started searching in earnest for a bear-filled radio collar. I reckoned I had a month or two before he got even.

This was the same bear that Dave had darted near the gift shop of Kingdom Come State Park , at the time a big male pushing 500 pounds. In the rush of finding the drugged bear before darkness, Dave tripped over a large log, tearing his right knee ligaments. While the bear was successfully collared, this was the end of field work for Dave, on injured reserve until today.

He now held the collar that had been deployed four months earlier. The fresh diggings into the rotten scarlet oak log suggested the bear had made a recent meal of red oak borer beetles (*Enaphalodes rufulus*) and their larvae. Apparently, while intent on crunchy coleopterans, the collar had simply slipped off his head, the result of winter weight loss. The dead tree was swollen at the base and had clearly been battling chestnut blight long before its colonization by the oak borers. These were simply the coup de grace of a process that had been started by the exotic disease from Asia. Sadly, the suitability of scarlet oak as a host for the blight means that restoring American chestnut to the center of its historical distribution will be difficult. I suspect that until the 1930s, the regular annual crop of chestnuts was the single most important black bear food in the central Appalachians.

By now, bear M12 had developed a reputation for frustrating and punishing researchers. Perhaps we deserved it for the inconveniences we caused him and his kin. He had frustrated Jeff and John, escaping their capture attempt in mid-February by the grace of a twig-deflected dart. His dropped collar not only meant another study animal subtracted from the total, but a drenching in some of the nastiest early spring weather I can remember.

He also showed how the combined intellect of three Ph.D.s can epitomize the opposite of efficiency. Just two days earlier, on March 31, Jeff, John, and I made the initial attempt at finding the collar at the beetle log. Pulling into the Hiram Pentecostal Church parking lot at 9 A.M. after leaving Lexington at 5 A.M., John asked if anyone had packed an antenna for the VHF receiver. The question was enough for us all to know that it had been forgotten.

We had the receiver, so I suggested that we fabricate something as an antenna. John recalled successfully walking in on a radio-collared elk some years ago in much less treacherous terrain and with nothing but a Leatherman tool attached to the end of the receiver's coaxial cable. Within seconds, the Leatherman tool was out and we were picking up a clear signal from M12's transmitter. Unfortunately, the small hunk of hinged steel was insufficient to obtain a direction to the signal source. But we thought that changes in our location would result in increases and decreases in signal strength such that we could meander eventually to the collar.

So we began our meandering – up, up, and higher. Through tangles of greenbrier, mountain laurel, boulders, fallen Virginia pines – all the stuff of Pine Mountain that we had come to know so well this winter. It seemed as though the signal strengthened with every 100 yards of ascent. Ruffed grouse were drumming in hopes of attracting mates, while newly arrived blue-headed vireos sang their intentions of future spring territories.

The higher we got, the more likely it seemed the collar would be on a bear, one that was sleeping soundly in a secure den. But the warmth of this morning (nothing like the snowy mess of two days later) should at least have had him moving his head and keeping the transmitter out of its mortality mode. The lack of directionality was frustrating. Eventually it became clear that we had no way of telling if we were within 100 yards or 1000. John and Jeff stopped, scanning the pastoral scene at the bottom of the mountain: brightly painted country homes, the Cumberland River, and a freight train rumbling toward Hazard. Somewhere, perhaps within a stone's throw, the bear had seen a similar vista. We agreed that it was time to head back down.

Inexplicably, I continued to wander about examining thick spots of vegetation and fallen pine trees. Finding a seam between a large Virginia pine and a laurel thicket, I stepped where a large animal had recently rested. Pine needles and leaves were mashed flat in an area that spanned perhaps three feet at its widest. On the downslope side, a dead pine trunk formed a wall, to the west a pine branch outlined this organic mattress. In the center, two ¾-inch stems of mountain laurel were nothing but bent stubs, chewed off then laid upon by the nest's occupant. Whatever it was had been big and it had sharp teeth – it was certainly no deer. Rather, this was a temporary winter bear den, likely that of a male.

I called for John and Jeff to have a look, as I began to pluck coarse black hairs from rough spots in pine bark, from leaves, and out of the underlying duff. We placed these in a plastic bag in hopes of matching the genetic code contained within the hair follicles to a known individual. Perhaps this nest belonged to M12.

Finishing the search of the den, I turned over a few oak leaves to find what at first appeared to be a bird beak. On closer inspection, however, the shiny gray tissue, shredded opposite the pointy end, was clearly the tip of a bear claw. Jeff had marveled, after his missed dart had deflected from a branch back in February, at how quickly M12 bailed his original winter nest in a rhododendron thicket, then easily scaled a 15 foot cliff as if he was part gecko. I wondered aloud if the toenail in this nest may have resulted from his ascent of the hard sandstone wall, tearing during his escape, but not detaching until subsequent grooming at a new den.

Regardless, we had another location that could be used to help characterize black bear winter dens, a data entry that would not have been possible without our bungling of the gear inventory. In 25 years of bear research, I had never just stumbled onto a bear winter den – occupied or otherwise. After securing toenail, hair samples, and field notes, we left an old radio collar at the den so Dave could return later to take his detailed measurements of the site. Talk about the blind squirrel finding the acorn.

* * * * * *

November 18, 2005

Whether it is a $200 electronic device or it is cobbled together with surplus string, duct tape, and leather, a radio collar's breakaway device provides no assurance of its hoped-for performance. This was why Dave Unger, Andrea Schuhmann and I were sipping hot coffee and munching Krispy Kreme donuts on I-75 at 6 A.M. Perfect weather, a spectacular sunrise, and John Cox circling 1000 feet over the bear in a Cessna 172, were too many good omens for our task – one that results in more misses than hits.

Exactly one week earlier, Dave approached yearling male M36 near Cumberland, Kentucky on Pine Mountain, but after a successful approach and delivery of 3 cc of Telazol in the air-rifle-fired dart, the bear simply ran off without showing the effects of the anesthetizing drug. Massive annual swings in body mass among adults can make the retention of a radio collar problematic. With enough weight loss, a perfectly good collar might drop off at the end of the winter denning period. Young animals, on the other hand, represent the opposite challenge because they often experience rapid growth that demands the temporary attachment of a collar. If the collar does not fall off, it could result in serious injury or worse.

M36's collar should have fallen off since its mid-summer deployment, and the signal was expected to quit in a matter of weeks, so we approached the bear with some urgency. This particular collar had been attached with cotton string and a layer of duct tape – normally a combination that lasts four to six months – at a cost of a few cents. The high-end drop off devices cost hundreds of dollars, normally to facilitate the retrieval of GPS collars that can cost thousands of dollars and can contain thousands of invaluable radio locations stored on a computer chip. Even the manufacturers of such devices warn their users to avoid placing complete confidence in them.

We parked the work-worn Bronco at the Cumberland Apartments complex, donned packs, and headed straight up the mountain. By noon, we had been trailing M36's radio signal for nearly three hours, with several false alarms of close encounters and a growing sense of frustration. The rugged topography was bouncing the radio signal all over the place, and the animal may have been on the move.

I had been carrying the loaded rifle for the last hour, thinking that an opportunity for a shot would present itself soon and with little warning. Our trek took us through rhododendron hells, mountain laurel thickets, and over downed trees and slick rock creeks. Witch hazel was in full flower, its wispy yellowish flowers glowing in the bright sunlight. On our closest approach to the bear, with John Cox circling above to confirm its location, we soon found his radio signal getting weaker. We were in the center of John's circle, but seemingly off the mark.

So we stopped for a ten-minute water and granola bar break before heading back downhill. Within 50 meters, we had drawn perpendicular to his signal. A rhododendron thicket was between us and the bear, so rather than make noise by crashing through it, we skirted around. Dave suggested the bear was within 50 meters, so we crept as quietly as possible. I held the rifle ready, checking twice and then again to make sure it was cocked and that I could quickly push the safety off.

Suddenly, there was the bear, downslope about 70 feet away at the base of a large northern red oak. For a moment, it appeared that we had approached unnoticed, but as I pulled off a glove (by now it was in the upper 30s), the bear detected a sound or a smell, and bolted out of sight. Fighting the urge to move in its direction, I remained silently still while Dave and Andrea wondered what was happening.

In about a minute, the bear was back at the base of the tree – perhaps looking for acorns. Though I could see the bear, he was mostly obscured with leaves and branches. Apparently he did not see us. There appeared to be an opening about the size of a Frisbee midway between the target and me. I raised the rifle and peered over the iron sights to judge how ridiculous the shot was.

As I steadied against a dead tree, I realized that I had this single shot – one opportunity before any additional movement on our part chased him terminally far away. I eased off the safety and squeezed the trigger. The dart's flight was miraculous, sailing in a slight arc, neatly through the leafy window, and into the bear's right rump. We heard it hit. The bear jumped slightly, then waited a second or two before running north, across a small stream that we had negotiated just a few minutes before, and uphill onto a laurel-covered slope. I thought to myself, "How unlikely." Then we waited a few minutes for the drug to take effect.

The bear's radio signal was getting steadily fainter as we scrambled through greenbriers and knee-grabbing shrubs. We stopped occasionally to look, listen, and catch our breath. Dave adjusted our course as we neared the bear, until we spied it wedged at the base of a rhododendron. He was out like a light, but breathing calmly – the dart still protruding from his rump. His body looked like a typical yearling, smallish and gangly. But his head was large – perhaps that of a three-year-old. His collar was very tight, the duct tape apparently protecting too well the string that held the two ends of the collar together. We worked quickly to remove it.

Andrea and Dave dragged the bear to a flat space to take measurements while I fabricated a new breakaway device – this time a thin leather spacer attached to the collar with string. No duct tape. During the workup, M36 became the first bear in Kentucky to receive a digital implant (a pit tag), a device that will allow his identification even without a radio collar or other marks. The day had suddenly become more beautiful as the last measurement was taken. We were done by 2:30 P.M., happy to be relieved of the worry of a growing neck and an inelastic tracking device.

On the way home, Dave received a cell phone call from KDFWR wildlife biologist Wes Hodges, who informed us that one of our radio-collared bears had been shot by a surface mine worker, who then loaded it into his truck and disposed of it in Virginia. Through John's tracking and other information, we concluded that the victim was another yearling male that had not made a habit of visiting mine sites (as far as our telemetry data indicated). The behavior of the "miner" was inexplicable – there was apparently no threat from the bear, and eyewitnesses saw the killing clearly and they apparently conversed with the poacher, who told them where he was taking the carcass.

Our hope was that he would be convicted of a Lacey Act violation – the transport across state lines of illegally obtained wildlife. It seemed ironic that in the face of the Kentucky Department of Fish & Wildlife Resource's keen interest in opening a bear-hunting season, one was already underway in eastern Kentucky.

Lt. Frank Campbell and KDFWR technician Travis Neal made a search for the bear's transmitter on November 21, using John's coordinates and directions. They found the bear with no difficulty: transmitter still attached, a bullet hole with no exit wound, and the carcass remarkably fresh despite nearly a week since the bear was shot. Apparently the miner was fired from his job, and the eyewitnesses were strongly encouraged to help with the investigation. A USFWS law enforcement investigator was scheduled to interview the suspect on November 22. In the meantime, the carcass was hauled to the UK Animal Diagnostics Lab for a thorough examination and a determination of cause of death. We await the outcome of this bizarre event...

* * * * * *

Patterns

North American black bears use a variety of structures and habitats for winter dens. Some have used road culverts, others have simply curled up on the ground to become snow-covered boulders. In Kentucky, we saw simple scrapes on bare ground, and nests in hollow trees. The most common were those in rocks: boulder piles, crevasses, and caves. Trees would likely be more commonly used in Kentucky, but there are not so many large trees as are found in the Smoky Mountains and some deep south swamps.

In my years of studying the black bear in Florida, I never found a bear den in a standing hollow tree. There, most of the forests were recently cut compared to Appalachia, plus the warmth of the subtropics reduces the importance of thermal cover for hibernating bears. One of the frustrations with winter den work in Florida was that female bears with cubs invariably abandoned their nests upon our approach (they would also return to the cubs upon our departure). Their nests were usually simple depressions on the ground in dense thickets of saw palmetto or some other dense vegetation. One old female that raised several litters over the course of several years used a cypress stump, cut in the 1940s during the extraction of the virgin timber from the Fakahatchee Strand, one of North America's largest hardwood swamps. She was the only female that allowed us to approach close enough to see her and not abandon her den. We speculated that this was because the solid walls of the stump created enough darkness and were sufficiently sound-proof that she was able to fall into a deeper hibernation. The only danger for her was the approach of stealthy, pesky researchers.

In Kentucky, we observed a range of behaviors in response to our 2005 disturbances. Those that abandoned dens before we could locate them tended to be out in the open. Those that allowed a close approach, but that were alert enough to escape after they were darted, tended to be in well sheltered sites (closed on three sides and protected from above), but not enclosed enough to resemble a cave or the cavity of a hollow tree. The one that stuck tight was 20 feet into a dark cave with a single, narrow exit. Clearly, the quality of winter dens is important, particularly to females with new litters. For males and solitary females, security is not so important for thermal reasons, but more so for protection from people.

The open dens that we found were always in remote settings that were far from areas of high human activity (though the general area around the den may have been highly altered by people). Females with cubs seemed capable of tolerating human activity – such as F3 and the rumbling coal trucks – so long as they had protected hibernacula, and the local human activities were regular in their patterns of time and space. Although it is impossible to formulate a description of the average bear den, I suspect that the combination of den availability, den quality, and human activity will be a contributing factor in the black bear's continued advance onto the Cumberland Plateau of Kentucky. Bears certainly appear to have plenty of options from which to choose.

More about Hibernation
from Bear Trust International
Bear Trust is solely responsible for the information in this section. Opinions about this information may vary.

Hibernation is a biological mechanism whereby animals conserve energy, especially during winter when food sources are scarce. During hibernation, stored body fat is used up at a slower rate. Hibernation is characterized by a state of inactivity and low metabolic functioning, lower body temperature, and slower breathing.

Many animals hibernate, including bats, ground squirrels and other rodents, mouse lemurs, many insectivores, monotremes, some snakes, and marsupials. There is some discussion as to whether the most famous hibernator, the bear, actually hibernates. During the bear's winter lethargy, his metabolic state is significantly less depressed than that of smaller mammals. As a consequence, many use the term "denning" to describe this state, rather than hibernation. However, a variety of physiological changes such as red blood cell shape and size, and the recirculation of metabolic water, make the bear's hibernation one of the most efficient in the animal kingdom. Dave Maehr, among others, considers the winter state of most black bears as true hibernation. During hibernation, the body temperature of a bear remains relatively stable at 31° C, down from 37° C. Additionally, the bear can be aroused easily.

Whether referred to as denning or hibernation, this period of time is a good opportunity for bear biologists to gather data about bears, put radio collars on their research subjects, and better understand the species. Bears living in warmer climates have no need to hibernate, as food sources remain abundant year around. However, all pregnant females hibernate in winter because reproductive events such as the delayed implantation of the embryo are linked to this physiological phenomenon that has its roots in a colder Pleistocene climate.

What Bears Dream When They Hibernate
Greywolf Elementary Third Graders

In Karen Sisk's third-grade classroom in Sequim, Washington, her students studied bears. Then Karen asked each student to write a story, imagining what bears are dreaming during their long hibernation. Children always seem to find the magic in wildlife, and remind us all why our natural world is so important to protect. Here are a few of these delightful stories, along with some terrific illustrations.

A BEAR'S DREAM GONE BAD

Once upon a time, there was a hibernating bear but before he went to sleep, he said, "I WILL HAVE A GOOD DREAM." And that did happen. The dream was about, well I'll just tell you.

It starts out not so happy. Once when a bear was playing in his dream, he saw a bush moving. A man came out. He did not like humans. Since it was a dream, he just poofed him away. But then there was another human, and the man was in a bulldozer.

He went up to that dozer and said, "AGARRARGGART." Another man came out. He was a poacher. All of a sudden, it started snowing. The poacher started pulling a trigger very slowly. He was sweating.

The bear wondered what this long, hollow stick was. The man finally pulled the trigger, and a rock-metal thing came out of the hollow area, and hit the bear on its throat.

But don't forget, it was his dream because if it wasn't his dream, he would be gone. So he put himself back to sleep.

But for some reason, it was warmer. So he woke up and looked outside, and it was SUMMER. He was so happy. I'm so sad to say, but my story is over. *Jacob*

* * *

BROWN BEAR: I think a brown bear dreams about spring and all the animals, and making new friends. But of course this is in hibernation. But his little brother was kicking and kicking, until he woke up his big brother. But he wanted to see the rest of his dream. So he went back to bed and lived happily ever after. *Tristan*

* * *

BEARS AND BEES

This black bear is dreaming of his family in the summer, and a bee hive. It was gray and brown, mixed with close to 170 bees and lots and lots of honey.

It's a good thing the black bear didn't dream of 1170 bees, or 170 bee hives! Anyway, he swallows the hive and the bees. In my opinion, it's not worth about one pound of honey. He also goes out and explores the world. And if he would get hurt in his dream, it won't hurt or kill him.

When he wakes up, he first has to go get food. Imagine if you slept for months. Wouldn't you be hungry? And I'll leave out the bear's business.

As you can imagine, that bear was thirsty. But in the forest, the only water they have comes from rain, a swamp, or a lake. Or a stream or river. So he chose the river. And that black bear lived happily (in his dream) ever after. *Brandon*

* * *

CUB'S FIRST HIBERNATION

Brown bears dream about food when they hibernate. Salmon. Yum.

"Auhhh, they're attacking me!" The fish were trying to bite him. The bear wakes up. "It was just a dream. Phew!"

The bear goes back to sleep. "Berries. Mmmmmm. "Yikes, they're zombies!" The zombie berries were trying to kill him. He woke up again.

"Go back to sleep, baby bear," said Mamma bear. "It was just a dream," she added.

So Cub went back to sleep.

"Yum, elk! Oh no, they're trying to buck me." He woke up. "Waaaaaa. Mommy, they broke my leg. I need an emergency ambulance," he said.

"What's an emergency ambulance?" asked Mamma bear.

"I got it off TV," Cub said.

"I thought I said no TV before hibernation. Remember?" Mamma bear said.

"Huh? Before hibernation? No, Momma, I forgot."

"Tee hee," Cub said, then went back to sleep.

"Lady bugs, my favorite. A swarm I will not tolerate. Gulp. Burp. Sting! Sting! Owww."

Cub woke up. It was spring. He told his mother, but she didn't believe him. She just said, "Now you've learned your lesson." *Becky*

* * *

THE POLAR BEAR DREAMS WHEN IT HIBERNATES

"It's my first hibernation!" said Squirt. I think the polar bear dreams about what he or she might do when they wake up from their hibernation.

For example, getting fish out of the ocean. If it's a female, it might have a baby cub. They might be dreaming of swimming down under water and getting food for their family. The family might even go together for a swim or just to play.

While the polar bear is hibernating, it also might be having a bad dream about drowning or getting polluted by what it ate. But first they have to fill their tummies until they are full.

DREAM: Crush, the dad polar bear, is walking with his wife, Dory and cub, Squirt on the ice. It was getting hot outside and the ice was starting to melt. Crush falls through an ice crack. He is stuck. The ice starts to break. Dory and Squirt run for land. When they got back, Dory was so sad!!! Meanwhile, Dory (in real) was trying to wake up Crush because his feet were waving in every direction you could imagine. When Crush woke up, he was so scared he said, "Am I alive?" "Yes, why?" Crush said, "I had a dream. A scary dream!"

The next day, Squirt had a bad dream about his first hibernation. Here is his dream:

"What is that big FAT thing in our den," said the wolf pack leader. Squirt was sleeping in the pack's den. Squirt was so scared, and he screamed so loud, that his mom and dad came running. "What is it, son?" "Oh, nothing, Dad." "Let's go get something to eat then." Okay. I'll race you!" said Squirt. *Melissa*

* * *

GRIZZLIES: Bears or cubs are sightless, and only the size of chipmunks. A mother can have up to 3 cubs in one litter and only keep their cubs for 1 or 2 years, then let them go explore. Sometimes the cubs even travel together. I think it's sad because people are clear cutting the forest so the bears have nowhere to go. The brown bear lives in the northern hemisphere. In North America, they're nicknamed grizzly bears because their fur is a little grizzled.

(In the cave while the dad is getting ready for hibernation.) "Dad, why are you sleeping. We have to go find some food to eat before hibernation. Let's go, Dad."

"But I don't want to right now!"

"If you don't do it now, we're not going to have time to do it later."

"Why, I'll do it later. I promise."

"Dad, wake up, you're going to do it right now."

"Fine, fine, fine."

Then they go out and the dad smells something. Then, all of a sudden a truck pulls up and a man jumps out and says, "A brown bear. I trailed all the way out here just to see a cub. "I thought that trail sign said deer trail. Man, I got to start wearing my glasses." *Colton*

* * *

BLACK BEARS: I think black bears are dreaming of a nice cold river swarming with fish, nice ripe blackberries, and a warm cave. And he might be thinking of having no humans for miles and miles. He was happy until he woke up. He said, "Darn it," and on the count of one, he was asleep. *Bailey*

SLOTH BEARS: Sloth bears probably dream about sucking termites out of mounds of dirt. Bathing in the sun. Seeing a large mound covering a whole field. Also seeing ants scattered in the savannah. Or having a nightmare about termite mounds getting destroyed by global warming, and ants getting killed by toxins. *Logan*

* * *

WHAT BROWN BEARS DREAM WHEN THEY HIBERNATE

Off in Dream Land . . .

"Ahhh, it's a wonderful day to read a book, isn't it Freddy? Freddy? Freddy, where are you?"

.

Meanwhile, in Freddy's dream . . "I win! I'm the win-aaah. Roar!" WHAP! (Other bear falls down.) "Oh-Ya, Boo-Ya," Freddy says, and shows his muscles.

Coming from off in the distance, "Freddy, where are you?"

"I'm over here, Mom! I just won my first battle and, and, and . . . uuuuuuuhhhh . . .Oh-Ya, I'm moving out!"

"WHAT! I can't believe you left in the middle of the book just to go FIGHTING! Wait, did you get a girl?"

"Ya," said Freddy.

"I'm going to be a Grandma!"

So the mother bear became a wonderful grandma and read stories to her two grandchildren every chance she could get (which was one a week). And Freddy is now a great husband <u>and</u> father.

Freddy suddenly woke up, looked outside, and saw it was spring. So he went out and decided he could write a story about his dream (which is the story you just read). *Sarah*

* * *

THE POLAR BEAR CUB THAT DID NOT WANT TO HIBERNATE

"Come here, little polar bear," called a mother bear to her cub. "Time for your first hibernation," said the mother bear proudly.

"I do not hibernate!" said the cub stubbornly.

Mother bear said, "Well of course, it's your first time."

"I mean my friends do not and I will NEVER hibernate! Did you hear me say NEVER?!" screamed baby bear.

"Look, there are your friends, going to hibernate, honey," said Mama Bear.

"They are not my friends; they hibernate," said little polar bear.

"Oh, let's just take a nap," said the mama bear, knowing her son would hibernate because it was hibernating season.

"OK, that sounds good," yawned baby polar bear. "I'm so tired."

So they went to a snow den to hibernate.

I do not know what baby bear dreamed when he hibernated, but I have a guess. One dream might have been that he was eating a seal.

"MMMMMM, seal! Mom is a good hunter."

Oh, yeah, the baby bear's name is Hunter. Hunter might dream that he lived in a warm place. Hunter loved that dream because he was sick and tired of just ice after ice. He also thinks that flowers might be a good change (even though he a rough boy bear).

He dreams about playing with his friends. "Let's go swim, friends!" Hunter said. That's what Hunter dreamed.

Mama bear dreamed she had three more cubs. They were all girls. Their names were Nala, Nataila, and Issabella. They were sweet and pretty cubs! When she woke up, she had three new baby cubs! All girls! She named them Nala, Nataila, and Issabella. Hunter liked his sisters and never fussed about hibernating again. *Maeve*

* * *

WHAT GRIZZLY BEARS DREAM WHEN THEY HIBERNATE

I think grizzly bears dream of salmon. Nice big salmon coming up the river and how good the juicy pink meat is they're going to eat.

I think she will be dreaming about all the poachers shooting her cubs with sleeping darts, and taking them away. She woke up startled by a truck. Then she saw one of her cubs was dead—in the valley. They loaded the cub into a cage, into the truck. It was the saddest hibernation of all.

She went back to her cave and went back to sleep without her cub. *Brandon*

* * *

SUN BEAR/HONEY BEARS

What would sun bear dream about? Well, here is what a third grader might say.

A sun bear was getting ready to hibernate in her dark, damp cave. Then she fell right asleep without a worry. She found herself in her cave (in her dream). Then she went to her friend's cave and said, "Denny, you in there?" No one answered.

Then she went to find her husband. But to her surprise, she found her husband skinned. She started to weep with sorrow.

"Cubs," she hollered.

She went searching for 20 days and 19 nights. Finally, she stumbled into a zoo. She found her cubs in the zoo. She climbed up, grabbed her cubs and ran out. Security was tight. She escaped right in time. The gates shut.

The four got back to the cave. Then mother said, "We're the only sun bears left."

The cubs started to cry. "It's OK," said mother bear.

She woke up and said these 5 words. *It was only a dream.*

To be continued. *Ashley*

* * *

POLAR BEARS

I think polar bear dream about family if the polar bear has no family. They might dream about new homes instead of living in an ice cave. They probably dream of food, like some delicious looking seals.

For example, a polar bear might have a dream like this—One day long ago lived a polar bear. He had no family. He was so sad. But one day he found a family.

The family had 2 kids. They want to go eat some delicious seals. He was happy now. If you were a polar bear, do you think you would dream about what I wrote? *Jared*

* * *

CHEWY, FISH HUNTER, AND SWIMMER DREAM OF GLOBAL WARMING

"Go in the den, Chewy, Fish Hunter, and Swimmer. Time for hibernation," said their mom to her three cubs. Chewy and Fish Hunter said, "No, no, no! We will have bad dreams. No, no, no!"

Swimmer, the oldest cub, rolled her big brown eyes. "It's not scary. It's just really boring. Wouldn't it be more fun if you could just swim in the water?"

"No, no, no," said Fish Hunter. "Let's go eat. I'm hungry."

Later when their stomachs were full, they waddled to their winter den. They forgot how scary it was going to be. They went to sleep as fast as snapping your fingers. They cuddled up next to their mom.

After quiet darkness, their mom was dreaming she was in Greenland. There were no people. However, there were fish in the skies and plenty of other fish.

Meanwhile, the cubs were having bad dreams. Swimmer was dreaming of falling in the water and drowning. Fish Hunter was dreaming about eating poisoned fish. Chewy was stranded on an ice berg surrounded by people.

The cubs were so close together that their dream bubbles slowly came together into one big bubble. "Plop!"

All three cubs heard a "Plop, plop!" All three cubs were in one dream bubble.

"What are you doing here?" said all three cubs to each other at the same time. "Clang, clang!"

Suddenly, the ice berg disappeared. "It's getting warmer!" Chewy said. "Global warming!"

"Global whata?" asked the two cubs.

"You'll see what I mean," said Chewy, worriedly.

"Everything's melting," said Swimmer.

"Help!" said Fish Hunter. He was caught in oily grime. "Help," he shrieked.

Fish Hunter plopped into the water. The waves started to sway harder until the waves swept away Swimmer.

"I'm all alone!" said Chewy.

"Or are you?" said a cold voice from nowhere.

"Who are you?" asked Chewy in a trembling voice.

"Wake up! Wake up!" said the voice again. Chewy woke up in his den.

"Mom!" all three cubs cried. They all embraced her.

"I can't wait until next hibernation," said their mom.

"We can!" said the cubs. *Katherine*

* * *

EL PATRON
Bonnie Reynolds McKinney
Chihuahuan Desert Black Bear

BonnieMcKinney is Wildlife Coordinator for Proyecto El Carmen in Coahuila Mexico. Here is the first of two remarkable stories about black bears of the Chihuahuan Desert, the incorrigible El Patron, followed by the story of Bonito, the bandit.

The story of El Patron *(the boss, or owner of land)* is how we would like many problem bear stories to end; unfortunately most problem bears are not as lucky as El Patron. In November 1998, I was with the Texas Department of Parks and Widlife, conducting black bear research in the Black Gap Wildlife Management Area. We were studying a small, reestablishing population of black bears. Black Gap is owned by Texas Parks and Wildlife and is located in southern Brewster County, Texas. The area is typical Chihuahuan Desert, low elevation scrub desert habitat, not your typical bear habitat. But then, Chihuahuan Desert bears are a bit different from other bears.

Chihuahuan Desert Black Bear

Black bears were extirpated in western Texas by the mid 1950s, but occasionally a bear would wander into west Texas from adjacent Coahuila, México. The situation began changing in the late 1980s when populations in adjacent mountains in Coahuila began dispersing northward into western Texas. With this reestablishment of small populations, the need arose for research and management techniques for a species that had been absent from its historic range for nearly 50 years.

My research was focused on the ecology of a desert population of black bears. This was by no means a large population of black bears, but a unique population since they were inhabiting low-desert habitat on a year-round basis and producing cubs. The information that I obtained from this study would be useful to Texas Parks and Wildlife for management of bears in other areas of west Texas.

The study at Black Gap began in September 1998. I had already captured and collared six bears, and in early November I began finding signs of a large bear using a major canyon system on Black Gap. This bear would roll barrel traps, try to demolish culverts, and pull snares right out of the ground, but I had not been lucky enough to catch him.

November 16 was a cold, windy west Texas day, and from high in Brushy Canyon, I could see a heavy bank of clouds in the north. I was rebaiting six barrel traps and one culvert trap. As I headed down the canyon, I saw the tracks of the large bear in the pea gravel in the creek bed; he was headed in the same direction I was. I reached the last trap, a culvert, at a small dirt tank that the bears used for water on a regular basis.

My husband Billy Pat drove up while I was baiting the culvert, and said, "Hurry up, you're running late, its getting dark. I'm hungry, and you aren't going to catch anything but a ringtail tonight." I hurried a little. It was cold and I was ready for a hot cup of coffee and dinner.

Early the next morning, I headed out to check traps. I met Dave Onorato at the Brushy Canyon gate. Dave was conducting a black bear study in adjacent Big Bend National Park, and would occasionally come over to Black Gap and spend a day in the field with me working on my project.

We headed up the canyon to check traps. The culvert trap was the first one, and sure enough, it was closed. I jumped out of the truck, with Dave close behind, and when we peered into the trap, a bear hit the wire mesh, slinging bear scat all over both of us. He was huffing and popping his teeth, and he had a huge frame, but was in poor condition. I darted him, and while we were waiting for him to go down, I called my husband on the radio and told him I caught a big male in the trap.

Billy Pat, Mike Pittman (Area Manager of Black Gap and co-principal investigator on the bear project) and Tom VanZant, (biologist) all came up to the trap site. They helped us work the big male up. He weighed 250 pounds even in his malnourished condition, and was definitely an old male, with worn teeth and many battle scars. I couldn't believe the size of this old bear. He was tall, long-legged and so skinny you could see his ribs. I could see why he was hitting all my traps and stealing bait every chance he got.

We worked him up, and the guys left. Dave and I stayed with him until he woke up and moved off into the brush. I named him "El Patron" because of his size, and the old battle scars and his nasty temper.

We finished running the rest of the traps, then rebaited the culvert and continued with daily telemetry and scat collection. We both kept talking about how big El Patron was, and how skinny he was. Over the course of the next month or so, I found him every day with telemetry. I could tell he wasn't going anywhere except where the traps were in the canyon.

And nearly every day, I found the barrels rolled and the bait gone. I tried tying them to small shrubs, as there are not many trees in the desert for anchors. But he would just tear up the bushes and roll the traps. On one trap, he pulled the rod completely out of the guides on the barrel trap, then rolled the barrel into the arroyo some 70 feet distant from the trap site. El Patron was aggravating me to no end. His favorite thing was to roll the barrel on its side, enter the barrel, eat the bait and leave. I did observe that he avoided the culvert trap, presumably because of his previous experience getting caught in it.

Christmas came and went, and bears were still moving around. The pregnant sows and sows with yearlings had denned. But the adult males and sub-adult males were still moving, and the weather was unseasonably warm. There wasn't much left for bears to feed on; the persimmons and acorns were gone, and they were feeding on their staple food, beaked yucca plant hearts, sotol hearts and insects. All was well and I was busy with telemetry and analyzing data from the first trapping season.

On December 28, a neighboring landowner called us up from Marathon, which is the nearest small town to Black Gap. Over the phone to my husband he said, "Billy Pat, a bear got in our hunting camps. He sure has made a mess, and Mamma and Daddy are sure mad."

Billy Pat assured him we would go check it out. This particular landowner and his dad had several tracts of land that bordered Black Gap and Big Bend National Park in the Brushy Canyon area. During hunting season, they leased out the land to deer hunters.

We headed up to see the damage. Brushy Canyon forks in several places. One of these forks leads to the private property. As we drove up toward the hunting camp, I was doing telemetry out of the pick-up window, and quickly picked up the signals on three adult male bears: El Patron, Chapo and Crockett. Which one was the culprit? All three were close, and I had no idea which bear to blame, or even if it was a collared bear that invaded the hunting camp.

We drove up to the camp, which was a series of small trailer houses with screen porches on them. It was evident a bear had been there. As we drove by a tin shack that housed equipment, there were several bear scats, and several empty three- quart oil cans with tell-tale bear tooth marks. But if this was all the damage there was, I was a happy bear researcher.

But no such luck. We stopped in front of the trailer houses, and it looked like a battle field. There were trash cans turned over, and they must have had been full to the brim with trash. There were window screens and porch screens with huge holes in them—it was very obvious that a bear had entered through a screen one way and exited another on the way out.

The landowner was mad, which is putting it mildly. He was swearing he was going to trap every bear on the mountain, even if they were listed as a Texas threatened species. He was describing how he been such a friend to the bears, and how he had put water in to benefit the bears and so forth, and that now the bears had repaid him only by betraying him. He didn't mention how he had liked seeing bears every now and then, and how he had told other people very proudly that he had bears on his ranch.

He ushered us into the first camp trailer, which was a wreck, to say the least. The bear had torn up the door to enter, then proceeded to demolish the inside of the trailer: furniture was overturned, all the groceries had been broken open, and there was flour and noodles everywhere. The bear also ate 12 small boxes of D-Con rat poison, drank a huge bottle of cooking oil (which may have saved his life), apparently ate everything else he could find, and broken bottles. There was glass scattered everywhere.

Then, perhaps running out of accessible food, the bear took the new, full-size, butane-gas-powered refrigerator and tore the entire front cover off of it, and ate much of the insulation. He then proceeded to carry the refrigerator out on the porch, from where he heaved it outside into the yard through another screen. There it was, lying on its side at the back of the house. He pulled gas lines out of the stove, turned over the gas tanks, ate more insulation, and downed many orange sodas.

The sight at the next trailer wasn't any better. Here, he couldn't get the trailer door open, so he went around to the end and pulled the air conditioner clean out of the window. Then he stepped up on the air conditioner, where he left his tracks, and crawled inside the trailer. Once inside, he proceeded to rearrange the contents of everything, with the exception of the new television which he didn't touch. When he got to the bathroom, he broke bottles of aftershave, and squeezed toothpaste everywhere. Then he headed to the trailer's single bedroom, where he rearranged the bed and moved the mattress to the opposite side of the room. At this point I assume he saw himself in the floor-length mirror, and demolished that. His exit was through another screen on the porch, but not before he demolished a rocking chair and ripped up a blanket.

It was clear he tried the third trailer, but didn't enter. He merely broke a small window and tore up one screen.

The landowner was furious, and his wife was even madder. In their rantings, the old, discarded furniture in the trailers suddenly became priceless antiques. We assured the landowner, who was a cousin of my husband Billy Pat, that we would catch the bear. With Billy Pat's help, we moved in barrel traps and culverts, and set snares. Surely, we would catch the bear tonight.

In the meantime, we had to figure out which bear was the culprit, and call our regional director, Ruben Cantu in San Angelo so he could advise Texas Parks and Wildlife headquarters in Austin. This wasn't looking too good for the bear. But, as all of us know who work with bears, if you leave trash and deer entrails lying about outside, unsecured food inside, birdseed on the porch, and attractants such as old cooking oil in pans, it is inviting disaster in bear country. And normally the bear loses.

I was taking up for the bear, felt he deserved some consideration, but I was getting nowhere fast. Relocating him was out of the question: we literally had no place to go with him, especially after he had broken into the houses, and now knew how easy it was.

We went back to Black Gap and made the necessary phone call to Ruben at home. It was late. Early the next morning, we headed out to check traps. Nothing, and still three bears were close to the area, according to telemetry. There was evidence the bear had come back to the camp, but he avoided all the traps and snares, and didn't harm anything.

Shortly, we got a radio call to go back to Black Gap and contact the regional director. The word from Austin was to catch the bear, and it looked as though we would have to destroy him. We still didn't know which bear it was. And of course I wasn't too happy with the prospect of destroying a bear in a very small, reestablishing population, when we didn't even know which bear it was. In this situation, every individual was important. I did telemetry all day, and was no closer to figuring out which bear invaded the camp than on the previous two days.

Early on the morning of December 30, we headed out to check traps. Nothing. Mike Pittman got on the phone with Austin, and had them fly the Cessna 206 out to Black Gap. We typically did aerial telemetry once or twice a month, and the pilots were familiar with the desert mountains. Tom flew telemetry while we searched from the ground. He got the same locations we did—two bears in the general area. He didn't pick up the signal on El Patron.

We continued to scout and do telemetry. In the late afternoon, we picked up El Patron's signal south of the area some five miles. At the time, we were driving in the direction that took us away from the demolished trailer camp. I said to Billy Pat, "You know, El Patron is headed up the canyon. Your cousins have another house on top."

We turned around and headed up the canyon, with the telemetry signal getting louder and louder. Then we started seeing bear scats, full of bright turquoise, digested rat poison pellets. It was incredible that the poison didn't kill him, but just passed on through. Next, we came to the landowner's bulldozer. Trouble. The bear had ripped the seat out and ate much of the cushion.

As we headed up the last big hill, which led to the very nice camp house we knew was up there, I was zeroed in on the radio signal. I said, "Well, if the bear isn't in the house, he just left."

We parked the truck, and immediately saw that the bear had tried to enter the back of the house through a high window. He must have abandoned this approach. As we walked around the front of the house, we saw the big plate glass window was broken out. And yep, inside, havoc.

There was no doubt now that it was El Patron. His signal was so loud, I knew he was only a couple hundred yards from us. Inside the house, he had pulled blankets off the beds, torn up pillows, and taken a foam mattress and blanket out on the porch. Bear hair and scratch marks were all over the foam mattress, and I could swear he must have taken it outside and slept on it.

And back inside: he had eaten another 12 boxes of D-Con rat poison, quaffed two bottles of wine and one of vodka, eaten cereal, flour, downed cooking oil, stuffed himself with noodles, root beer, strawberry jam, and an assortment of crackers and cookies. I could just visualize a drunken bear careening around in the house, sampling everything edible.

This house perches right on the edge of a bluff, and a short distance away is Coahuila, México and the Maderas del Carmen mountain range. I was hoping this bear would head over there and never return. But no such luck.

There was one scraggly acacia at the end of the porch, which was all we had to tie the snare cable to in order to catch the bear. Billy Pat started setting the snare, and I was looking for the bear. He was very close and getting closer.

Then, just across the canyon, I saw him, all tall, lanky and skinny. He stopped, looked directly at me, and settled himself on a flat shelf of rock, where he put his head on his paws and watched us set the snare. I figured we would catch him, but we didn't have much bait with us, just a half jar of strawberry jam from the house he had somehow missed. And I had two old doughnuts in the truck. We placed the bait at the snare.

We left the area quickly, but I don't think we could have scared him off if we had wanted to. He was a bear on a mission, to seek and destroy. I still felt sorry for him, poor old guy. He had probably been born in Coahuila, and had been in this mountain for years. Food was scarce, and he thought he had found the land of milk and honey for sure when he hit the camp trailers. He had chanced upon a real smorgasbord, from birdseed to bacon grease to jam and vodka, with a bit of rat poison thrown in.

Early the next morning, we headed out in two trucks. We stopped by one of my trap sites, and hooked up the culvert trap to my truck to take it up the mountain to the house. Then we took Billy Pat's truck up to the landowners' hunting camp to check the other traps, but there was nothing there.

Back down the canyon, I hopped in my truck and followed Billy Pat up the mountain. This is a four-wheel-drive road that snakes through a creek, goes up a mountain, and ends some 17 miles on top at the house. All the way, I was doing telemetry, and got signals on the other two bears. Both were in the same general area they had been in for the last week or so.

El Patron's signal came from the camp house area. I knew we had him caught. It was 8:30 A.M. when we drove up. There he was, trying with all his might to break free from the snare cable. The acacia bush was now a single stick, and most of the root was above ground. Thank the gods that acacias have deep roots.

He had also demolished a huge prickly pear cactus, and the ground was literally bare in the radius of the snare cable. I prepared the injection, and Billy Pat decided he would dart him. I was to bring the rifle in case we needed it.

We eased out of the truck. This was one mad bear. He was lunging and popping his teeth, and huffing for all he was worth. And to make matters worse, he wasn't caught very well. The cable had only caught a couple of his toes, and the acacia bush was slowly giving up more root to the surface. There's nothing like a little drama.

I slid the bolt on the .357 rifle, jacked a shell in the chamber, and flipped on the safety. Billy Pat remarked that he didn't know which was more dangerous, a loaded rifle in my hands or the bear. Then Bill darted him with a capture pistol, and shortly the bear went down.

But we weren't through. We still had to load the bear into the culvert on the truck. Unfortunately, he was in a bad position for doing this, on a downhill slope right at the edge of the bluff. And it was a long, long way down from there.

We got him untangled, and Billy Pat backed up the culvert as close to him as we could get. We took the cable off his foot, and proceeded to try and load him. This turned out to be darn near impossible—a 250-pounds-plus bear immobilized was like loading 250 pounds of loose macaroni. We huffed and puffed, and pulled and pushed, but this approach wasn't working. The problem was, because he was on that downhill slope, we would have to lift him several feet straight up to get him up and into the culvert. To add to our problems, the culvert was built high off the ground, so we could haul it in the backcountry.

We were getting nowhere fast. And the immobilized bear he was starting to move just a little. We didn't have much time. At this point, we came up with the idea of putting a rope around his middle, just behind his front legs, and use the small pulley on the trap door to lift him. We theorized that if Bill would pull the rope, I would then lift the bear, and we could get him inside.

While Billy Pat was rigging up the rope, El Patron and I were slowly, inch by inch, sliding downhill toward the edge of the bluff. He would move his head a little, his body would push into mine, and I would slide down a little; then he would move a little more, and I would slide down a little more. At this point, the bluff edge was only about ten feet away. Now, I certainly didn't want to lose that bear over the bluff, but I sure didn't want to go over the side either. A 127-pound woman is no match for a 250-pound bear sliding downhill.

Finally, Billy Pat threw me the rope and we cinched it around El Patron, hoping the small pulley would hold. Bill started pulling, and I started pushing the bear uphill. Slowly he went up; our theory was working. Then, when we had him bumping against the culvert gate, Bill tied off the rope and we both lifted the bear's front end inside the culvert. The rest of him went in easier.

We took off his rope harness, shut the gate, and headed down the canyon. By the time we were halfway down the canyon, I could see El Patron sitting up in the culvert. By the time we reached the highway, I couldn't believe it, he was wide awake. And hungry. He had already eaten the bait I had in this trap.

We took him straight to Black Gap headquarters, and put him in the only thing we had to hold him: the gooseneck trailer we used for hauling desert bighorn sheep. I put water, dry dog food and cut up apples in the trailer for him. He immediately started eating, and cleaned the big tub of every scrap of food (about 20 pounds of dog food and ten apples). Then he took a drink of water, curled up, and went to sleep.

Meantime, Billy Pat called the landowner in Marathon, and told them that we had caught the bear. It's an hour drive from Marathon to Black Gap, and it was December 31, New Year's Eve. Nevertheless, within an hour, people started driving in to see the bear. The previous day, there had been several articles in the local newspapers about the "rogue bear" that had torn up the landowners' house and camps, and destroyed all those antiques. I couldn't believe the newspaper articles, and I certainly couldn't believe that people were driving so far to see the bear.

They finally all left, home to celebrate the holiday. We finally had the bear, but nobody knew exactly what we were going to do with him. We had called and left messages with Texas Parks and Wildlife offices that we had caught the bear. The last word we had, which was before we caught the bear, was that we were going to have to destroy him. I fretted and worried all night.

The next morning it was New Year's Day. I was sure nobody was anywhere near their offices at Texas Parks and Wildlife or anywhere else. Billy Pat said to me, "If you think anything of this old bear, you better find a home for him, because he is going to be destroyed otherwise."

I had very little hope that on a holiday I was going to find anyone in an office, much less anyone who wanted to take this old bear. I was thinking hard when I remembered that Carlsbad, New Mexico had a living desert zoo and garden, and that they had bears. This was a natural-type setting; it would be perfect for El Patron.

I was much too agitated about the bear to leave it until after the holiday, so I called in hopes of at least being able to leave a message. But the gods were with me. Mark Rosacker, Wildlife Culturist, answered the phone on the third ring. I launched straight into the explanation for why I was calling. I will never forget his response.

"This is a real Chihuahuan Desert bear?" was his question.

I assured him that El Patron was about as Chihuahuan Desert as you could get.

He said, "Well, our old bear died last week and we are looking for another one. Yeah, we would like to have him."

Things moved rapidly from there on. Phones were ringing off their hooks, and people were moving and shaking to get this done. We had to have permits from Texas Parks and Wildlife, U.S. Fish and Wildlife Service, and New Mexico Game and Fish. As hard as it is to believe, we got the permit process going that very day. I sent emails, and phoned Texas Parks and Wildlife bosses right at home, and relayed the news that we had found a home for El Patron.

I still have copies of those two important permits: #STP0199 014 for transport of one tagged black bear from Texas to New Mexico, and permit #1148, Importation Permit from New Mexico Department of Game and Fish.

Billy Pat and I had to leave on January 2 for San Diego, California to attend our son Matt's graduation from U.S. Marine Corps Boot Camp, so we were not going to get to take El Patron to New Mexico. Mike Pittman, Tom Vanzant and others transported El Patron to Carlsbad. Mark Rosaacker met them at the Living Desert facility, and they ushered El Patron into his new quarters with the radio collar still on him.

Then the Texas guys headed back home. It appeared all was well. But the very next day, Mark Rosacker called to report that El Patron had escaped in the early hours of the morning. He was heading for downtown Carlsbad (where they have a nice HEB grocery store). Fortunately, they were able to locate him with his radio collar, dart him, and haul him back to the facility. All I could to was to imagine this bear on the loose in a city with all the temptations.

One thing Mark said stuck in my mind.. "He was headed due southeast, which is the exact direction he would have taken if he was headed home to west Texas." Mark went on to say that they had housed several bears over the years, and had never had a problem with a bear escaping, or even trying to escape.

Well, this escape wasn't too much of a feat for an old Chihuahuan Desert veteran like El Patron. He took one look at that 12-foot-high, slick cement wall, climbed right up it, and he was off and running. He had been climbing up slick rock for years in west Texas and Coahuila, México. No, not so hard to believe that he had escaped, but thank goodness his radio collar was still on him.

Mark and other staff at the facility decided they needed a complete remodel of the bear facility in order to keep El Patron inside. So off went El Patron to the Roswell, New Mexico Zoo, still with radio collar intact just in case. He stayed there over a year in a large cage, eating and taking it easy.

Meantime, the staff at Carlsbad Living Desert Zoo were not idle. They started a huge campaign to raise funds for El Patron so he could have new living quarters, in a natural setting, but quarters that he couldn't escape from.

I kept up with El Patron's progress in Roswell. He had to have several treatments of Vitamin K to return his liver to normal after the D-Con rat poison ingestion, but he was gaining weight and doing well.

Mark kept me up to date on his progress raising funds and building the new quarters at the Carlsbad Living Desert Zoo. Among their many events, they had a "Dia de El Patron" (El Patron day), when hundreds of people visited the facility, donating time, money, and other resources to build this old bear a great facility. He was their bear now, and they wanted the best for him.

In 1999, while El Patron was still in Roswell, New Mexico in solitary confinement, we visited him on the way to Ruidosa, New Mexico. By now, he was one big, aggressive black bear, over 350 pounds. It was good to see him again, looking so fit.

In 2000, the Carlsbad facility was set for a big anniversary celebration. They called and invited me to be the guest speaker at the celebration. The new facility was ready, El Patron was back at Carlsbad, and he was doing great. The zoo had raised funds from donations large and small, and from the sale of T-shirts sales and clay figures of bears made by an artist in

Mata Ortiz, Chihuahua, Mexico. A local band wrote a song about El Patron. He was a regular feature in the local newspaper, and everyone loved "their bear."

We arrived at Carlsbad, and when Billy Pat and I entered the zoo in our Texas Parks and Wildlife uniform shirts, people immediately started coming up to me and saying, "Oh, you're the woman who caught El Patron. He is our bear, we love him, he is doing great."

The zoo was festooned with El Patron items. School kids had made colored drawings of him, and there were El Patron T-shirts everywhere. The people of Carlsbad were incredibly attached to this old bear. It was very touching.

I gave a presentation on Chihuahuan Desert bears, and the staff and volunteers showered gifts on me: T-shirts, one of the Mata Ortiz clay bears, a beautiful, hand- painted tile of a black bear, lunch, dinner and a night's stay. After lunch, the band tuned up, and the first song they did was the "Ballad of El Patron," an incredibly true song about an old bear that was born in Coahuila, Mexico, who crossed the Rio Grande, and then lived a long time as a desert bear. But then he got in trouble and was transported to Carlsbad, where he found a new home.

After the facility closed for the day, Mark took us to see El Patron and his new facility. I couldn't believe how big he was. He was lying down in his very natural rock cave, there were native desert plants inside his very large open air enclosure, a running creek, and a pool to swim in. El Patron was living in the lap of bear luxury.

I noticed a hot wire along the top of the enclosure. Mark chuckled and said it was for extra security, and that El Patron tested it several times before he was convinced that it was better to be inside than trying to escape.

El Patron watched us intently as we stood there, then slowly got up and walked over, moving within millimeters of the hot wire. He sniffed, huffed at us and walked back to his cave and lay down. Not much of a show of gratitude for saving his ornery black hide.

I watched him a long time. He was sure fat. And he didn't have to be destroyed. He had lived a long time in the Chihuahuan Desert, and here he was, still in the same desert. I wondered, as I watched him, if he dreamed of roaming the mountains in west Texas and northern Coahuila, México. I hoped he was somewhat content. He could never be released into the wild again; that fate was sealed when we captured him. But at least he was where he was well taken care of and cherished by the local people.

I continued to check on him, and sent Mark information on diet, home range, habitat, measurements and general information on black bears. The zoo would use this information in its first-rate educational display about Chihuahuan Desert bears. El Patron had helped bring awareness to many people about the plight of many bears that become habituated to garbage and people.

**Photo courtesy of staff,
Carlsbad Living Desert Museum**

This is El Patron, a year after capture in Texas and relocation to Carlsbad, New Mexico, 1999.

Matson's lab aged Patron's premolar. He was 16 years old when I captured him on November 17, 1998. Today, as I write this, he is 23 years plus and still doing well.

*Saludos and Viva
El Patron.*

BONITO, EL BANDIDO DE LA SIERRA
Jonás A. Delgadillo Villalobos
and Bonnie Reynolds McKinney
Chihuahuan Desert Black Bear

Jonás A. Delgadillo Villalobos is Assistant Wildlife Coordinator for Proyecto El Carmen; Bonnie McKinney is the Wildlife Coordinator. Proyecto El Carmen is owned by Mexican cement company CEMEX. The following account takes place in the 250,000-acre area CEMEX has dedicated to habitat and native wildlife restoration in the northern part of Coahuila, México, in the Maderas del Carmen mountain range.

This story takes place in Coahuila, México, in the Maderas del Carmen, which lie directly south of the Big Bend Region of Western Texas. The Maderas del Carmen mountain chain was one of the last strongholds for the black bear when populations began a rapid decline in México in the 1940s and 1950s. The population of bears here, and in adjacent mountains in northern Coahuila, has been the source of bears dispersing to other areas in México and reestablishing small populations in historic range. Additionally, bears from these mountains have crossed the Rio Grande and reestablished populations in western Texas.

We began a long-term study of the black bear population in the Maderas del Carmen in 2003 (*Dinámica Poblacional y Movimientos Del Oso Negro Mexicano en el Norte de Coahuila, México*). During 2005, weather patterns changed and we had a very early, warm spring. Grasses were already green in March. From March onward, rain was very scarce, which was unusual for this big mountain chain. Normally, the altitude and mountains trapped the clouds, and we received abundant rainfall in

237

summer and fall. 2005 was the exception. As a consequence, food sources for bears were not as plentiful. We were kept busy chasing bears with telemetry, the bears moving all over the mountains searching for food.

Late April at Campo Uno, a beautiful research setting high in the mountains, looking more like a picture postcard than a facility dedicated to wildlife conservation. The camp has a small lake, and a beautiful new log cabin and caretaker quarters. Bear movement had begun to increase in the area of the camp. We had a few incidents with black bears chewing water hoses, or taking a nip out of a log on the camp's lovely new cabin. Just normal bear mischief, nothing to get really excited about.

Then, in June, the incidents began to get more frequent. One day, we drove up to check traps in the area, and the "Bandido" had been back. This time, he'd sampled several logs on the new log cabin. We smoothed things over as best we could, and wondered why this bear wasn't getting in our traps. In fact, he would walk right by them.

July brought a few more incidents, but still no bear in the traps in the area of the camp. There were lots of signs, and it appeared that more than one bear was using the area. The latest incident in July involved the "Bandido" cutting on all the water faucets outside the new cabin and leaving them to run. When we drove up, the whole area was standing in about an inch of water, with water running off the hill from the cabin down into the lake. We muttered and mumbled about bears not taking baits, how this bear was sure trap wary, doing all this mischief but avoiding the traps.

Our luck changed later in July when we starting catching bears in this area. We caught the first one just a little beyond a cabin at the camp that the men used when they were working on projects. We named this bear "Tecate," and figured the trap experience scared him enough to keep him away from the house. A couple of days later, we caught another bear in the same place, and we named him "Pacifico." Both were about two-to-three-year-old males in excellent condition. Neither had any sign on them, however, indicating that they were the camp bandit who ate logs and turned on the water.

Nearly every day now there were tracks around the camp and the big log cabin. We were still trapping in the area, but not having any luck. August brought the ripening of acorns, wild plums, and other fruits. The bears were really on the move in response to the food. We were running in circles doing telemetry and trapping.

September was very hot and dry. Many of the creeks that flowed year round in the sierra were drying up. No rains fell and food sources were scarcer than in previous years. Acorn production was lower than normal, as was the fruit production.

During this dry month, we caught bears of course. One in particular was very gentle. In fact, when we walked up to the barrel trap he was caught in, he didn't huff, or even move. He just seemed to be very content inside the trap. We collared him and dubbed him "Bonito," because of his conformation and jet black coat. Through his signal, we observed that he moved around quite a bit. In fact, we picked up his signal several times near Campo Uno, and up the mountain in an area that has a natural laguna.

In early October, the workers were camped at Campo Uno while building a new caretaker's cabin. One of the guys called us on the radio and said that there was a bear that had just walked through their camp. He said that the bear walked right by one of our barrel traps, and that he had a collar on. Later that day, we were in the area doing telemetry and checking traps, and got the signal on four different bears in this area: Tecate, Don Pedro, Pacifico, and Bonito. A lot of bears.

The next week, the men were pouring the new slab for the cabin and had it all smoothed out at the end of the day. Early the next morning Salvador, the boss of the work crew, called on the radio. He was just a little upset to tell the boss that a bear had come into camp and walked all over the new cement slab. He reported that the bear's footprints were all over it.

That was the beginning of a continuous run of incidents with the Campo Uno bear that the workers had named Bandido. Nearly daily there was a bear coming into the camp. He'd get in the garbage dump, even though the workers were instructed to burn the trash daily to prevent the bears becoming habituated to garbage. Better yet, we told the workers to sack it all up and bring it down the mountain to headquarters. Salvador assured us they wouldn't leave it again.

The work crew continued to see a medium-sized bear in the area nearly every day, but when we were in the area, the signals were always up the canyon, or we didn't even pick up a signal. Then no major damage from bears occurred for a while and we were hoping the "Bandido" had moved out of the immediate area.

In mid-November, we left for our days off. I headed to Del Rio, Texas and the biologists, Jonás and Hugo, left for their respective homes in México. We have a base station radio so we can talk to the project personnel if we need to. Early the day after I arrived in Texas, I was having coffee on the patio and looking southwest toward the Carmen Mountains in Mexico at some dark clouds. I was hoping we were getting the needed rains over there.

Just as I took a sip of coffee, I heard Locario, one of the workers, calling from Campo Uno into headquarters. Locario asked my husband Billy Pat to send along a jacket with Salvador when he came back, that it was very cold on the mountain. Billy Pat asked, "Locario, where is your coat?" Locario answered that he had left it hanging outside the night before, and the bear had taken it. I thought, "Oh no, here we go again. That bear is back."

A few days later, I heard this conversation on the radio: Rogelio was complaining to Salvador that the bear had taken a pair of pliers, and some other tools. Now I had a vision of the bear, wearing a heavy jacket, with pliers and other tools sticking out of the pockets, walking away from camp. Of course, the truth was that it wasn't funny at all. The bear, whichever one he was, was getting bolder and bolder, and I didn't like that at all.

We returned to work, and again were trapping bears all over the mountain for our study. Trapping was really good; in fact, one day we caught four bears. We also recaptured several, and one of them was the bear we named "Bonito."

Again, Bonito was very gentle. When we opened the barrel trap to release him, he didn't want to leave the barrel. Then, when he finally did, he walked off a little ways, stopped and turned around. He just looked at us with the most quizzical expression on his face. Jonás and I both remarked how gentle he acted, and how he wasn't afraid of people. He was the only bear that acted this way.

About a week later, the workers had their days off and left for town. We were still trapping in the area, so were checking traps daily in the sierra and doing telemetry. We drove into Campo Uno and were going to have lunch at the workers' camp. Then, just as we walked up, we began to notice things out of place: at the back of the cook cabin, we noticed the gas tank to the stove inside was turned over, the connections pulled off and a hole bashed in the wall of the cabin. All of the gas had leaked out of the tank. The water lines running inside the cook house to the sink had been pulled completely out through the wall of cabin to the outside, leaving another hole in the wall. The buckets that the men use every day and then neatly stack up in the evening, were strewn about.

But at least the bear hadn't broken down the door and entered the cabin. We went inside, and put a bucket under the sink to catch any drips. Then we plugged the holes in the wall. We went up to the big cabin, which is a guest house for our project as well as the property of Alberto Garza. All was well there, but there were bear tracks everywhere, and two sets of tracks on the back screen door. We re-baited all the traps in this area and moved two more barrels into strategic areas the bears were traveling in.

Two days later, we had a big group coming in to Camp Uno for a weekend visit. Our special cooks, who work when we have VIPs or other special guests, arrived and we shuttled them up the mountain to Campo Uno.

David and his wife Elvie live in a cabin near the big house, and are caretakers of the property. David met us when we got there and said, "Come see what the bear has done now."

So, we followed David over to an open-air building that serves as a garage, and that houses David's truck and the Kawasaki mula he uses for work on the mountain. The bear had paid a visit. He had opened the door on the mula and bitten chunks out of the seat cushions. There were muddy paw prints all over the truck, even on top.

So we moved more traps closer. We located the trail most recently used by the bear, and also set a trap there. But the funny thing was, we were not getting any radio signals in this area. Telemetry is difficult in these mountains because of the huge boulders and rock piles, and the very thick forest and tight canyons. But if the bear was here nearly every day, as the evidence seemed to indicate, why were we not picking up his signal?

David and Elvie reported seeing him daily going down to the lake for water, or just sashaying across the parking area or down the road. In fact, the men were now so used to seeing him they didn't pay him any attention when he strolled on by. And likewise, he didn't pay any attention to them, nor did the construction noise at the camp seem to bother him.

Turning our attention back to the group coming in, we settled the cooks in and headed back down the mountain. The guests flew in and were shuttled up the mountain.

Billy Pat called me early the next morning and said, "Bonnie, you and Jonás need to catch this bear right now. He came right up to the kitchen door at the big cabin. We couldn't run him off. He isn't afraid of anything."

I explained to my husband that we had traps all over the area, but that we would be back up there shortly. It takes two hours to reach the cabin from the lower elevations. Jonas and I headed out with new bait and the telemetry equipment. We couldn't raise even a beep in this area. Two bears were up the canyon several miles, but there was nothing close. This bear was beginning to be a real nuisance. He didn't act as though he was aggressive, but he was too close to houses and people, and worse, he wasn't a bit afraid.

When the bear had come to the kitchen door, one of our guests took a digital photo. We were really surprised at how close the bear had come. He was a beautiful bear, in excellent condition. But he had no special marks, just his radio collar. And since we don't use ear tags in this study, there was no way to identify him as a specific bear. We had several in the study that were the same size, with a radio collar. We assured everyone at camp that we had traps out, and hoped to catch him that night. Jonas and I went back down the mountain.

Early the next morning, Billy Pat, who was staying up on the mountain with the guests, called and said, "I want something done about this bear. He was at David and Elvie's house last night, looking in the window."

So back up the mountain we go, and we hear the story from our cooks, Veronica and Yoli. Veronica said, "I was lying in bed and looked up because I heard a noise. The bear was gently tapping the screen on the window and looking directly at me." Naturally, she jumped up screaming, "A bear, a bear." The cooks' bedroom has bunk beds, and Yoli, the other cook, a short, rotund lady, leaped off the top bunk, prepared to leave the mountain under her own steam.

David and Elvie were asleep, but the shouting from the cooks woke them up. They jumped out of bed. Now, everyone in camp is running around in their pajamas trying to chase the bear off. But the bear didn't want to leave. He just stopped right behind the house and watched them. David threw rocks and chased after him, yelling. Finally, he wandered off.

We assure everyone that we will catch the bear, and then relocate him to another property that is miles away, but still in the conservation project. Soon, all of the guests depart, and everything is back to normal. There were no bears in the traps the next day.

Bandido de la Sierra

Bandido near the big log cabin, Campo Uno

Two days later, we went up to run our daily route on traps and do telemetry. We had a small sow caught at Campo Cinco, so we worked her up and then headed down to Campo Uno. Now we hear what is the last straw with the bear: David and Elvie tell us about the latest escapade, which has just happened a few hours ago. Elvie had baked a cake and decided to set it outside on the porch rail to cool so she could frost it by the time David got in for dinner. She put the cake on the porch, walked straight back into the house, and as she went by the window, she sees the cake is gone.

She thinks the cake must have fallen off the porch rail, so she goes back outside and sees the bear with the collar running off with her cake. Elvie is not happy. At this point, we are pretty concerned about the bear's boldness.

So back down the mountain we go, another two-hour, low-range, four-wheel-drive trip. We gather up snares and head back up the mountain.

Our Mexico permit stipulates that we are to use barrel traps, but at this point we are willing to risk bending the rules a little and bring in a little heavier artillery. It's obvious the bear is not going to visit a barrel trap.

We set three snares, one practically at the back door of David and Elvie's cabin, tied to a big pine tree, and the other two on fresh trails the bear was using. We checked telemetry; nothing. David and Elvie were leaving for their days off, and followed us down the mountain.

Early the next morning, we call Rogelio on the radio to ask him to check the snares for us. We told him that we were leaving headquarters to check traps for the study, and that we would be up there later unless there were bears in our traps. He called back on the radio in a few minutes, and we could tell by his voice we had a bear caught.

He said, 'Si, hay un oso en el lasso muy cerca de la casa." So, we had a bear caught at the back door, and he had a collar.

We headed for the mountain, and when we got there, sure enough, there was the bear in the snare. He was lying down, asleep, not a bit concerned he was in the snare.

The word had spread around the camp, so when we drove up, all of the men from the work project came over to watch us work the bear up. It was incredible. The bear got up, shook, and stood up on his hind feet. He latched on to the tree with his front feet, turned, and just looked at all of us.

He got a little huffy when we closed in to jabstick him, but not in the way a normal bear does who is caught in a snare. Once he was unconscious, we took the snare off, checked him all over, checked his microchip and signal, and then double checked it. We couldn't believe it. This bear, Camp Uno's "Bandido," was none other than "Bonito."

We put him in a barrel trap and hauled him down the mountain, then across the desert flats to another mountain range. This is still in the project area for the study, but it doesn't have people, houses, or anything else a bear can get into trouble with. And although this wasn't so far away that a bear couldn't potentially move back into his home range, we knew the weather forecast over the next few days called for temperatures to turn colder. We were hoping he would decide to stay and hibernate in this area.

When we reached the area where we were going to release him, we had to literally dump him out of the barrel. He just didn't want to leave the barrel. To get him moving, we finally resorted to chasing him and throwing rocks. Even with this, he would run a little ways, stop, and look back at us with that same quizzical look. When we left the area, I fully expected to look behind and see him running behind the pickup, trying to hitch a ride back.

Now, at Camp Uno, the incidents stopped abruptly. There was no more mischief from Bonito, El Bandido de la Sierra. I hope he will set up a new home range in the Sierra Encantada and not return, or if he does, I hope he comes with a new attitude.

As to this bear's gentle behavior, after much thought we figured that this might not have been the first time our paths had crossed. He might have been a bear that we released in the Maderas del Carmen several years ago as a yearling.

The Governor of Coahuila, Enrique Martinez Martinez's wife had adopted two small cubs that were rescued from a forest fire in the mountains adjacent to the Maderas del Carmen. The cubs grew quickly, making things difficult for their adoptive mother, who needless to say had no experience dealing with bear cubs. We were asked to take the cubs and, when they were older, release them.

We had rehabbed several cubs previously, so we took the two, a male and a female, from the governor's wife. They were released into the wild when they were about 12 months old. We were told not to put a collar on these cubs or mark them, since the governor's wife wanted to be assured that they were really in the wild. We named them Enrique and Malena.

Possibly Bonito was the little male Enrique we had released several years ago, or maybe he was just a gentle-tempered black bear. Either way, a bear this gentle is a threat to people. When a bear has no fear of people, there are bound to be problems. Bonito, Bandido de la Sierras, was living proof of this.

HIKING AND CAMPING IN BEAR COUNTRY

The Center for Wildlife Information shares the following safety techniques to help hikers and campers enjoy their experience in bear country. In addition to providing brochures and other educational materials, the Center has a Train the Trainer Program for teachers, youth group leaders for organizations such as the Girl Scouts and Boy Scouts, and others. The following information is designed for those hiking and camping in North America. For more information, visit the Center's website at www.BeBearAware.org.

Each year, more and more of us are venturing into the backcountry to enjoy the great outdoors. New safety techniques are available to make these forays safe and fun. The Center for Wildlife Information has designed an instructor's guide to empower teachers, youth group leaders, hunters, outfitters and guides with the information needed to train others. Participants learn the latest safety techniques for hiking, camping, viewing and photographing wildlife. By putting these techniques into practice, participants engage in wildlife stewardship, helping to keep wildlife wild.

The Girl Scouts have taken advantage of the Bear Avoidance and Wildlife Stewardship Training Program. At the Girl Scouts National Training facility in New York State, training programs are being offered to local Girl Scout councils. The program involves high school and college age Girl Scouts who have been previously trained in bear avoidance and wildlife stewardship techniques, who then teach other Girl Scouts and the public how to recognize bear signs, and avoid encounters with wildlife while hiking and camping.

The participants learn to be aware of their surroundings and identify signs such as diggings, claw marks and overturned rocks that may indicate the presence of a bear in the area. They also learn the importance of taking time to study the trail ahead and making their presence known by calling out "hey bear, ho bear' when sight is limited or sound is muffled.

A few tips from the program:

Why do bears attack humans?

- Mother bears are protecting their cubs from possible threat
- The bears are protecting their personal space or food
- The bear is surprised when people don't make their presence known

Special precautions to take are—

- Watch for signs of a bear's presence such as bear scat, claw marks and torn stumps
- Make your presence known by talking, singing, etc., especially in areas with low visibility or where this is noise from water or wind
- Before proceeding down a trail, especially with areas of dense brush and low visibility, view the area carefully and make additional noises. And be sure to stay on the marked trail.

What if you encounter a bear?

- Regardless of the distance, never approach a bear.
- If the bear doesn't see you, keep out of its sight, and detour a far as possible, downwind of the bear. Avoid entering dense brush.

- If the bear sees you, but is not confrontational, retreat or bypass the bear, slowly leaving the area as soon as possible.

If you have a sudden encounter at close range—

- Do not panic—your safety may depend on remaining calm.
- Do not run, shout or make sudden movements.
- You cannot outrun a bear! Bears run up to 40 mph.
- Remain still, avoid direct eye contact, and talk quietly and calmly to the bear.
- Climbing a tree to avoid an attack is often impractical. Bears can climb trees too.
- Stand still if a bear charges you. Charging bears often veer away or stop abruptly (bluff charge).
- If you carry pepper spray, point it at the bear and discharge it if the bear charges to within 20 to 30 feet.

Tips on Camping, Food, and Garbage Handling in Bear Country

- Use an open meadow. Food, storage and dining area should be 100 yards from the campsite.
- There should be no signs of food or cooking equipment in the campsite. Put ONLY sleeping bags, pillows, clothing, flashlight and bear pepper spray inside the tent.
- Don't put tents in a circle, but in a line so if a bear comes into camp it does not feel trapped.

- Remember, personal hygiene products, including lip balm and toothpaste, have odors that may attract bears. Do not bring these products into your tent.

- Hang your food and other supplies from a tree limb at least ten feet off the ground and four feet out from the trunk or side support, or store them in bear-resistant containers that are properly latched.

Some local resources you can contact to learn more:

- Local land or wildlife agency
- Backcountry Horsemen chapter
- Outfitter and Guide Associations
- Zoos and nature centers
- Outdoor gear retailers
- Taxidermists
- Camera retailers and clubs
- Hunting organizations
- Outdoor sports stores
- Nonprofit wildlife organizations

BEAR ATTRACTANTS AND BEAR-RESISTANT CONTAINERS

The Bear Trust Adopt-a-Dumpster Program promotes the installation of bear-resistant containers at campgrounds, trail heads, and in residential areas in bear country. Properly securing trash protects both wildlife and humans. Sponsorships for the program are available through the Bear Trust website, www.beartrust.org.

As the saying goes, "A fed bear is a dead bear." Bears can be attracted to just about anything that has a scent, from tooth paste in a tube to an empty, discarded French fry container, across great distances. Additionally, bears that are found around campsites are likely to have become habituated to humans and human food, losing their natural fear in the process.

The presence of bear attractants is the leading cause of nuisance bear incidents. Bears are experts at opening containers such as ice chests and cans, and have no trouble getting into a tent. Don't crawl into a sleeping bag at night with a snack. And when you leave a campsite, think of the next campers and secure any trash. In residential areas that abut wildlife habitat, everyday items such as bird feeders and dog food can call bears. Fruit orchards are prized attractants. At hunting camps, even a frying pan can signal food to a bear.

In bear country, the solution is to be aware of what comprises a bear attractant—that is, practically anything (remember the story of El Patron and his taste for D-Con rat poison). It is important to be conscious of this when considering what to secure at a campsite. In residential areas, it is necessary to seasonally eliminate what can be eliminated, such as bird feeders, which can be put back out during the winter in areas where bears are hibernating. Orchards should have electrical fencing installed around them. Dog food should be kept inside in a secure container, not stored in a garage or on a porch.

Two-cubic-yard bear-resistant container

Human trash is bear treasure. Trash should be discarded in bear-resistant containers—containers that are specifically designed to foil a strong, persistent bear—with the lids securely fastened. As housing development expands into bear habitat, many communities are now looking into bear-resistant municipal solid waste management systems.

GLOSSARY

Bear Trust hopes the following definitions are helpful, and enhance the reader's enjoyment and understanding of this book. Bear Trust is solely responsible for the content of this glossary.

Acacia—Warm region plant, member of the mimosa family, widely found throughout both hemispheres.

American black bear—(*Ursus americanus*). Most common of the eight bear species, found from northern Canada and Alaska south into Mexico, in 40 of 50 states in the U.S. and all provinces of Canada except Prince Edward Island. (*Views from the Bear Den; In the Louisiana Canebrakes; El Patron; Bonito*)

Andean bear—See **Spectacled Bear**.

Annamites—Western Indochina mountain range, 700 miles long, running through Laos and Vietnam. (*In the Market for Bears*)

Arctodus—Short-faced bear, a genus of extinct bear that lived in prehistoric North America until 12,500 years ago as the largest land predator during the Ice Age. (*In the Market for Bears*)

Asiatic black bear—(*Ursus thibetanus*). Also known as the Tibetan black bear, Himalayan black bear, moon bear, and found throughout the Asian continent. Closest relative of the American black bear. (*In the Market for Bears*)

ATV—All terrain vehicle, designed for off-road use, with low pressure tires, usually designed for a single rider.

Baiting a trap—Putting a bear attractant, typically food, into a trap in order to capture a bear for research purposes, such as taking measurements and putting on or replacing a radio collar, or to relocate a bear. (*El Patron*)

Banyan—Large tropical tree that usually starts as a seed growing on another tree.

Barrel trap—Trap the size and shape of a large storage barrel, with a trap door on one end that is activated when a bear or other wildlife species enters a barrel that has been baited. (*El Patron*)

Bayou—Small, slow-moving stream, usually located in low lying areas such as the Gulf Coast of the United States. (*In the Louisiana Canebrakes*)

Bear attractants—Anything remotely edible or that smells like food, including but not limited to processed and unprocessed food, outdoor grills, toothpaste, bird feeders, apple orchards, chicken coops, unsecured trash, unlocked outbuildings, etc.

Beaufort Sea—Part of the Arctic Ocean, to the north of Alaska, frozen for much of the year. (*Hunting the Russian Bear*)

Boar—Adult male bear (adult female is a sow).

Bromeliads—Genus of tropical plants with hard, dry, gray foliage, that typically grow on trees or in rocks, common in South America. (*Yinda*)

Brown bear—(*Ursus arctos*). Found in both Eurasia and North America. DNA testing shows that brown bear subspecies, including the European brown bear and grizzly, are very homogeneous (see **DNA**). (*Bear Baiting, In the Market for Bears*)

Burl—Knot in a tree that is overgrown with bark. (*Views from the Bear Den*)

Bushmeat—Meat of wild land animals killed for subsistence or for commercial sale. (*Nelun*)

Canebrakes—Dense thicket of cane plants. (*In the Louisiana Canebrakes*)

Captive breeding—Process of breeding rare or endangered species in environments controlled by humans, such as zoos or wildlife preserves. (*The Day Mei Xiang Disappeared*)

Chaparri Ecological Reserve—35,000-hectare area in northern Peru, donated by the local community to protect the spectacled bear and other wildlife. (*Yinda, a Strange Family Member*)

Chauvet Cave—Cave in southwestern France decorated with Paleolithic art work. (*Visiting with the Ancestors*)

Color phase—In zoology, a group within an animal species sharing similar coloring and markings. For example, the American black bear may be black, brown, tan, blue-grey, or other colors depending upon the group. (*In the Market for Bears*)

Culvert Trap—A large, cylindrical trap made from a culvert or resembling a culvert, frequently on wheels for easy transport, that functions like a barrel trap although larger (see **Barrel Trap**). (*El Patron*)

DNA—Deoxyribonucleic Acid, the molecule that contains the genetic instructions for the development and functioning of living organisms, often compared to a blueprint.

Ecosystem—A self-sustaining relationship among plants, animals, and their physical environment in which species are often studied.

Electric fence—A barrier designed to create an electrical network when touched that is used to impede animals from crossing a boundary. (*Yinda*)

El Nino—Anomaly in the sustained sea surface temperature in the tropical Pacific Ocean that impacts rainfall conditions.

Endangered species—Population of an organism (species or subspecies) in danger of becoming extinct due to a very low population, a change in the environment, or a change in the predation pattern.

Endemic—Native to or prevalent in a place, or exclusive to an area.

Escarpment—Geologically, a transition zone, found most commonly in sedimentary rocks of a different age or composition, or formed by faults.

European brown bear—*Ursus arctos*. (See **Brown Bear**). (*Bear Baiting*)

Evolutionary biology—Field of biology focused on the origin and descent of species, and the ways in which species change over time. (*In the Market for Bears*)

Fauna—Collective term for animal life. **Flora** is the collective term for plant life.

Giant panda—(*Ailuropoda melanoleuca*—black and white cat foot). Native to central western and southwestern China, and listed as endangered. 99 per cent of its diet is bamboo (see **Captive Breeding, Omnivore**). (*The Day Mei Xiang Disappeared*)

Grizzly—(*Ursus arctos horribilis*). Subspecies of the brown bear, inhabiting uplands of western North America. Color ranges from blond to brown to black (see **Brown Bear, Color Phase**). (*How I Learned about Bears*)

GPS—Global position system that uses a constellation of medium Earth orbit satellites which transmit precise radio signals, enabling the GPS receiver to determine the location, speed, and direction of an object, such as a bear with a radio collar. (*Views from the Bear Den; El Patron*)

Hectare—Unit of measurement frequently used in agriculture, equal to 10,000 square meters, which is equivalent to approximately 2.5 acres.

Hibernaculum—Location chosen by an animal for hibernation. (*Views from the Bear Den*)

Hibernation—State of inactivity and metabolic depression in certain species, including some bear species in colder climates, characterized by lower body temperature, slower rate of breathing, and lower metabolic rate, to conserve energy in periods of food scarcity. (*Views from the Bear Den, More about Hibernation*)

Inupiat Eskimo—Inuit people of Alaska's northwest Arctic, the North Slope, and the Bering straits, including Barrow, Alaska. (*The Great Nanuq*)

INRENA—National Institute of Natural Resources, Peru. (*Yinda*)

Ivory-billed woodpecker—Large member of the woodpecker family, known as the iconic bird of the US bayou country, officially listed as endangered but now widely believed to be extinct despite reports of periodic sightings. (*In the Louisiana Canebrakes*)

Kamchatka Peninsula—1250-kilometer-long peninsula located in Russia's Far East between the Pacific Ocean to the east and the Sea of Okhotsk to the west, noted for its wildlife, including brown bears, and its volcanoes.

KDFWR—Kentucky Department of Fish, Wildlife Resources. (*Views from the Bear Den*)

Kermode bear—Canadian subspecies of the North American black bear, also known as the spirit bear. About one in ten Kermode bears is white (see **Color Phase**).

Khmer Rouge—Ruling political party of Cambodia between 1975 and 1979 known for its brutality toward the Cambodian population. (*In the Market for Bears*)

Komatik—Baggage sled pulled by a snow scooter

Lascaux Caves—Complex of caves in southwestern France famous for Upper Paleolithic cave paintings made between 15,000 and 13,000 BCE. (*Visiting with the Ancestors*)

Leopold, Aldo—1887-1948. Considered to be the father of wildlife management in the U.S., and influential in the development of modern environmental ethics. Founder of The Wilderness Society and author of *A Sand County Almanac*.

Maderas del Carmen—Mexican biosphere reserve in the northern state of Coahuila. (*El Patron, Bonito*)

Mestizo—Term of Spanish origin used in Latin America for people of mixed European and indigenous non-European ancestry.

Microclimate—Local atmospheric zone where the climate differs from the immediate surrounding area.

Midden—Dump for domestic waste, such as bones, feces, shells and botanicals, typically studied in relation to archaeology.

Monotremes—Mammals that lay eggs, such as the platypus and the short-beaked echidna.

Mortality mode—Period of time that a radio signal from a research animal is completely immobile, typically four hours, when it is assumed the animal is either dead or has lost its transmitter. (*Views from the Bear Den, Bibi and the Python*)

Muir, John—1838-1914. Founder of the Sierra Club. One of the first wilderness preservationists, credited with saving Yosemite.

Moon bear—*Ursus thibetanus*. See Asiatic black bear. (*In the Market for Bears*)

Olfactory—Related to the sense of smell.

Omnivores—Species adapted to eating and digesting both plant and animal matter, as opposed to meat-eating **carnivores** and plant-eating **herbivores**. Bears are omnivores.

Paleolithic—Archaeological time scale dating back 2.5 million years, distinguished by the development of stone tools and ending at the introduction of agriculture in approximately 10,000 BCE. Typically divided into Lower, Middle, and Upper. (*Visiting with the Ancestors*)

Pampas—Vast area of lowland plains of South America.

Peary, Commodore Robert—1856-1920. American polar explorer claiming to be the first man to reach the geographic North Pole in 1909. (*Hunting the Russian Bear*)

Pleistocene—Geologic time scale, following the Pliocene (see **Pliocene**), covering the epoch of recent glaciations dating back 1.8 million years. The end of the Pleistocene is generally considered to be concurrent with the end of the Paleolithic period (see **Paleolithic**).

Pliocene—Geologic time scale dating 5.3 million to 1.8 million years ago. Hominids first appeared in the late Pliocene.

Polar bear—(*Ursus maritimus*). Species of bear native to the Arctic. A semi-aquatic marine mammal.

Pressure ridge—Ice formation, essentially a large crack, appearing on a frozen lake as a result of alternate heating and freezing on the surface.

Radio collar—See **telemetry**.

Rip rap—Coarse rock or other material used in stabilizing shorelines and to reduce water erosion. Also known as revetment.

Rostrum—Anatomical feature resembling a bird's beak, sometimes used to describe a snout.

Scat—From scatology. The technical term for feces.

Sendero luminosa—The Shining Path. A Maoist guerilla organization in Peru since 1980. (*Yinda*)

Shaman—Person who practices as an intermediary between the natural and spiritual world.

Sloth bear—(*Melursus ursinus*).   Small, solitary bear with a shaggy coat inhabiting forested areas and grasslands in India, Sri Lanka, Bangladesh, Nepal, and Bhutan.   Baloo from Rudyard Kipling's *Jungle Book* is a sloth bear. (*Nelun*)

Slovakia—Land-locked area in Central Europe, formerly part of Czechoslovakia and since 1993 the Slovak Republic. (*Bear Baiting*)

Slurry—Liquid waste, often toxic, a byproduct of surface mining. (*Views from the Bear Den*)

Sow—Adult, female bear (adult male is a boar).

Spectacled bear—*Tremarctos ornates*. Also known as the Andean bear and Ucumari. Native to South America, and closest relative to the giant panda. (*Yinda)*

Sun bear—*Helarctos malayanus*. Species of bear found in the tropical rainforests of Southeast Asia, with short, sleek fur. (*Bibi and the Python*)

Taxonomy—Practice and science of biological classification, used to group species in the following hierarchy for bears: Kingdom Animalia, Phylum Chordata, Class Mammalia, Order Carnivora, Family Ursidae, Genera, Species. (*Primer on Bear Species*)

Telazol—Anaesthetizing agent used in veterinary medicine as an injectable anaesthetic.

Telemetry—Wireless communication technology used to take remote measurements and other information, typically using a radio-frequency system. In wildlife research, for instance, wildlife such as bears are often fitted with a **radio collar** that provides information on location and movement. See also **Mortality Mode**. (*Views from the Bear Den, El Patron*)

Terror Birds—Large, carnivorous, flightless birds of the Cenozoic Period, 62-2 million years ago.

Threatened species—Any species vulnerable to extinction in the near future (compare to endangered, critically endangered under the World Conservation Union—IUCN).

Ucumari—See **Spectacled Bear**.

Understory—Area of a forest that grows in the shade of the forest canopy, including saplings of canopy trees, shrubs, fungi, etc. The understory has lower light and higher humidty.

Ursa Major—(Great Bear). Constellation visible in the northern hemisphere. The seven brightest stars in the constellation are often referred to as the Big Dipper.

Ursa Minor—(Smaller Bear). Constellation visible in the northern hemisphere that contains Polaris, the North Star. Also referred to as the Little Dipper.

Ursus—Latin for "bear."

USFWS—United States Fish and Wildlife Service, a federal agency under the Department of the Interior.

Velvet Revolution—Nonviolent Czechoslovakian revolution in 1989 that resulted in the Communist Party of Czechoslovakia relinquishing power. (*Summary of Current Bear Situation in Slovakia*)

Vertebrate—Species with backbones or spinal columns within the Phylum Chordata (see **Taxonomy**).

Wrangel Island—2800-square-mile Russian Island in the Arctic Ocean that is a breeding ground for polar bears. (*Hunting the Russian Bear*)

Notes on Contributors

Gilbert T. Adams (*Bear Tale from the Big Thicket*), a fifth generation Texan, is an attorney, rancher and wildlife enthusiast. He has been involved in ranching in East Texas virtually all his life, and is a member of the East Texas Black Bear Task Force. He is also on the board of Bear Trust International.

Chuck Bartlebaugh (*How I Learned about Bears*) is founder and director for the Center for Wildlife Information. Chuck's path to bears has not been a direct one. He started out driving racing cars, then started a marketing agency. But when he became interested in grizzlies, the trajectory of his life was sealed. He became an advocate for educating the public on how to behave in the presence of bears and other wildlife. Today, in addition to being an accomplished wildlife photographer, Chuck heads up the Center for Wildlife Information, where he works with agencies, NGOs, organizations such as the Girl Scouts of America, and the public, providing teaching materials, brochures, and other educational resources.

Leon Chartrand (*In the Nearness to the Nothing: Revelations from a Dying Bear*) is a Ph.D. candidate in environmental phenomenology at the University of Toronto. His dissertation is entitled, "An Originative Perspective of Wildness and its implications for dwelling alongside grizzly habitat: A Phenomenological Case for Bear Wise Communities in the Yellowstone." He is also the State Bear Wise Community Planner for Wyoming Game & Fish Department and is responsible for bear conflict management in the Jackson Region. Chartrand holds two masters degrees. He and his wife Amy live in Jackson Hole, Wyoming.

Monte Dolack (*Visiting with the Ancestors*) is a popular wildlife artist whose depictions of the western landscape and wildlife enjoy a national reputation. After studying art at Montana State University and the University of Montana, Monte opened his first studio in 1974, beginning a successful career in fine art and graphics. His best known early works – wild animals wreaking havoc in human homes – comprise his "Invaders Series." Monte has been the recipient of a number of prestigious awards, and his work is part of the collection of the Library of Congress, the American Association of Museums, the National Wildfire Foundation and numerous other museums and corporations. He was selected at the turn of the century by the *Missoulian* as one of the 100 most influential Montanans of the twentieth century.

Gabriella Fredriksson has worked in Indonesia since 1994, initially on orangutans but later on Malayan sun bears. She is finalizing her Ph.D. on sun bears and is now focusing on protected area management in Kalimantan and Sumatra, Indonesia. She is co-chair of the IUCN/SSC sun bear expert team.

Jean Craighead George (*The Great Nanuq*) is a much beloved children's author who has written over sixty books and received numerous awards for her writing, including the Newberry Award for her contributions to American literature for children.

Bob Lange, Jr. (*Trail Crew Days*) graduated from Colorado State University with a degree in Veterinary Medicine. He went on to have a long agency career working with wildlife, and spent two years as a Peace Corps volunteer in El Salvador from 2002 to 2004. He recently retired from the U.S. Forest Service, and is currently working on a novel.

David S. Maehr, Ph.D. (*Views from the Bear Den*) is Professor of Conservation Biology at the University of Kentucky, Department of Forestry, where he teaches and conducts research on a restored elk population, black bears in Kentucky and Florida, and imperiled neotropical migrant warblers. Dr. Maehr has also been a technical advisor on three black bear studies in northern Mexico and helped initiate the first study of the southernmost population of the species in North America. He has published over 100 technical papers and book chapters, has created artwork for wildlife-related books and publications, and is the author of three books, *Florida's Birds* (1990, 2005), *The Florida Panther: Life and Death of a Vanishing Carnivore* (1997), and *Large Mammal Restoration: Ecological and Sociological Challenges in the 21st Century* (2001). Maehr received his B.S. in wildlife management from The Ohio State University, and M.S. and Ph.D. degrees in wildlife ecology from the University of Florida.

Tom Mangelsen (*Photo Essay*) is an award-winning wildlife photographer. In 2005, Tom was named one of the 100 most important in photography by American Photo Magazine, as well as being honored with Nikon's Legend behind the Lens recognition. He has received an Honorary Fellowship from The Royal Photographic Society in 2002, named North American Nature Photographer Association's (NANPA) Outstanding Nature Photographer of the Year in 2000 and in 1994, Mangelsen received the prestigious Wildlife Photographer of the Year Award, sponsored by the British Broadcasting Corporation (BBC) and British Gas. Mangelsen's work has been published in National Geographic, Audubon, National Wildlife, Smithsonian, Natural History, Newsweek, Wildlife Art, American Photo, National Wildlife and other publications.

Downs Matthews (*Hunting the Russian Bear*) is a writer and editor who finds inspiration in the Arctic. Eight of his 11 books and scores of feature articles draw upon his travels to the Far North, which have taken him beyond the Arctic Circle 40 times. His 1989 *Polar Bear Cubs* (Simon & Schuster) received Parenting Magazine's Certificate of Excellence for nonfiction. In 1992, Matthews joined with wildlife photographer Dr. Dan Guravich to found Polar Bears International, a nonprofit conservation group seeking to improve conservation through education. Matthews continues his affiliation with PBI as a director emeritus. Matthews' compass points south as well, with his 1999 book *Beneath the Canopy, Wildlife of the Latin American Rain Forest* (Chronicle Books). Now 82, Matthews makes his home in Houston, Texas.

Bonnie Reynolds McKinney (*El Patron*) is Wildlife Coordinator at Proyecto El Carmen and investigator of the research project "Population Dynamics and Movement of Black Bears in Northern Coahuila, México. Previous to moving to Coahuila, McKinney conducted black bear research and handled problem bears for Texas Parks and Wildlife in western Texas. McKinney and co-contributor Jonás Delgadillo Villalobos are authors of the first black bear field guide published for México (Manual Para El Manejo Del Oso Negoro Mexicano: Guía Para Manejadores). The manual was published by CEMEX, owner of the Proyecto El Carmen. Both McKinney and Delgadillo are members of "Subcomité Consultivo Para la Protección, Conservación y Recuperación del Oso Negro en México," and Mexican representatives for Bear Trust International.

Sterling Miller, Ph.D. (*A Cautionary Tale*) is senior biologist with the National Wildlife Federation. He previously worked as a bear research biologist for the Alaska Department of Fish and Game for 21 years. He is a former President, Vice President (Americas), and Secretary-Treasurer of the International Association for Bear Research and Management (IBA). He is an affiliated faculty member of the University of Montana and the University of Alaska-Fairbanks, a former President of the Alaska Chapter of The Wildlife Society, and has some 50 peer-reviewed publications to his credit, mostly on bears. He received his BS at the University of Montana, and MS and Ph.D. degrees in wildlife biology from the University of Washington.

Sy Montgomery (*In the Market for Bears*) is a prolific wildlife writer and commentator for National Public Radio's *Living on Earth.* Her *Journey of the Pink Dolphins* was a top ten Sci-Tech book for 2000 on *Booklist,* and a finalist for the Thomas Cook Travel Book Award. She makes her home in New Hampshire.

Brenda Morgan (*The Day Mei Xiang Disappeared)* is a zookeeper at the National Zoo in Washington, D.C., where she looks after the zoo's famous giant pandas.

Bernie Peyton, Ph.D. (*Yinda*) is a wildlife biologist and spectacled bear expert who conducted field research on bears from 1977-1987. He worked on kangaroo rats and kit foxes until 1997 before returning to his earlier career in art. You can see his origami bears at www.eco-origami.com.

Shyamala Ratnayeke, Ph.D. (*Nelun*) grew up in Sri Lanka, and moved to the United States 15 years ago. She was an assistant professor at Spelman College for four years. In 2002, she returned to Sri Lanka to study sloth bears. She is currently publishing the results of her research as an adjunct assistant professor at the University of Tennessee, Knoxville.

Robin Rigg (*Bear Baiting*)**,** who has an M.Sc. in zoology**,** is with the Slovak Wildlife Society's BEARS Project (Bear Education, Awareness, and Research).

Jonás Delgadillo Villalobos (*Bonito, El Bandido de la Sierra*) is Assistant Wildlife Coordinator at Proyecto El Carmen located in the Maderas del Carmen in Coahuila, México and investigator of the research project

"Population Dynamics and Movement of Black Bears in Northern Coahuila, México." He completed his M.S. at Universidad Autónoma de Nuevo León, Linares, Nuevo León,México on Ecología nutricional del oso negro en la Sierra Maderas del Carmen." Previous to working at Proyecto El Carmen he worked with black bears on other research projects in Mexico and various wildlife projects in his home state of Sinaloa, México.

Notes on the Editorial Board

Jack Ward Thomas is a consultant, writer, and speaker in the conservation arena and is Professor Emeritus at the University of Montana. He was the Boone and Crockett Professor of Conservation at the University of Montana (1997-2005), Research Scientist for the U. S. Forest Service from 1967-1993, Chief of the Forest Service 1993-1996, and served the Texas Parks and Wildlife Department from 1957-1966. He holds degrees from Texas A&M University (B.S.), West Virginia (M.S.), and the University of Massachusetts (Ph.D.), and has been named a distinguished alumni by each. He has published over 500 articles and books in the general areas of wildlife ecology and management, range management, forestry, fisheries, natural resources policy and politics, ecosystem management, land-use planning, and economics. Thomas has received numerous recognitions and awards, including the Aldo Leopold Medal from The Wildlife Society and the Award for Distinguished Service from the Government of the United States.

Karen Noyce is a bear researcher at the Minnesota Department of Natural Resources. She is Vice President for Americas with the International Association for Bear Research and Management (IBA).

Harry Reynolds is formerly with the Alaska Department of Fish and Wildlife, where he was brown bear biologist, and is the current (2007) President of the International Association for Bear Research and Management (IBA). Harry literally grew up with bears; his father was a park ranger in Yellowstone National Park. Following his retirement from Alaska Fish and Wildlife, Harry has been part of an international team studying brown bears in the Gobi Desert in Mongolia.

More about Bear Trust International

Bear Trust International is a 501(c)(3) nonprofit wildlife conservation organization founded in 1999 to protect all eight species of bears through three program areas: wild bear research, habitat protection, and conservation education. Taken together, these programs address the many contexts that are necessary for effective wildlife conservation. Bear Trust International envisions a world where wildlife prospers in its natural habitat while coexisting with environmentally sensitive economic development.

Bear Trust Mission
Bear Trust International is conservation organization working for wild bears and wildlife. We believe that wild bears in their natural habitat are key indicators of ecosystem health. Their ability to sustain themselves is therefore critical to wildlife. Bear Trust strives to reinforce ecosystem viability through habitat conservation and education projects that build on available research.

Bear Trust Goals
- Conserve and enhance wild bear populations, other wildlife, and their natural habitat
- Promote sound management of wild bears
- Foster cooperation among governments, federal and state agencies, public and private organizations, and individuals in wildlife management and habitat conservation
- Educate the international public about wild bear and wildlife management, and habitat conservation

- Promote international research and program funding for wild bear and habitat projects
- Educate the general public about the impact of the world's human population on wild bears, other wildlife, and natural resources

Program Purposes

- Promote sound stewardship of the world's bear populations
- Promote large, linked bear ecosystems, where the concept of bear habitat is increasingly defined from the point of view of the bear, rather than being limited by geopolitical boundaries
- Publish information about bears and their habitats in easily accessible formats so that critical, basic information is available to a broad international base
- Develop international, grassroots support for bear conservation
- Develop a presence in international decision-making circles to impact policies that affect bear populations
- Provide the public with contacts and information that assist them in minimizing property damage and nuisance-related problems

The Bear Book has been made possible by generous donors who express their concern for wildlife by financially supporting organizations such as Bear Trust. You can make a tax-deductible donation to Bear Trust International and help protect wild bears. Mail a check today to:

Bear Trust International
PO Box 4006
Missoula, Montana 59806